English Linguist
from Below

CRITICAL LANGUAGE AND LITERACY STUDIES

Series Editors: Professor Alastair Pennycook (*University of Technology, Sydney, Australia*) and **Professor Brian Morgan** (*Glendon College/York University, Toronto, Canada*) and **Professor Ryuko Kubota** (*University of British Columbia, Vancouver, Canada*)

Critical Language and Literacy Studies is an international series that encourages monographs directly addressing issues of power (its flows, inequities, distributions, trajectories) in a variety of language- and literacy-related realms. The aim with this series is twofold: (1) to cultivate scholarship that openly engages with social, political, and historical dimensions in language and literacy studies, and (2) to widen disciplinary horizons by encouraging new work on topics that have received little focus (see below for partial list of subject areas) and that use innovative theoretical frameworks.

All books in this series are externally peer-reviewed.

Full details of all the books in this series and of all our other publications can be found on http://www.multilingual-matters.com, or by writing to Multilingual Matters, St Nicholas House, 31–34 High Street, Bristol, BS1 2AW, UK.

Other books in the series

CRITICAL LANGUAGE AND LITERACY STUDIES: 28

English Linguistic Imperialism from Below

Moral Aspiration and Social Mobility

Leya Mathew

MULTILINGUAL MATTERS
Bristol • Jackson

DOI https://doi.org/10.21832/MATHEW9141
Names: Mathew, Leya, author.
Title: English Linguistic Imperialism from Below: Moral Aspiration and
  Social Mobility/Leya Mathew.
Description: Bristol, UK; Jackson, TN : Multilingual Matters, [2022] |
  Series: Critical Language and Literacy Studies: 28 | Includes
  bibliographical references and index. | Summary: "The book shows how
  English has been newly constituted as a dominant language in post-market
  reform India. Political economic transitions experienced as radical
  social mobility fuelled intense non-elite desire for English schooling.
  Rather than English schooling leading to social mobility, new
  experiences of mobility necessitated English schooling"—Provided by publisher.
Identifiers: LCCN 2021061177 (print) | LCCN 2021061178 (ebook) | ISBN
  9781788929141 (Hardback) | ISBN 9781788929134 (Paperback) | ISBN
  9781788929158 (PDF) | ISBN 9781788929165 (ePub)
Subjects: LCSH: English language—Political aspects—India. | English
  language—Social aspects—India. | English language—Study and
  teaching—India. | English language—Study and teaching—Foreign
  speakers. | Imperialism.
Classification: LCC PE3502.I6 M38 2022 (print) | LCC PE3502.I6 (ebook) |
  DDC 306.442/21054--dc23/eng/20220314
LC record available at https://lccn.loc.gov/2021061177
LC ebook record available at https://lccn.loc.gov/2021061178
Library of Congress Cataloging in Publication Data
A catalog record for this book is available from the Library of Congress.

British Library Cataloguing in Publication Data
A catalogue entry for this book is available from the British Library.

ISBN-13: 978-1-78892-914-1 (hbk)
ISBN-13: 978-1-78892-913-4 (pbk)

Multilingual Matters
UK: St Nicholas House, 31–34 High Street, Bristol, BS1 2AW, UK.
USA: Ingram, Jackson, TN, USA.

Website: www.multilingual-matters.com
Twitter: Multi_Ling_Mat
Facebook: https://www.facebook.com/multilingualmatters
Blog: www.channelviewpublications.wordpress.com

The policy of Multilingual Matters/Channel View Publications is to use papers that are
natural, renewable and recyclable products, made from wood grown in sustainable forests.
In the manufacturing process of our books, and to further support our policy, preference is
given to printers that have FSC and PEFC Chain of Custody certification. The FSC and/or
PEFC logos will appear on those books where full certification has been granted to the
printer concerned.

Typeset by SAN Publishing Services.

Contents

Figures and Tables

Acknowledgments

My greatest debt is to the mothers, children and teachers who shared their struggles with me. The book is a record of our journey. Raghu Eraviperoor, MA Khader and R Meganathan were co-travelers. Along the way, Nancy Hornberger and Nelson Flores patiently introduced me to Applied Linguistics. Special thanks are also due to Rama Mathew and R. Amritavalli. Getting this book out was hard; it swims against some powerful currents. I am grateful to Anna Roderick and the series editors at Multilingual Matters for seeing value in the book. Thanks also to Flo McClelland, Stanzi Collier-Qureshy and Mythili Devi for shepherding me through the production process.

I gratefully acknowledge funding from the following sources: preliminary research was made possible by a summer travel award from the Center for Advanced Study of India at the University of Pennsylvania. I am also thankful to the American Institute of Indian Studies, whose Junior Fellowship funded part of the fieldwork. A write-up grant from the National Academy of Education/Spencer Foundation was crucial for the completion of the project.

Before I came into academia, I worked in film and television. Ajay Raina and Sai Paranjpye taught me to value the everyday long before I had heard of ethnography. Once I made the shift to academia, Kathleen Hall taught me how to wrestle with theory meaningfully, and I am forever grateful for that. Ritty Lukose continued to engage with the project long after I finished my dissertation. John Jackson provided support throughout. Fellow graduate students provided friendship and conversation: Matthew Tarditi, Arjun Shankar, Gabriel Dattatreyan, Audrey Winpenny, Sofia Chapparo, Mariam Durrani, Julia McWilliams, Emmerich Davies, Roseann Liu, Kathy Rho, Talar Kaloustian, Mustafa Abdul-Jabbar and Scott Cody.

At the National Institute of Advanced Studies, Bengaluru, Jeebanlata Salam urged me to get started on the book. I have learned much from her. Savitha Suresh, Anu Bittianda, Krupa Rajangam, Varun Bhatta, Abha Rao, Keya Bardalai, Priya Gupta and R. Maithreyi helped me navigate the waters. Special gratitude is also due to Sundar Sarukkai, Carol Upadhya, Hemangini Gupta, Cheshta Arora, Anamika Ajay, Janaki Balakrishnan, Shivali Tukdeo, M. Mayilvaganan, Narendar Pani, Anitha Kurup and Srikumar Menon.

At Ahmedabad University, Patrick French provided much needed support. Karthik Rao Cavale, Aparajith Ramnath, Mary Ann Chacko, Karishma Desai and Tejaswini Niranjana provided valuable feedback. Aditya Vaishya, Aparajita Basu, Ashwin Pande, Apaar Kumar, Aditi Deo, Divita Singh, Keita Omi, Manomohini Dutta, Manish Datt, Murari Jha, Neha Jain, Ratna Ghosal, Samuel Wright, Sarthak Bagchi and Maya Ratnam made the GICT basement the most fun place to be on campus. Soon after, the pandemic closed everything down. Special thanks are also due to Priyana Vidhani, Munzerin Qureshi, Vijay Bhavsar, Shahul KT, Abrar Saiyed, Pratishtha Pandya, Saumya Malviya, Suchismita Das and Darshini Mahadevia.

My greatest debts are to my family, who endured the many moods of writing: Ajay, Mariem, Amma and Achachan. And Leny, Betty, Dikutty, Shreya, Leanne, Cibu, Sindhu, Simona and Ruhaan made Philly and Upper Darby home for the years that I was there. Thank you!

A part of Chapter 1 was previously published in 'Pedagogies of Aspiration' in *South Asia: Journal of South Asia Studies,* an earlier version of Chapter 3 was published as 'Aspiring and Aspiration Shaming' in *Anthropology and Education Quarterly,* Chapter 6 as 'Betrayed Futures' in *Anthropological Perspectives on Student Futures* and Chapter 7 as 'Mandated Resistance, Embodied Shame' in *TESOL Quarterly.*

Series Editors' Preface

This book takes us to the heart of a contemporary dilemma: what sense do we make of aspirations to learn English in contexts of poverty? A number of years ago, an article in the *EL Gazette* (English language, 1999) (a publication aimed at 'the English Language Teaching industry and international English-medium education') argued that the widespread introduction of English into elementary education around the world should lead to the alleviation of poverty. Next to a picture of laughing children on the front page is the claim that 'English is key to a better life for the poor' while an editorial on the next page explains further that 'for many of the world's poorest people, English can hold the key to escape from grinding poverty' (Pennycook, 2007). Such claims raise several questions for English language education: certainly, better education in poor communities can help, particularly if girls are ensured equal access. Such educational provision needs to take into account the lives of the children and their parents: if children provide work and income for the family, alternative forms of income and support need to be provided.

Such education also needs to be highly relevant to their lives, both to keep children in school and to encourage their learning. A key aspect of that relevance is education in the first language(s), not so much education in a prescribed mother tongue but rather education in whatever varieties, multilingual mixes, or vernacular styles the children use. To suggest that English should be part of this is a strange and unsubstantiated claim. For many of the world's poor, English language education is 'an outlandish irrelevance', and 'talk of a role for English language education in facilitating the process of poverty reduction and a major allocation of public resources to that end is likely to prove misguided and wasteful' (Bruthiaux, 2002: 292–3). This issue of resource allocation is important: it is a question not only of providing teachers and materials, but also of considering what will *not* be taught in order to include English. While in some contexts, education and English may provide certain advantages to some students (an escape from poverty, perhaps), it is unclear how such an education can be advantageous to poor children in general.

This raises the question of what such claims actually focus on: is this about the possibility of some children escaping the bonds of poverty via an English education, or is it a question of largescale economic change, of the transformation of the lives of a whole class of people? Are we considering poverty alleviation in terms of individual escape from poverty or in terms of larger social and economic change, and if the latter, how might English be related to such change? While on the one hand it is possible to look at an 'English divide' between those who have access to English and those who do not, it is important to consider the role of English in its relations to class, curriculum and inequality. As Tollefson (2000: 8) warns, 'at a time when English is widely seen as a key to the economic success of nations and the economic well-being of individuals, the spread of English also contributes to significant social, political, and economic inequalities'. Grin (2001) points to the question of diminishing returns, since the more people learn English, the less the skill of knowing English will count. Arguments for access need to be set against an understanding of the broad effects of educational provision in all their complexity. 'Any discussion of English as a global language and its socioeducational implications', Rubdy (2015: 43) reminds us, 'cannot ignore the fact that far from being a solution to the dismantling of "unequal power" relations in the world, English is in fact often part of the problem'.

And yet, of course, people around the world want access to English. In April 2010, in the village of Banka in Uttar Pradesh in India, a temple was consecrated to the English language. Angrezi Devi – the English goddess – is a two feet tall bronze statue, modelled after the Statue of Liberty, and inspired by a desire for English among Dalit (the lowest castes) in India. 'Goddess English is a family deity of liberation from poverty, ignorance, and oppression for the Dalits... The Downtrodden believe that there is nothing possible for them without English, She is the goddess of Hope for equity' (Ganvir, 2013: 161). Some of this discussion of Dalit English education goes so far as to laud the infamous 1835 Macaulay's Minute on education, as well as British colonialism more generally, for instigating change in favor of India's lower castes (Ilame, 2020). Yet Macaulay's Minute was not so much a policy that inaugurated English education as a piece of grandiloquent Anglicist posturing, denigrating the languages of India, and announcing European (White) superiority. Colonial authorities remained extremely reluctant to promote English for a range of pragmatic, financial and educational reasons: they feared English education would lead to opposition to colonial rule and were more interested in the provision of vernacular education as a means to improve loyalty to empire and cultivate a work ethic within colonial capitalism (Pennycook, 1998).

Leya Mathew's wonderfully careful and close ethnography of poor communities in Kerala (South India) enters this difficult space with a critical eye. This book is particularly important because of its deep ethnographic work, and its readiness to deal with the complexities of the everyday, as well as its engagement with questions of class and caste in India (a topic often still deemed only for discussion within India). It helps us grasp not just the desire for English but the ways this is entangled with a set of moral aspirations, with mothers' affective labor for English education for their children: this is also about being a 'good mother'. The women who are central to this study are from impoverished backgrounds and see education as a means to overcome the intergenerational poverty and class and caste-based segregation and marginalization that has defined their lives. In aspiring to a new lifestyle, as the expansion of a new consumer society in India starts to touch their lives, these women, particularly those of Dalit background, desire for themselves a position away from the stigmatized labor that is so often their lot, and instead hope to look after a home and tend to the educational needs of their children.

Such aspirations are sometimes dismissed as misguided, ideological delusions of neoliberalism. Our capacity to understand such desires has not been helped by the language commodification literature, which purports to provide a political economy of language, but fails to distinguish between language commodification as discourse and as a product of labor (which it isn't) (Petrovic & Yazan, 2021; Simpson & O'Regan, 2021) while also denigrating those who see language learning in such materialist terms. The focus on neoliberalism, to which language commodification is usually closely tied, also often fails to do more than attend to the macro-structures of domination and economy – pro-market agendas, deregulation, privatization, and so on – and to see their local take-up only as ideological reflexes of these broader structures. Such approaches miss the importance of local action, of the ways that people may follow neoliberal agendas through informal economies, entrepreneurship and subaltern politics around accumulation, and fail to address the kinds of affective intensities that often drive local economic activity yet elude top-down policy directives.

Park's (2021: 3) focus on subjectivity partly bridges this gap by arguing that Koreans do not pursue English only because of the economic opportunities it affords, but also for a range of 'feelings, longings and imaginings' for a different self, a sense of moral responsibility, anxieties about failure, insecurity about levels of English and frustration at the impossible goals that have been set. English becomes an 'index of an ideal neoliberal subject' prepared to engage in self-improvement and self-management (2021: 4). Park's (2021: 7) interest is on 'the subjective experiences of English rooted in the materially specific conditions of neoliberalism'. These 'affective, emotional, and moral dimensions of how we pursue, acquire, and value English in the political economy' point to the 'thoughts actions and struggles' of people as they try to make sense of English in a neoliberal world (Park, 2021: 7). Mathew's focus in this book, however, is particularly on the affective labors and desires of mothers hoping to haul their families out of poverty.

The role English plays at this grassroots level takes us to the need to understand neoliberalism from below (Gago, 2017). Like other discussions 'from below,' the point here is to understand local practices without seeing them as only a reflex of larger structures. Globalization from below, for example, looks at informal networks and economies, 'flows of people, goods, information, and capital among different production centres and marketplaces' across different regions of the world (Ribeiro, 2012: 223). This is by no means to glorify neoliberalism from below as liberating or independent – far from it – but it is to see how people negotiate profits in the 'context of dispossession, in a contractual dynamic that mixes forms of servitude and conflict' (Gago, 2017: 5). The aspirations for English education and all it is hoped to deliver for the non-elites is partly a form of resistance – going against the advice of experts for mother tongue (Malayalam-medium) education – while also providing a moral response to the development of a new consumer society. English is perceived as a route to escape intergenerational poverty, which drives the business of low-fee private English-medium schooling, and which in turn reasserts the dominance of English and the social inequalities that it maintains.

One of the problems that Mathew identifies and describes in close detail is the kind of education these students receive. In ways similar to the divide that Ramanathan (2005) identifies between more affluent English education and the impoverished and often stultified vernacular education, the cheap English education these mothers can afford for their children is itself an impoverished education. While wealthy Indians can provide resource-rich classrooms, those of the rural poor are much less well provided for. The elites who already have access to English – a mixture of critical educators, textbook writers and policymakers – respond to such aspirations negatively, undermining these aspirations as irrational consumption that jeopardizes the democratic possibilities of education. While the non-elites put their aspirations for social mobility – or at least a shift from the hardships of a subsistence life to the relative comfort of life within a consumer economy – into practice through English education, the elites become increasingly insecure at the possibility of such social change.

We have, therefore, a desperate cycle of hope, desire, disappointment and inequality. The disenfranchised want access to English, which they see as a means for social mobility for the next generation. Those who already have such access advise against this, promoting first language education. But the poor spurn education in the first language, and instead find themselves paying for poor quality rote English that may not provide the ticket to change that is hoped for. The book therefore shows how the hegemonic role of English in a postcolonial context like India is constantly reproduced, and that the agents of this reproduction may be Dalit women as much as Brahmin men. English for these mothers becomes, at least in their eyes, a tool for emancipation from class and caste-based segregation and subjugation. And yet, English language education and policies also serve to maintain these inequalities. The English these students get is an impoverished variety that may not do much for the non-elites. This also indicates the need to consider carefully what we mean by 'English' in these different contexts: it is a very different thing depending on whether it is a school subject, a language policy, or a hope for a better life.

This book points to the need to understand English language education on the ground, at the grassroots level, in the Global South. This is part of a turning away from the expertise of the academic institutions in the Global North, who have for too long insisted on expertise in knowing what is good for the world (see e.g. Ndhlovu & Makalela, 2021). This book is a really important addition to this series. This is not the first time we've been to India (Vandrick, 2019) and more specifically to Kerala in this series: Pennycook (2012) recounts travels to the tea and rubber plantations where his mother grew up, but there are more important relations here to questions of gender, mobility, ELT and development discussed in other books. The close ethnographic study continues our commitment to the position that, as Blommaert (2013) showed, we need ethnographically-informed research if we are to grasp the workings of language. The relations among neoliberalism, education and English continue to be of great importance to our understanding of language education (Flubacher & Del Percio, 2017).

Gender, ELT and development, as Appleby (2010) shows, are intertwined, and ELT and development have a far more complex relation than one of more English leading to greater development (Erling & Seargeant, 2013). Takahashi (2013) explores complex intersections of gendered identity negotiation and desire through English language learning in her contribution to the series. Gender, English, mobility and aspirations for a better life also play out in a range of contexts, as Lorente (2018) shows in her study of domestic workers from the Philippines. This book from Leya Mathew adds a layer of complexity that gives us further grounds for critical reflection on what English is and does in the world. It adds weight to key aspects of this series: we have to examine local conditions of language and education, preferably ethnographically; this has to be done with a critical eye on questions of class, caste, race and gender; and all this occurs within much wider forces of inequality.

Alastair Pennycook
Brian Morgan
Ryuko Kubota

References

Appleby, R. (2010) *ELT, Gender and International Development: Myths of Progress in a Neocolonial World.* Bristol: Multilingual Matters.

Blommaert, J. (2013) *Ethnography, Superdiversity and Linguistic Landscapes: Chronicles of Complexity.* Bristol: Multilingual Matters.

Bruthiaux, P. (2002) Hold your courses: Language education, language choice, and economic development. *TESOL Quarterly* 36 (3), 275–296.

EL Gazette (1999) English language could be the key to a better life for the underprivileged. *EL Gazette*, 237 (October), p. 3.

Erling, E.J. and Seargeant, P. (eds) (2013) *English and Development: Policy, Pedagogy and Globalization*. Bristol: Multilingual Matters.

Flubacher, M.-C. and Del Percio, A. (eds) (2017) *Language, Education and Neoliberalism: Critical Studies in Sociolinguistics*. Bristol: Multilingual Matters.

Gago, V. (2017) *Neoliberalism from Below: Popular Pragmatics and Baroque Economies*. Durham, NC: Duke University Press.

Ganvir, A.J. (2013) The English language teaching and the Dalits in India in the present scenario. In D.D. Shete (ed.) *Teaching English language: Modern approaches* (pp. 161–162). Khaparakheda: B.S.W. College, Khaparakheda.

Grin, F. (2001) English as economic value: Facts and fallacies. *World Englishes* 20 (1), 65–78.

Ilame, V.R. (2020) The English language as an instrument of Dalit emancipation. *International Journal of English Literature and Social Sciences*, 5 (4), 998–1002.

Lorente, B.P. (2018) *Scripts of Servitude: Language, Labor Migration and Transnational Domestic Work*. Bristol: Multilingual Matters.

Ndhlovu, F. and Makalela, L. (2021) *Decolonising Multilingualism in Africa: Recentering Silenced Voices from the Global South*. Bristol: Multilingual Matters.

Park, J.S.-Y. (2021) *In Pursuit of English: Language and Subjectivity in Neoliberal South Korea*. Oxford: Oxford University Press.

Pennycook, A. (1998) *English and the Discourses of Colonialism*. London: Routledge

Pennycook, A. (2007) The myth of English as an international language. In S. Makoni and A. Pennycook (eds) *Disinventing and Reconstituting Languages* (pp. 90–115). Clevedon: Multilingual Matters.

Pennycook, A. (2012) *Language and Mobility: Unexpected Places*. Bristol: Multilingual Matters.

Petrovic, J. and Yazan, B. (2021) Language as instrument, resource, and maybe capital, but not commodity. In J. Petrovic and B. Yazan (eds) *The Commodification of Language: Conceptual Concerns and Empirical Manifestations* (pp. 24–40). London: Routledge.

Ramanathan, V. (2005) *The English-Vernacular Divide: Postcolonial Language Politics and Practice*. Clevedon: Multilingual Matters.

Ribeiro, G.L. (2012) Conclusion: Globalization from below and the non-hegemonic world-system. In G. Mathews, G.L. Ribeiro and C.A. Vega (eds) *Globalization from Below: The World's Other Economy* (pp. 221–235). London: Routledge.

Rubdy, R. (2015) Unequal Englishes, the native speaker, and decolonization in TESOL. In R. Tupas (ed.) *Unequal Englishes: The Politics of Englishes Today* (pp. 42–58). Basingingstoke: Palgrave Macmillan.

Simpson, W. and O'Regan J. (2021) Confronting language fetishism in practice. In J. Petrovic and B. Yazan (eds) *The Commodification of Language: Conceptual Concerns and Empirical Manifestations* (pp. 7-23). London: Routledge.

Takahashi, K. (2013) *Language Learning, Gender and Desire: Japanese Women on the Move*. Bristol: Multilingual Matters.

Tollefson, J.W. (2000) Policy and ideology in the spread of English. In J.K. Hall and W. Eggington (eds) *The Sociopolitics of English Language Teaching* (pp. 7–21). Clevedon: Multilingual Matters.

Vandrick, S. (2019) *Growing up with God and Empire: A Postcolonial Analysis of 'Missionary Kid' Memoirs*. Bristol: Multilingual Matters.

1 Moral Aspiration

Contesting Moral Worlds

News agencies in the southern Indian state of Kerala reported in September 2014 that a teacher had locked up a kindergarten student in a doghouse on school premises for talking in class. The Kerala state responded promptly. It ordered the closure of the low-fee private English-medium school and the transfer of enrolled students to neighboring state-funded schools. In an unexpected turnabout, the transfer decision provoked school parents to protest against the state. Parents insisted that if students had to be transferred, they be transferred to English-medium, not Malayalam-medium schools. In Kerala, as in much of India, the medium of instruction in state-funded primary schools is the regional language.[1] In contrast, low-fee private schools promise English-medium instruction. In what quickly became known as the 'doghouse controversy', parents accused the state of 'playing with the futures of their children [kuttikalude bhavi vachu panthadukaya]'. Parental anger was re-directed at the state for its attempts to reconstruct vernacular futures for non-elites.

Non-elite private schooling is at the center of public as well as scholarly debates about ethical-moral educational opportunity in India. The state and critical educators assert that one, very young children should not be subjected to instruction in a foreign language, and two, aspiring parents should not be left to the mercy of the profit-seeking market. These publicly circulating moral assertions attempt to reform non-elites.

In a TV news panel about the doghouse controversy, Fr Philip of Childline Services[2] and Dr Nirmala, a child psychologist, joined Jomon, the father of the child who had been locked up in the doghouse (Asianet News, 2014). During the discussion, Dr Nirmala expressed astonishment and sorrow at the event and then went on to admonish Jomon for sending his child to such a 'cruel' educational space. As if in defense against Dr Nirmala's insinuation that he was to blame for the abuse his child had suffered, Jomon remarked that his older child ranked first in her class. He reiterated, on air, his request to the education minister to transfer his son, the younger child, to an English-medium school. For Jomon, marks and English are the most visible expressions of love he can provide his children, and what he *should* or *could* provide so that they can escape intergenerational poverty. As Black (2018: 81) explains, morality/ethics emerges 'first and foremost in the realm of social action and possibility', 'providing guidance for how one should or could act in the course of everyday encounters'.

Non-elite ethical-moral assertions, however, immediately evoke correction. Riled over Jomon's misplaced priorities, Dr Nirmala exclaimed:

> Education is not just about marks and ranks; education has to nurture good character [*nalla swabhavamulla vyaktitvam*]. … Your child may get good marks, but he will not learn how to love. As long as a child does not know how to love, that child cannot become a good person [*nalla vyakti*], I am certain schools like this will not be able to present him [*pradanam*] to society as a good person. (Asianet News, 2014)

For Dr Nirmala and the Kerala state, education *should* be about 'good character', not marks and definitely not English. The state-subsidized Malayalam-medium school is assumed to be the default ethical-moral nurturing space, one that teaches practical pedagogies of love in the mother's tongue (also see Pennycook, 2002). According to this logic, private schools cheaply and brutally commodify marks while promoting new linguistic imperialisms.

Meanwhile, the ethical-moral worlds of non-elites remain invisible, undocumented. Parents like Jomon inhabit a new consumer society that is profoundly different from the deprivations they grew up in. The context is key here. Non-elite Indians are turning to educational projects with unprecedented urgency in a particular sociohistoric context. As described in this book, their own childhood was marked by hunger, deprivation and the myriad labors of subsistence living. But the present is a new world. Food, clothes, cooking gas, fridge, phone, TV – all of these are available, relatively cheaply. It is as if non-elites had emigrated *en masse* without leaving home, to inhabit a new consumer society. Rather than English education leading to social mobility, political economic transitions experienced at the personal level as radical social mobility led to intense parental desires for English education for children.

Linguistic Imperialism from Below

In his influential book, Robert Phillipson (1992: 47) proposed the notion of English linguistic imperialism to unravel the ways in which English is constituted as a dominant language. His analysis focused chiefly on British and American institutions and ideologies around development aid and the English Language Teaching (ELT) profession. It revealed how English was abstracted out of deeply unequal social, economic and political relations into a language that should be learned by everyone but taught by a few. Actually existing postcolonial classrooms complicated this reading. Suresh Canagarajah's (1999) work in Sri Lanka showed that rather than rejecting or celebrating English, learners and teachers reconstituted it in contradictory ways. In the two decades that have passed since these debates, much has changed. Though imperialism is over, the political, economic and cultural subjugation of social life through English has only intensified (Hardt & Negri, 2000; Phillipson, 2013).

With linguistic imperialism from below, I draw attention to how English is newly constituted as a dominant language in a rearticulated political economic context through the fervent aspirations of non-elites and the zealous reforms of postcolonial ELT experts. Veronica Gago (2017) proposes that we distinguish between 'neoliberalism from below' and 'from above'. She argues that reducing neoliberalism to pro-market agendas, practices and policies such as financialization and deregulation (neoliberalism from above) risks losing sight of widespread informal economies, mass self-entrepreneurship and subaltern politics around accumulation (neoliberalism from below). Gago (2017: 45) cautions that neoliberalism from below can 'function in terms of self-management, mobilization, and insubordination and *also* as a mode of servitude, submission, and exploitation'. This book documents a similar unfolding in the context of marketization in India.

The title 'moral aspiration' holds together two contesting moral worlds that together produce new English linguistic imperialisms from below. The aspirations of non-elites like Jomon function in terms of insubordination (to experts) as well as submission (to markets). Non-elite aspirations for English-medium education were a moral response to the possibilities of a new consumer society. Escaping intergenerational poverty seemed possible, and the pursuit of English necessary. This reasserted the dominance of English. Meanwhile, well-intentioned policymakers and critical educators had diverging moral aspirations. They wanted English to be taught in decolonizing, non-oppressive, child-friendly ways. Like Dr Nirmala, they wanted to craft 'good' humans. This required the assembling of resource-intensive classrooms, which became the prerogative of wealthy Indians. As the book explains, reform calls for ethical-moral pedagogy reconstituted English from a literacy practice to an oral performance. What constituted English itself was restructured, in ways that subjugated aspiring non-elites.

It is important to clarify how I use the terms ethical and moral. Though some anthropologists in the Foucauldian tradition distinguish between ethics as everyday embodied practice and morals as abstract, prescriptive norms (Mahmood, 2005: 28), non-elite mothers in Kerala 'evoked abstract moral principles at the very moment they engaged in embodied affect and action, thus irreducibly intermingling the two' (Muehlebach, 2012: 19). Therefore, I use morality/ethics interchangeably. Additionally, I do not argue that non-elites have a special claim to ethics. Instead, I argue that (1) the context of marketization engendered a

4 English Linguistic Imperialism from Below

particular kind of moral politics and (2) the effects of ethical-moral action are uneven.

To hold the contesting moral worlds together, the introductory chapter reviews literature on consumption and the middle classes in India. Since English education is central to middle-class formation, the fragmentation of the middle classes and its discursive unification into a middle class are directed through English. Scholarship on consumption explains the unprecedented emergence of non-elite aspirations for English in a new consumer society. The following sections detail how moral discourses are mobilized to manage the new middle classes.

Universalization of Aspiration: Consumption and Affective Labor

The liberalization of the Indian economy in the 1990s triggered a definitive shift from an austere socialist economy to a full-blown consumer society. Literature on liberalization is vast, attempting as it does to understand the restructuring of the state and the society in a new political economy. This section offers a selective review of scholarship on non-elite consumption in liberalizing India to situate the aspirational worlds of parents like Jomon.

To begin with, rather than merely a possession of commodities, consumption is a social practice and cultural performance through which notions of the self and one's place in society are negotiated (Appadurai, 1986). To give an example, Lukose (2009) describes how young, lower-caste men in Kerala asserted a jeans-shirt inflected masculinity to rework stigmatized caste locations that were earlier marked by strict codes of dressing and presentation. The consumer practices of liberalization interrupted existing caste and gender norms and enabled citizens to embark on new 'social value projects' (Nakassis & Searle, 2013: 2). The social value of jeans-shirt here relates to the ways in which lower-caste youth revalued the self, social relations and possible futures. Appadurai (2013) calls such rearrangements 'capacities to aspire'. The future is transformed from a predetermined embodiment organized along caste and gender lines into the realm of possibility and potential (Adam, 2008: 111–116). Consumer practices animated a political consciousness among non-elites as they learned to aspire.

Importantly, the self-making entailed in consumer practices are not just individual claims to social recognition but also a central mechanism of capitalist accumulation (Irani, 2019). The scale of change is not limited to the local or the individual. It was as if a generation of Indians had 'emigrated without leaving [home]' (Berdahl, 1999: 202). To fully grasp the breadth and the depth of this large-scale transition, the notion of affective labor is useful. Labor in its earlier Marxist conceptualizations was understood as the physical effort that produced material things for profitable exchange, typically in factories, to propel industrial capitalism. Affective labor alerts us to the enticing imaginative and affective work of aspiring which in turn drives contemporary capital accumulation. As Mazzarella (2003: 20) explains, capitalist consumer societies incorporate aesthetic and affective production into commodity production and generate value out of enjoyment, play, seduction and vulnerability.

The affective labors of consumption are especially pertinent for those on the margins. For instance, young, urban, non-elite men 'wandering' in malls in the National Capital Region cultivate 'commodity-oriented aspirations and pleasures' that promise inclusion and participation 'in an otherwise segregated city' (Zabiliute, 2016: 273). They rehearse their fraught inclusion in the city by wandering through malls. In another striking example, Zyskowski (2020) documents how attending a basic computer training center teaches young Muslim women to aspire for fantasy IT futures in a job market that is hostile to Muslim female bodies. The very impossibility of the dream spurs frantic affective labors. As Lukose (2009: 3) reminds, those on the margins of capitalist articulations are yet 'fully formed by its structures of aspiration and opportunity'. Scholarship on affective labor tends to focus on self-making work that is oriented toward but cannot be reduced to wages, but as the next section explains, it has long been central to middle-class formation.

The massification of the middle class in liberalizing India has generated much debate, with markets aggressively targeting imaginary numbers rather than real population groups (Searle, 2016) and scholars debating the numbers of the real middle class versus those aspiring to be middle class (Kapur & Vaishnav, 2014). While markets and scholars in India struggle to quantify the middle class to predict trends and profits, citizens leverage affective rather than economic resources to claim middle-classness. If aspirational self-making and affective labor are key characteristics of becoming middle class, objective indicators such as income are necessary but insufficient to explain middle-class formation.

The Affective Labors of the Middle Classes

In the pre-liberalization decades, the middle class in India was relatively small but influential, organized around particular forms of cultural capital including English education and professional work. The dispositions accumulated in the body and misrecognized as respectability, and therefore accorded disproportionate opportunity, is what Bourdieu (1986) calls cultural capital. Rather than a straightforward exchange of affective labor for economic profit, the labors of the middle classes are routed through cultural capital to define debates surrounding the distribution of resources and opportunities. With the liberalization of the economy, the Indian middle class was massified, diversified and fragmented, and earlier routes of social mobility were unsettled.

Historically, the 'middle class' was not an income category but a social group that had an ambiguous relation to capital and processes of production and therefore competed internally for distinction and externally for moral legitimacy (Fernandes & Heller, 2006; Liechty, 2003). The social groups comprising the middle class are not merely sellers of labor (laborers) or owners of capital (capitalist elite) but are simultaneously sellers of labor and owners of cultural capital who have to market their skills, services and accomplishments in the capitalist 'free' market. This makes cultural-moral-affective work central to middle-class production. Gyan Pandey (2009: 323) explains:

> The ideal society would be a society in which no one had the benefit of aristocratic wealth or the afflictions of inherited poverty. The emergence and strength of the middle-classes appeared to be the measure of human equality, of the possibility of self-fashioning, of individual achievement and capability—the very signs of the modern. It is merit, not inherited wealth or sectional loyalty or networks, that counts in the making of the middle-class world, we are told. It is improvement, and self-improvement, through education and moral reform, individual effort, and sheer determination that brings advancement for society, family, and individual.

In an insightful example, Ajantha Subramanian (2019) explains how the Tamil Brahmins, a privileged caste group, transformed itself into a middle-class group. Central to this story is their pursuit of higher education, subsequent professional employment and self-narratives about education, merit and distinction. English-medium schooling, family networks of professionals and histories of government employment mediated their disproportionate access to premier state-funded higher educational institutions such as the Indian Institute of Technology (IIT) (Subramanian, 2019). The cultural capital that accrues from an IIT degree is convertible into spectacular economic capital in the form of fantasy salaries (Henry & Ferry, 2017). But their 'characterization as a middle-class fighting with only one weapon—education—disregards the long and multifaceted history of Tamil Brahmin capital encompassing ritual authority, land ownership, and state employment' (Subramanian, 2019: 226).

As alluded to in the IIT example, English education and its links to higher education and professional work has been a constitutive element of middle-class formation in India. Since the era of British colonialism, English has been a central vehicle for achieving economic security and social recognition, but colonial and later national educational policies reserved English-medium schooling and subsequent higher education for privileged groups (Ramanathan, 2005). After independence, English became the primary language in the expanding realms of academic work, science and technology, and intellectual and management activities. The initiation of federal state-funded English-medium schooling systems such as Kendriya and Navodaya Vidyalayas for diverse and even contesting groups of elites consolidated and expanded their privileges (Nambissan & Batra, 1989; Rajan, 1992). Ramanathan (2005: 112) explains that English-medium students could '*assume* that the system will work for them' not just because all prestigious disciplines at the postsecondary level were taught in English but also since the 'thought structures' of institutions were aligned with their 'cultural models'. Non-English-medium students faced cultural alienation and academic marginalization (Faust & Nagar, 2001) that accrued as a 'backwardness of mind' requiring reform and correction. Critiquing the 'double standards' of education policy that valorized mother tongue medium education for the 'masses' while facilitating English education for the children of elites, Naik (1997: 86) writes that 'in the philosophy of our elite', mother tongue education is the 'best education for other people's children'.

It is with the liberalization of the economy that these enduring pathways of middle-class formation came undone. Previous pedagogies of middle-class culture were typically unavailable to class others. But now, the sites where one can learn to become middle class have proliferated: coaching institutions, basic computer classes, Spoken English classes, calling customer care, learning to use a cellphone, viewing films, wandering in malls, working retail jobs, all of these offer lessons in middle-class culture. At the same time, the more formal institution that defined the Indian middle class – English education – has escaped from elite schools to all consumer segments.

For non-elites, the possibility of abstraction from stigmatized caste and gender locations through new consumption practices has profound significance. As Kapur *et al.* (2010) report from their survey among Dalits (former untouchable castes) in North India, new grooming, eating and ceremonial consumption practices have become commonplace and discriminatory processes that stigmatized Dalits have eroded considerably. Meanwhile, Heyer (2015) notes that Dalit women are increasingly retreating from stigmatized wage labor to 'become housewives'. Claims to middle-classness are now made from previously unlikely caste locations.

This also brings us to the profoundly gendered nature of middle-class formation. Feminist work has elaborated how respectable femininity is central to becoming middle class (Skeggs, 1997). For women in India, respectability is defined around their ability to protect and nurture the domestic space and structured around the upper-caste home and its preoccupations with child crafting, endogamy and upholding male superiority (Devika, 2008; Donner, 2008; Krishnan, 2014). Lower-caste women have historically engaged in waged work and were seen as 'unable' to adequately nurture the home. Newer forms of patriarchy emergent in the context of liberalization oblige upper-caste women to work but in class-segregated, respectable professions (Amrute, 2016; Radhakrishnan, 2011) even as lower-caste women reorient themselves toward the home rather than stigmatized workplaces (Heyer, 2015). Since scholarship on affective labor continues to be oriented toward participation in waged work, the implications of shifting gender formations for education have been largely ignored. The few that foreground education focus on elite women's parenting struggles in hyper-competitive contexts (Donner, 2006; for China, see Anagnost, 2008; Kuan, 2015). Similar inquiries into non-elite women's affective labors are scarce (for an exception, see Jakimow, 2016), especially the ways in which their aspirations and work intersect with language education.

From the Middle Classes to the Middle Class

With liberalization, the middle class in India became diverse and fragmented. The more privileged among the new middle classes, whom Leela Fernandes and Patrick Heller (2006) call the hegemonic fraction, found that their natural order of dominance had been disrupted. To continue to consolidate privilege, the privileged fraction had to establish new meanings. Amita Baviskar and Raka Ray (2011: 7) explain that the 'power of the middle-class' resides in their ability to conjure up 'a universal, unifying identity that summons up legitimacy for projects that favor elites'. The hegemonic fraction becomes the ruling bloc by 'translating relations of domination into the language of legitimation', that is, by transmuting elite interests into national agendas. It is through these processes that the diverse and fragmented middle classes of liberalizing India are transformed into a discursively coherent middle class.

To illustrate, I go back to the IIT example. Subramanian (2019) notes how the rise of the coaching industry made the IITs accessible to new social groups such as the Kammas, a non-Brahmin but dominant, landowning community. Meanwhile, with the reservation of seats for historically marginalized communities extended beyond the Scheduled Castes and Tribes to the Other Backward Classes in 2006, the opportunity structure offered by the IITs was redefined. Faced with eroding opportunities, Tamil Brahmins reworked definitions of merit to create new hierarchies between boutique and mass coaching, with the Kammas relegated to the mass category. Alongside, ranks in the hyper-competitive entry exams (IIT-JEE rank) were inserted into exit opportunities (job offers) to distinguish privileged groups from those entering the IITs through lesser-ranked, affirmation action quotas. That is, Kammas, who gain entry to the IIT through factory like coaching institutions, and historically marginalized groups who are admitted through reserved quotas do not really represent the exceptionally meritorious student that the IIT is assumed to admit and train. Older hierarchies were reclaimed anew as privileged groups worked frantically to redefine the meanings of actions in ways that legitimized their agendas and resources. The boundaries of the hegemonic fraction of the middle class were thus reassembled to distinguish them from the 'aspirers'.

In many domains, this boundary work now relies on Western cosmopolitan cultural capital. Tuxen (2017: 91) explains cosmopolitan cultural capital as the 'bodily and mental predispositions and competencies which allow individuals to engage confidently in globalizing social arenas'. In postcolonial schooling spaces, Western cosmopolitan cultural capital has retained its unambiguous dominance over other formations including Asian cosmopolitanism (Tanu, 2017). English fluency is of course a constitutive element of Western cosmopolitan cultural capital, but much more is layered onto language proficiency. 'Fluencies in the vocabularies and civilities of global technocratic cultures' include interactional styles (brainstorming), familiarity with Western pop-culture, transnational social networks, expressive verbalization and experimental hobbies (Irani, 2019: 89).

Desirable self-making increasingly requires transnational resources, and this is mirrored in the educational landscape. In comparison to the forced austerity of earlier nationalist, elite schooling (Srivastava, 1998), contemporary elite schooling is marked by an array of resource-intensive, exclusive activities including study abroad opportunities and spectacular theatrical performances (Rizvi, 2014; Sancho, 2015). But the intensification of material resources is folded into a premium on moral citizenship, including service competitions, projects about social issues and adoption of villages (Chacko, 2020; Chidsey, 2020). Service opportunities are exceptionally useful for elite projects of distinction on the transnational stage. Arathi Sriprakash, Jing Qi and Michael Singh (2017) explain that service, and its promise of (deferred) equality, teaches elite subjectivities such as benevolence, confidence and independence even as it documents these on CVs required for college applications in the US.

This resource-full, active and moral framework of elite education is posited as the properly ethical framework for all educational projects, and distinguished from conventional pedagogies, or rote, which has circulated far and wide with the democratization of schooling and coaching. Describing the performances of students enrolled at an elite school in the Western Indian city of Ahmedabad, Lilly Irani (2019: 58) documents how schooling and mothering organized around rote pedagogies are presented as a 'mass alienation machine' that operates through 'the routine, the mechanical, the repetitive, the unemotional, the uncreative'. Rather than subjection to the time and bodily discipline of an earlier idiom of middle-class achievement, children now have to be trained in naturalized, interactive, cosmopolitan English cultures. In the world of international schooling, rote is conclusively inimical to creative, genuine, deep learning. Meanwhile, extending 'deficiencies' in teaching-learning methods into judgments about character, students at an elite school in Hyderabad distinguish themselves from those enrolled in lower-fee-charging schools through the binary of rote and exposure. Gilbertson (2016: 308) writes:

Nandini suggests that those who do not have communication skills and the ability to mingle have a lack of exposure and an inability to think for themselves. This lack is presented as something that just happens rather than as indicative of durable inequalities that ensure that the odds are stacked in favor of upper-class students. The problem is the character of the disadvantaged, who choose not to participate, who, through their own closed mindedness, fail to seize opportunities that are open to them.

Non-elite discomfort in interacting with wealthier counterparts and inhabiting affluent social spaces is thus articulated as 'shyness', which easily slips into judgments about their interactional skills as well as their intellectual ability and moral worth. Thus, the diverse middle classes are reduced into the properly moral middle class through discourses about moral-pedagogic hierarchies that legitimize their economic resources.

While sociologists and anthropologists of education have provided us with insights about the strategies pursued by the middle class to reclaim and consolidate privilege, this scholarship has largely skirted policy and subject-specific pedagogic analysis. Meanwhile, critical analysis of policy and pedagogy tends to focus on educational provisioning for non-elites. To put it bluntly, research has not adequately examined the ways in which policy and pedagogy, and even critical education research, dovetails with middle-class strategies of distinction. The book explicates how well-intentioned, critical language interventions inadvertently drive national policies and pedagogic standards in ways that legitimize the resources of the privileged middle class.

Prescriptive Moralities and Illiberalism

Since there is substantive scholarship on the phenomena described in this book, this section reviews existing research on non-elite English schooling and explicates the contributions made to this body of work. Private schooling has historically been an elite phenomenon, and its recent democratization has animated development scholars, who enthusiastically look to the private sector to meet development goals. A few clarifications are needed. Much of this literature uses the term 'low-fee' or 'low-cost' to indicate historic shifts in the private sector from elite to non-elite provisioning. But low-cost private schooling is not experienced by the non-elites who patronize them as low cost. Therefore, I use the term non-elite private schooling. Additionally, the phenomenon itself is largely a primary school level (Grades 1–4) expansion.

Debates about non-elite private schooling in India (low-fee private schooling) have chiefly been between development economists and critical education scholars. The primary bone of contention is this: is the efficient market or the redistributive state the ideal, desirable provider of education? The moral tenor of this debate has invisibilized other urgent questions, including those pertaining to English language pedagogy. Furthermore, the aspirational mobilities that emerged in the context of liberalization are a blind spot for both. While development economist research mimics what good consumers *should* do – compare and calculate the utility of various offerings in the market – critical scholars emphasize what democratically oriented citizens *should* do: recognize market engendered subjectivities as detrimental to the social aims of education. Neither explores the ethical-moral imperatives that drive non-elite mothers' consumer practices.

I will begin by tracing scholars' discovery of the phenomenon of non-elite private schooling. Net enrollment in primary schooling in India increased from around 77% in 1990 (UNESCO, 2017) to near universal enrollment in 2014–2015 (MHRD, 2016). Crucially, a substantive segment of the universalization of primary education transpired in the private sector. In 2014–2015, 49% of primary school-going children in urban India and 21% of their rural counterparts attended fee-charging private schools (Kingdon, 2017). Early research had to struggle to establish the phenomenon as significant since private schooling immediately conjured up the image of elite, high-fee-charging public schools in the British model.

This basic, foundational work was fraught with difficulties. Statistics collected by the education department was grossly unreliable, and researchers turned to large-scale household surveys such as the National Sample Survey (NSS), the National Council of Applied Economic Research Survey (NCAER), and later, the India Human Development Survey (IHDS) designed by the NCAER in collaboration with the University of Maryland to calculate the size and nature of non-elite private schooling (Desai *et al.*, 2008; Kingdon, 1996a). Where school-level information was required, researchers conducted their own census surveys, especially in order to include unrecognized private schools that are not enumerated by the government (De *et al.*, 2003; Kingdon, 1996b; Muralidharan & Kremmer, 2006; Tooley *et al.*, 2007). This trajectory eventually culminated in the yearly Annual Status of Education Report (ASER) surveys, initiated from 2005 onward. ASER is a rural household survey that not just collects information about school enrollment and household assets but also tests children in each household to generate data on academic proficiency.

Since much of the early research was undertaken by development economists, they computed the relative efficiency of public and private educational provision, focusing on correlations between inputs and outputs. Though 'school achievement is a complex area where school input combines with parental support and the willingness/aptitude of the individual child' (De *et al.*, 2003: 5232), school quality, defined by some outcome of schooling, was computed on the basis of 'inputs into the education process such as students' characteristics, their home backgrounds, and school and teacher variables' (Kingdon, 1996b: 3). On school-based inputs including building and infrastructure availability and maintenance; facilities such as toilets, drinking water and fans; and teacher presence and teaching activity (De et al., 2003; PROBE, 1999; Tooley et al., 2007), low-cost private schools were found to be relatively better than government schools. In addition, parents too are documented as highlighting the appalling state of state-funded schooling to explain their preference for private schooling (De et al., 2003; Muralidharan & Kremmer, 2006; Srivastava, 2007).

Meanwhile, researchers consistently considered home-based inputs as equally or perhaps even more significant variables for schooling success (Desai et al., 2008; Kingdon, 1996b). Proxies for home inputs include household assets, number of books at home, mothers' education, homework help at home, private tuition, caste, religion, number of siblings, gender of siblings and distance from school (Kingdon, 1996b). As for outputs, the consensus among economists and development scholars has been student learning proficiency as defined by standardized tests (Desai et al., 2008; Kingdon, 1996b; Muralidharan, 2013). The definition of standards – what counts as English proficiency, for whom, and how this intersects with pedagogic methods – is left unexamined. Expanding outputs beyond standardized tests to socioeconomic relations, Srivastava (2007) notes low-fee private schooling as producing new kinds of financial negotiations between parents and education providers. In her account, however, the pedagogic-social is reduced to the financial.

The more reductive strands of economic research shrink efficiency to cost efficiency and, to compare relative cost of provision, they disregard the social and cultural capital of the home and focus singularly on school-based economic inputs, specifically, teacher salaries (Kingdon, 1996b; Tooley et al., 2007). In particular, they note the salaries of state-funded schoolteachers as irrationally high, and laud the minimal wages private schools give their teachers as the hallmark of efficiency. In their corrective, Bhatty et al. (2015) note that state-funded schoolteachers are remunerated on four to five scales, and the top scale is a civil service post that has salaries comparable with other civil service positions. However, a large section of state-funded schoolteachers do not fall in this category and are paid like their private school counterparts.

A significant landmark within the efficiency framework is the Andhra Pradesh School Choice Research, a randomized control trial undertaken by a Harvard education economist in collaboration with the Azim Premji Foundation (APF, 2013; Karopady, 2014). Here, rather than controlling for student home backgrounds statistically, a treatment and control group was devised empirically over 180 villages. While children in the treatment village were given scholarships to attend a low-fee private school of their choice, the children in the control village were not. In addition, within the treatment villages, those who applied for but were not awarded scholarships and non-applicants from government and private schools formed other comparable groups. While the ethical implications of such provisioning are debatable, here too, quality was defined by student outcomes on standardized tests. The study concludes that only students who would have attended private school regardless of scholarship did better in tests. That is, home background was identified as more significant than school-based inputs in accessing education and doing well at school. Interestingly, the Andhra Pradesh School Choice Project notes with surprise that parental satisfaction is based on 'soft factors' such as uniforms, discipline, attendance and relative social standing rather than on the purely pedagogic as defined by standardized test scores (APF, 2013). The study had isolated the pedagogic out of its aspirational context.

Meanwhile, critical educationists and sociologists of education argue that frameworks of and advocacy for efficiency are themselves rooted within a neoliberal market logic that prioritizes the economics of minimalist provision over pedagogic concerns (Kumar, 2010; Nambissan, 2011; Nambissan & Ball, 2010; Sarangapani & Winch, 2010). Foregrounding the complexity of the pedagogic and situating it within specific political economies, Sarangapani's (2018) and Jain's (2018) census like surveys in Hyderabad and Delhi complicate the distinctions between state-funded and private schools empirically and conceptually. School-based inputs are expanded beyond the infrastructural to include processual accounts of the pedagogic including school expectations regarding learning, home-school relationships, teaching learning methods and techniques of discipline. Further, rather than a public-private distinction in terms of management, schools are classified according to management ethos, aims of education and pedagogic styles, that is, data are linked to social experiences of *poverty* rather than to school type (public and private).

In Hyderabad, schools that catered to the poorest, whether they be state-funded (50%), or private (aided, unaided, unrecognized) (20%), were found to be poorly maintained. Pedagogy is similarly related to the social class of the clientele rather than the management type of the school. Coming to outputs, Sarangapani and Jain (2018: 224) differentiate between basic literacy, rote-based reproduction, drill-based reproduction, textbook learning with understanding, conceptual learning of math and science with emphasis on skill and accuracy, all round development and proficiency in religious values. It is important to note that though their outcomes take into account dominant socioacademic expectations, for instance, the valorization of science and math, they do not engage with consumption-inflected, non-elite aspirations for status and recognition of the kind documented by the Andhra Pradesh School Choice Project. Nevertheless, the processual, embedded conceptualization of inputs and outputs makes the computation of relative cost-effectiveness and ascription of causality challenging, which is perhaps what is intended.

Despite their differences, economic and critical perspectives and their respective pedagogic expectations elide how parents subject themselves to aspiration and, thereby, reanimate social processes. While development scholars diminish parental negotiation of shifting educational landscapes into rational economic choices or standardized test scores, critical scholars reduce parental life worlds into false consciousness about marginalization. Though Sarangapani's (2018: 188) account presents a much more nuanced account of the emerging schooling landscape in Hyderabad, her reduction of non-elite pedagogic experiences into techniques of governance erases non-elite ethical-political projects. For instance, she writes that the pedagogy of the poor, rote, teaches marginalized children to conform, be obedient and be controlled. In doing so, she reduces learning to technologies of domestication.

Consequently, the contesting perspectives seek to correct and reform parental 'lacks'. Development scholars advocate for accreditation services that bridge the 'information gap' between standardized tests and school-based tests since parents don't seem to understand or value what standardized tests measure (Tooley & Dixon, 2003). Meanwhile, critical perspectives too seek to educate parents in ways that help them understand the real meaning of education, which will reorient them away from 'commonsense' quality and aspirations that are 'heavily influenced by dominant value systems' (PROBE, 1999: 26). Education research has thus become a 'politically prescriptive project' that offers diagnosis of issues and prescriptions for change and, in the process, forecloses comprehension of the forms of life it so passionately wants to remake (Mahmood, 2005: 198).

Educational policy and pedagogy in its idealist socialist imagination has been the preserve of the academic Left, and they are now called on to defend this imagination against marketization and privatization. They do so by locating ethical-moral pedagogy and aspiration outside the sphere of the market, engendering a prescriptive moral politics and illiberalism that has disastrous effects for non-elites. The last section elaborates this market-moral divide.

Markets and Morality

The concept of a moral economy is typically traced to EP Thomson, particularly his 1971 article titled 'The Moral Economy of the English Crowd in the Eighteenth Century'. In this article, Thompson examined how the poor, pre-market English crowd of the 18th century rebelled against an amoral market economy. This approach tends to posit the moral economy as antithetical to a market economy (Arnold, 2001). That is, morality is assumed to lie outside the sphere of the market.

As Andrea Muehlebach (2012) explains, this split between the market and the moral is fundamental to liberalism. The (masculine) liberal subject was understood to be a split subject, who was the rational actor required for economic activity in the public sphere and the compassionate but stern family man who upheld values in the private sphere. This split between the economic and the affective/moral is constitutive of the political philosophy of liberalism. However, the split between the public and the private, between the rational economic and the affective moral, has become untenable under contemporary capitalism. Earlier distinctions have come undone as newer work and consumer practices require passionate labor across public-private divides. While this has led to an 'affective turn' in critical scholarship, to find the analytic tools necessary to explain the affective turn of the market, the significance of morality has been less explored.

The book explains how moralities are a scaffolding frame that defines meaning, value and hierarchy in the educational market. First, the assembling of ethical-moral learning opportunities demand increased market participation as every aspect of learning is commodified but differently for different consumer segments. Second, new standards 'humanize' the allegedly immoral educational market through moralities that denigrate rote, but these legitimize economic privilege as humanizing pedagogy. Inequality is *managed* through the production and circulation of moral norms (Ahmed, 2004). Third, parental aspirations and affective labors are evaluated, both by the self and others, on the basis of their ability to negotiate an expanding and intensifying educational market. The market is an unavoidable site for the enactment of ethical-moral claims.

With specific reference to English education, long-cherished ideals such as decolonization, which counter earlier dominant discourses of native supremacy and monolingualism, became new prescriptive moral norms that reproduced enduring inequalities. Braiding constructivism, active learning and decolonization under the rubric of natural acquisition, oral proficiency was posited as a humanizing pedagogy even though *literacy* rather than oracy is the more readily available local resource. This requirement of scarce (and enjoyable) resources translates privilege into ethical, moral registers. Like Jomon's children in the opening vignette, those who cannot afford expensive resources such as English-speaking instructors and glossy picture books also learn English (literacy) through more laborious methods, but their pedagogy and proficiency is rendered suspect. Equally important, their aspirations and labors are read as repulsive and even dangerous for an egalitarian democratic society. The book illustrates how this spawns a prescriptive moral politics. Furthermore, the book also explains how standards of English language proficiency are neither universal nor static but redefined in specific historic moments. But at the heart of these transformations is a story of desire, that of non-elite mothers for their children.

An interdisciplinary book such as this will be of interest to scholars from diverse disciplines, and I will briefly map the chapters by discipline before introducing them. Chapters 3 and 6 present a detailed analysis of mothering and the intersections of gender, class and caste in liberalizing India. These draw from and contribute to anthropological and sociological theory and South Asia Studies. Chapters 4, 5 and 7 present the classroom ethnographies and analyze English language pedagogy. They are rooted in TESOL (Teaching English to Speakers of Other Languages), applied linguistic and sociolinguistic scholarship. While these chapters explain policy implementation, critical scholars of language policy will also find detailed accounts of policy production in Chapter 8. The historical formations that direct contemporary policy production is elaborated in Chapter 2, which details localized colonial, postcolonial and communist histories and its intersections with language policy.

Chapter Outlines

Chapter 2 traces English-vernacular hierarchies from 1894 to 2014 in the fieldwork site as diversely positioned residents negotiated localized center-periphery relations. Their efforts were governed by the regional state, which during the colonial period was the princely state of Travancore and during the postindependence period is the state of Kerala. The chapter traces how governing mechanisms instituted by the colonial state (modernity) and the postcolonial state (development) were translated into concrete institutions and educational opportunity. That the Communist Party has been the ruling party in Kerala has profound implications; they loudly oppose the neoliberalization of the contemporary. This opposition takes on specific pedagogic forms as described in later chapters. The historical and methods chapter also introduces the primary ethnographic sites – a failing state-funded Malayalam-medium school and a neighboring non-elite private English-medium school. The schools are located in Pathanamthitta, the district with the highest percentage of 'uneconomic' or 'failing' state-funded Malayalam-medium schools in Kerala. To set up the analysis that follows, the chapter also delineates the state and market agencies that support and govern English pedagogy and the methods of data collection employed to understand English language pedagogy.

Chapters 3 and 6 tell two related stories of aspiration that emerge out of the transitions of liberalization. At the English-medium school, mothers had migrated from the hardships of a subsistence economy to the relative ease of a new consumer society. Those left out of this temporal migration, all former slave castes (Dalits), were congregated at the Malayalam-medium school. If at the English-medium school, the radical experiences of mobility prompted mothers to pursue English education for their children in order to become 'good mothers', Dalit mothers at the Malayalam-medium school turned to education to manage despair. Unlike Tamil Brahmins in Ajantha Subramanian's (2019) study who *claim* to only have education at their disposal, the obsessive hopes and punishing love of Dalit mothers at the uneconomic Malayalam-medium school illuminate what happens when education is the only way out of intergenerational poverty.

The latter halves of the chapters analyze how the dominant fraction of the middle classes responds to and manages non-elite aspirations. Educators' as well as policy accounts mobilize the figure of the bad (subsistence) consumer and the animalized (non-elite) child to delegitimize non-elite mothers' aspirations. The bad consumer mistakes immediate social recognition rather than pedagogic proficiency and subsequent social recognition as the core utility of education. This dovetails with rote pedagogies, which allegedly animalize children. Together, these discourses dismantle the ethical claims of non-elites.

Chapters 4, 5 and 7 expand the moral compass of educational aspiration to focus on pedagogic labor. Specifically, Chapters 4 and 7 focus on the pedagogic labor of English users, that is, mothers, schoolteachers and after-school tuition teachers who can read and write but not speak English. Their pedagogic labors and literacy practices, commonly glossed as rote, taught young children reading readiness and trained them to struggle toward academic literacy in deprived circumstances. Meanwhile, English reforms equated proficiency and pedagogy with oracy rather than literacy and normalized English speakers as potentially competent, and English users as already-always lacking.

Chapter 5 shifts the focus to the pedagogic labor required to teach oracy in what Tickoo (1990, 1995) calls an acquisition-poor environment. Examining the Spoken English class I taught at the non-elite private school, I analyze the extensive resources and enterprising labor I expended and the outcomes these produced. I suggest that what I taught students was the verbalization of personalized, individualized opinions and feelings on request. Though rote laid the foundational proficiencies for my enterprise pedagogy, education reforms defined communication skills around the negation of rote.

The last data chapter complements the pedagogic analysis offered in earlier chapters with an analysis of the political contexts and policy processes that constitute education reforms. It explains how differing assumptions and objectives converged to promote oracy as properly ethical-moral English pedagogy and proficiency. The three English reforms that governed classroom English learning at the two school sites were the 1988–1997 central board (CBSE) reforms, the 2005 national (NCERT) reforms and the 1997–2014 Kerala English reforms. The Kerala English reforms were undertaken by a communist state struggling to rearticulate socialist democracy, in particular, through schooling reforms. Sustained funding assembled a tight-knit cadre of English-speaking, activist professionals, who offered participative, expressive citizenship as the alternative to consumer citizenship and the privatization of primary education. Their pedagogic reforms mandated oracy (in English) in primary classes as the pedagogic route to build a socialist democratic society. The NCERT (National Council of Educational Research and Training) reforms too had activist aspirations but were caught up in institutional structures that served middle-class interests. The contradictions fragmented and trivialized pedagogy, but reformers expected oral interaction to bring it into coherence. Diverging from its activist counterparts, the CBSE (Central Board of Secondary Education) sought to make domestic social interaction amenable to transnational standards. The most obvious modality of commensurability was proficiency in English-speaking skills. The unlikely convergence of activism and transnationalism thus assembled the conditions under which interaction became pedagogic commonsense even though literacy rather than oracy is the most readily available local resource.

The concluding chapter explores the concept of linguistic imperialism from below as it revisits how English aspiration unfolds in a new consumer society. Shifts in political economy have upturned value, meaning and politics. In fact, the moral debates around aspiration and pedagogy alert us to the contradictory shape of politics in the contemporary political economic context. Non-elite discontent manifests as aspiration rather than as resistance, and it assembles domination. While British imperialism is no more, the empire of English has extended beyond borders, history and diversity to produce new inequalities and subjugations. 'Critical' pedagogues urge non-elites to pursue ethical but vernacular futures. When ethical-moral action is defined through market participation, privileged groups discursively place morality outside (lower income segments of) the market. At the intersections of aspiration, labor and morality, the dominations of English are produced anew as learners, teachers and policymakers go about their everyday lives.

Notes

(1) For new exceptions, see Dey's (2019) analysis of the Andhra Pradesh government's promise to provide English-medium instruction in state-funded primary schools.
(2) An outreach emergency phone service for children in need of care and protection.

2 Development and its Afterlives

This chapter introduces histories of development and education in the fieldwork region in order to situate contemporary non-elite aspirations for English schooling in longer desires for progress and dignity. The southern Indian state of Kerala has an unusual relationship with development, both in terms of how it fared on modernization efforts and the zeal with which such efforts were measured and articulated. The construction of Kerala as a development model is typically traced to a 1975 United Nations report that presented for Kerala high levels of literacy and life expectancy along with low levels of fertility and mortality, achieved on unusually low levels of per capita income (Dreze & Sen, 2002; Tharamangalam, 2006). Within the polarized discourses at the time, of whether capitalist industrialization or socialist centralized planning was the preferred path toward equitable development, Kerala's development profile acquired international prominence. Parayil and Sreekumar (2003: 469) note that the initial scholarly response to Kerala's development indicators 'was of admiration or bewilderment'. The Kerala model of development, as it later came to be called, presented an alternative to rapid capitalist industrialization and socialist revolution since neither had been determinant factors for its development experience. They add that 'optimistic assessments of the Kerala model' have to be understood 'in the historical conjecture where a stalemate on future path of development in Third World countries became the central theme of development debate' (2003: 470).

While narratives of 'exceptional' development have overdetermined how Kerala is read transnationally, critical development scholars explain that this exceptionalism was one, the ability to appropriate dominant notions of development like European modernity, and two, generative of new caste and gender discriminations. This chapter traces the unfolding of these contradictions across the English-vernacular divide in the fieldwork region.

Fieldwork was conducted in 2013–2014 in a village in Pathanamthitta, the district with the highest percent of failing Malayalam-medium schools. I call this village Edanadu.[1] Since the district of Pathanamthitta was formed only in 1982, the chapter traces histories of a north western taluk in the district, Thiruvalla. It is important to note Thiruvalla's proximity

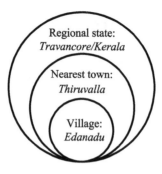

Figure 2.1 Relational geographies of the fieldwork region

to Kottayam, where the Church Missionary Society (CMS) had established the first college in the princely state of Travancore in 1817. The expansion of modern schooling in Thiruvalla owed much to its proximity to the CMS. Villagers in Edanadu organized their schooling in close relationship with the events unfolding in Thiruvalla town. Figure 2.1 shows this layered geography of desire.

Figure 2.2 and the sections that follow elaborate how the relationships between the village, town and the state unfolded through educational desire.

Colonial Modernity, Socioreligious Reform and the Expansion of Modern Schooling

The oldest modern school established in Thiruvalla is the Thulakasherry English Middle School. It was established in 1848 by the CMS through the efforts of Rev. Hawksworth.

The CMS had come to the south of India to reform native Christianity which professed ties to the Syriac tradition. Vlad Naumescu (2019) writes that the colonial missionary encounter with Syrian Christians in Kerala was a work of purification, aimed to 'purge their faith of all false beliefs, fetishes, and idolatrous customs of Hindu and Catholic origin that tarred it'. Even if it was 'an ancient Christian community', it was only through purification of rites that the Syrian Christians could be taught to 'rediscover their true Oriental roots and create a modern, rationalized faith' (2019: 396–397). Unlike in the allegedly 'secular' contemporary, where the religious is notionally separated out from the state and civil society, these were intricately entangled for the colonial state (which listened to Christian missionaries), the princely state of Travancore (which employed only high-caste Hindus in prominent administrative positions) and communities (for whom social reform was inseparable from religious mobilization).

School reports available at the Thulakasherry School, Thiruvalla, include missionary letters, and one such letter by Rev Andrews notes that that six of the children who attended school in 1889 came from 'chief'

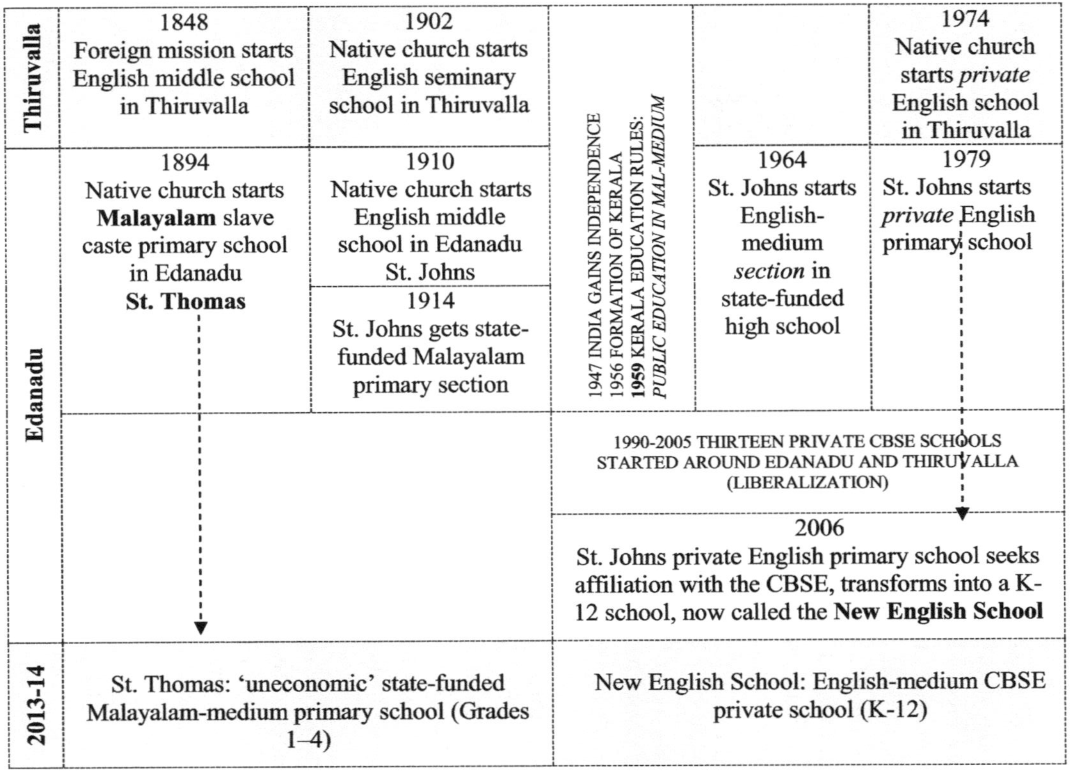

	Thiruvalla	Edanadu	2013-14
1848	Foreign mission starts English middle school in Thiruvalla		
1894	Native church starts **Malayalam** slave caste primary school in Edanadu **St. Thomas**		
1902	Native church starts English seminary school in Thiruvalla		
1910		Native church starts English middle school in Edanadu St. Johns	
1914		St. Johns gets state-funded Malayalam primary section	
1947 INDIA GAINS INDEPENDENCE			
1956 FORMATION OF KERALA			
1959 KERALA EDUCATION RULES: *PUBLIC EDUCATION IN MAL-MEDIUM*			
1964		St. Johns starts English-medium *section* in state-funded high school	
1974	Native church starts *private* English school in Thiruvalla		
1979		St. Johns starts *private* English primary school	
1990-2005 THIRTEEN PRIVATE CBSE SCHOOLS STARTED AROUND EDANADU AND THIRUVALLA (LIBERALIZATION)			
2006		St. Johns private English primary school seeks affiliation with the CBSE, transforms into a K-12 school, now called the **New English School**	
2013-14			St. Thomas: 'uneconomic' state-funded Malayalam-medium primary school (Grades 1–4); New English School: English-medium CBSE private school (K-12)

Figure 2.2 Relational timelines of the school sites: St. Thomas and the New English School

Syrian families and that most of the slaves attending school belonged to 'these masters'. The principal of the CMS Thulakasherry School during 2013 explained that the English middle school was converted into a Malayalam middle school in 1893 to focus more carefully on the education of the depressed classes, the colonial English term for slave castes. The Malayalam term in use, especially in slave title deeds was *adimakal* (slaves), but school reports use *sadhujanangal*, a literal translation of depressed classes. The Thulakasherry School's conversion from English to Malayalam is the only instance in the region of a decision taken at the school level which foregrounded the welfare of the most marginalized *over* that of the dominant groups. The more common practice was the establishment of separate English middle or high schools for dominant castes and Malayalam primary schools for the slave castes.

Influenced by the reformations advocated by the CMS, the native Evangelical Church established several Malayalam lower primary schools for slave castes in and around Thiruvalla and one English seminary school for upper castes in the town proper. Local parishes such as the one in Edanadu established Malayalam schools for upper castes in their parish region. The 1908 annual report of the Evangelical Church describes the educational project among the slave castes during the early 1900s. The report describes that as slave castes were expected to work, not attend school or study, they were kept busy at work during harvest season and starved through the other seasons. The annual report suggests that if schooling had to take root among depressed classes [*sadhujanangal*], there must be some provision for food and clothing.

The 1911 annual report of the Evangelical Church reports with sorrow [*sangatakaramayi*] that lower-caste students are disallowed from enrolling in higher classes. Lower primary schools received grant-in-aid from the Travancore government, but middle and high schools were financed through tuition fees and church funds, which were beyond the purview of the slave castes. Unable to enroll for higher studies, lower-caste learners eventually gave up on schooling. Evangelical work with the slave castes focused on functional literacy that would enable them to read the scriptures in translation.

It is important to note that evangelical literacy also engendered new resources through which the slave castes could refashion their social selves. The case of Prathyaksha Raksha Daiva Sabha (PRDS), a religious-political movement that emerged near Thiruvalla, is instructive. Sanal Mohan (2005) notes that the PRDS folded Dalit experience of slavery into colonial modernity to project new social possibilities. The founder of PRDS, Yohannan,[2] integrated the local cultural world of the slaves into the Christian life-world, particularly that of the liberation of Hebrew slaves from the Pharaoh of Egypt, to actively imagine liberation from slavery. While Christian churches continued caste-based segregations between the privileged Syrians and slave castes, the PRDS critiqued these hierarchies through Christianized content (egalitarianism) and form (spiritual awakening). However, though spiritual awakening allowed slave castes to imagine a life of freedom, they continued to face acute discrimination from dominant castes. Even as late as 1942–1943, the Evangelical Church annual report laments that Christian parishioners practice slavery and do not look kindly on their slaves attending Christian schools.

Meanwhile, for dominant castes, school education especially English education opened up the world of salaried employment in the government bureaucracy or prominent positions in the Evangelical Church hierarchy. The Seminary School was established in 1902 by the Evangelical Church to prepare upper-caste Christians for seminary study and the matriculation exam. The primary justification for English study was religious, but, in practice, the justifications were expansive enough to include caste and class counterparts (Hindu Nairs and Ezhavas) but not religious counterparts (Christian slave castes). Slave castes were actively discouraged from enrolling at the seminary school for post-primary education even though they were actively pursued at the primary level.

According to the 1908 annual report of the Evangelical Church, 18 students from the Seminary School, Thiruvalla, sat for the matriculation exam in 1908, but only one passed. By 1916–1917, of the 40 students who sat for the English Secondary School Leaving Certificate exam, 19 became eligible for college study and 'most of the others' became eligible for government employment. Further, in 1916–1917, a Nair student from the Seminary School came first in the Travancore English School Leaving Certificate exam. By 1940, total enrollment at the Seminary School was 579.[3] The sixth form (Grade 10) had 78 enrolled students of which 61 were sent for the school leaving exams. A total of 27 students passed. A 44% pass percent in the English School Leaving exam was no mean feat. This select minority went on to become professionals and prominent leaders both in the church and the administrative bureaucratic system of the colonial princely state.

The Slave School and the English School in Edanadu

The primary fieldwork sites of this book are two schools located about 10 kilometers from the town of Thiruvalla. I was allowed to conduct research at a failing state-funded Malayalam-medium primary school and a neighboring low-fee-charging English-medium school to which many families had migrated in the present generation. The Malayalam-medium primary school, which I call St. Thomas, and its elite English school counterpart St. Johns are products of the colonial period.

St. Thomas School was one of the slave caste schools established by the Thiruvalla Evangelical Church during the religious reformation of the 1890s. Situated on a hill as befitted a church, St. Thomas was both church and school for the slave castes, and the vicar doubled up as the headteacher. Dalit elders reminisce that the church was a thatched shed in its early decades and could have been one of the churches where the founder of PRDS, Yohannan, preached. In 2013, the school building stood separate from the church, but the cemetery view from classrooms reminded one of the religious beginnings of the school. St. Thomas School admission registers, available intermittently from 1914, reveal that new students enrolling into Class 1 at St. Thomas averaged around 28 from 1914 till the late 1980s, with only a few exceptional years where the enrollment fell to 11 (1929) or spiked to 51 (1916). Parental caste and family names from admission registers also reveal that Dalits and low-status upper castes – who had minimal land holdings and lived relatively proximate to Dalits – had historically patronized St. Thomas.

Most agricultural landowning upper castes in the school neighborhood had studied at St. Johns primary school in Malayalam-medium but segregated from lower castes. St. Johns is the pride of Edanadu. It was established in 1910 as an English middle school, and offered primary schooling in Malayalam from 1914. Three cousins, all parishioners of the Edanadu Evangelical Church, bought a two-acre plot in the center of the village [kavala] from two Ezhava brothers and set up the school. In keeping with the social milieu of the time, the parish priest of the Edanadu Evangelical Church was requested to head the educational trust that owned and managed the school. Four years later, they heard about the grant-in-aid policy of the Travancore government for lower primary schools and established a lower primary Malayalam school that came to be called the Grant School. The Grant School began getting three rupees annually as government aid. The English school ran on student fees.

By 1938, the middle school was upgraded to sixth form, the equivalent of 10th grade, and prepared students for the English School Leaving Exam. In 1952–1953, a total of 705 students paid an annual fee of Rs. 54 over the course of eight installments. A student from the early 50s remembers that families without paddy fields, who survived mostly on tapioca cultivation, wouldn't have paid any of the installments on time and would most likely have ended up paying fines for late payment. They survived on 'half-stomach meals [ara vayaru]' of tapioca and looked forward to weddings in the community to eat a full meal [kalyanathina nirachunu]. Cash was hard to come by. Food was scarce. In addition to the full-fee-paying families, 75 students paid 'half-fees' and 70 students from the Scheduled Castes were enrolled under a 'no fees' category. First form (Class 5) had two sections totaling 81 students. Second form had 92. Third form had three sections, of which one was for girls. Fourth form had three boys sections and two girls sections, with a total of 233 students in all. Fifth form had similar sections and numbers. The matriculation class, sixth form (Class 10), had one girls section with 51 girls and two boys sections with 50 boys each.

These local developments should be read in connection with what was happening in the princely state under colonial rule. That is, why would communities pursue English education so fervently in the early 1900s?

During the 1860s, in part to thwart the annexation threats of the British, Maharajah Ayilyam Tirunal and his Dewan Madhava Rao established a successful system of fee-paying government English and vernacular schools, linked the education in these schools to all government employment and, through this process, reorganized the administrative infrastructure of the state to mirror British systems.

After government employment became explicitly linked to educational certification, the Syrian Orthodox, Romo-Syrian, reformed Syrian protestant and Anglican churches started educational institutions of their own (Tharakan, 1984). Not to be left behind, the Nair Service Society took to establishing educational institutions, also partly to counter the decline upper-caste Nairs faced in a 'modern' society that found their matrilineal traditions archaic (Jeffrey, 1994). Meanwhile, the simultaneity of opportunity and discrimination propelled non-elite mobilizations. One prominent example is the anti-caste mobilization undertaken by the most populous untouchable caste group in southern Kerala, the Ezhavas. English-educated Ezhavas like Dr Palpu were barred from government employment despite eligibility (Panikkassery, 1970). Dr Palpu came together with the charismatic Hindu reformer Narayana Guru and acclaimed poet N. Kumaran Asan[4] to form the Sree Narayana Dharma Paripalana Yogam (SNDP) to promote the Ezhava cause. The SNDP not only encouraged Ezhavas to access education but also started educational institutions to enable access where denied (Tharakan, 1998).

It is important to note that while Ezhavas (former untouchable caste) are located as the 'starting point' from which the Kerala development narrative unfolds, Dalits (former slave castes) have been systematically excluded from the Kerala model of development (Thiranagama, 2019: 11). In the face of extreme hostility to any work that accrued benefits on the slave rather than the owner, missionary schools became a crucial space where slave castes reworked their social selves into devout and dignified bodies. The affordances of religious modernity were most acutely evident in the case of slave castes, but acute dispossession and discrimination disallowed the accrual of substantive benefits such as government employment or land ownership.

To summarize, modern schooling expanded in the region as diversely positioned individuals and communities negotiated colonial modernity to re-make themselves as civilized under colonial rule. The reorganization of economic, political and social life under colonialism proceeded such that the Travancore state, privileged communities such as Hindu Nairs and Syrian Christians, and former untouchable communities such as Ezhavas were able to garner and mobilize resources to generate favorable social locations for themselves. In particular, the transformation of an untouchable caste into a dominant, modern community lies at the core of what is now recognized as successful development. Alongside, caste hierarchies in relation to the slave castes were reworked in modern registers of inequality, including disproportionate access to schooling.

Independence, Development and Universalization of Schooling

As the struggle for independence gained momentum across the subcontinent, leading members of the Congress Socialist Party created their own particular brand of indigenous socialist communism in what is now the state of Kerala (Jeffrey, 1978). In 1937, four prominent Congress Socialists – P. Krishna Pillai, K. Damodaran, N.C. Sekhar and E.M.S. Namboodiripad (three Nairs and one Malayali Brahmin) – secretly joined the Communist Party of India (Nossiter, 1982). The strong support base the Communist Party generated for itself translated into electoral victory, and in the first elections held in Kerala in 1957, the Communist Party was elected into power and E.M.S. Namboodiripad became Kerala's first Chief Minister.

The social and economic changes the Communist Party attempted in its first tenure, particularly the 1957 Education Bill that universalized access to school education and the land reforms that benefited tenants and small landowners consolidated the new state's tryst with development. The allegedly radical land and education reforms, which also established Kerala's place as a model of egalitarian development in subsequent decades, were able to garner wide participation from different communities. But the reforms were aligned with the interests of the more privileged from among subjugated populations. The education reforms privileged the needs of educated and employed but beleaguered teachers rather than the aspirations of the 'uneducated' for equitable educational development (Lieten, 1977). The Kerala Education Rules 1959 legislated secure tenure and decent work conditions for teachers by shouldering the financial liability of all schools. The rules also ensured schooling access to all children by subsidizing tuition since the primary expense of teacher salary was now borne by the state. Similarly, in the land reforms, the 'peasant' was not the landless laborer but the tenant farmer facing eviction threats and unfair rents (Radhakrishnan, 1981).

Meanwhile, the inclusion of 'others' in the development experience was negotiated through the distribution of minimum entitlements, which nevertheless had immense symbolic significance, such as fragments of unproductive homestead land distributed to landless laborers or schooling access for students from marginalized communities. This uneven redistribution of resources was accompanied by rearrangements of power and culture that replaced traditional ways of performing caste hierarchies – derogatory treatment of lower castes, eating separately, untouchability or lack of social interaction among different castes – with new cultural performances that Communist leaders purported as radically egalitarian (Devika, 2010; Lindberg, 2001). Thus, older caste hierarchies were modernized and normalized into newer practices of inequality.

Responses to the Kerala Education Rules (KER) 1959 in Edanadu provide one example of such re-formations of inequality. The KER regularized all fee-charging schools, and the state took over schools' financial liabilities, specifically teacher salaries. This eliminated student fees. In return, St. Johns was forced to comply with state rules regarding teacher salary, tenure and conditions of work. Only the power to recruit teachers was retained by the school management. Furthermore, linguistic requirements in the KER obliged St. Johns to become a Malayalam-medium school. What had once been the pride of Edanadu became just another Malayalam school. But not for long. Five years later, in 1964, St. Johns opened a fee-charging English-medium section in fifth and eighth grades. Titus, now a doctor nearing retirement, was one of the 26 students who enrolled in the English-medium section of eighth grade in 1964. Titus remarked that the Rs. 50 non-installment, admission fee was a princely sum in those days and 'the English-medium section was not intended for a lot of people [*adhikam peru cheranda ennulla rithiyillayirunnu*]'.

The tensions around the founding of the Malankara School in Thiruvalla, established in 1974, provide a similar but different example. The Malankara School was established by prominent professionals in Thiruvalla, especially lecturers attached to the recently instituted Thiruvalla College. The 1960s saw the establishment of federal state-funded English-medium Central Schools for the children of transferable central government employees. Around the same time, the KER declared Malayalam as the 'ordinary' medium of instruction in all state-funded schools (Government of Kerala [GoK], 1959: 51). Thiruvalla's prominent citizens became concerned about their children falling behind counterparts in central schools.

The professionals floated a proposal in their local parish to establish a private English-medium school which would prepare students for the Indian Certificate of Secondary Education exams (ICSE). The ICSE was the postcolonial version of the Senior Cambridge examinations, earlier conducted by the British government. In the discussions which ensued, Left-leaning parishioners strongly opposed the proposal. They argued that a fee-charging school was elitist. Further, they insisted that the primary language of the region had to be the medium of instruction in order to ensure an inclusive, egalitarian educational agenda. Leftist factions within the church began a hunger strike opposing the school proposal. Regardless of the opposition, the proposal went through, and the Malankara School began functioning out of a hostel premises rented from the parish church for a modest fee. Teaching staff was recruited from educated women parishioners, who were exhorted to contribute to the welfare of their parish community on a humble salary.

The egalitarian agenda of development is marked, here too, by its constitutive exclusions. Ten years prior, and less than a kilometer away, the first ICSE school had already been established in Thiruvalla. This school, however, was established by the Seventh-Day Adventist (SDA) Church, which worked mostly among 'poor people' in the Travancore region. The Principal of the SDA School in 2013 clarified that Thiruvalla elites and professionals did not want to mingle with the 'converted Christians' of the SDA Church, a euphemism for former slave caste Christians.

In addition, gender posed its own paradox. As Devika (2006: 50) reminds, female education prepared privileged women to participate in development through an extension of their domestic modernity, the modern mother seamlessly blending into the ideal teacher. The development trajectory and its constitutive exclusions rested at least in part 'upon the agency of the "Kerala model woman" – the better educated, more healthy, less fertile, new elite woman' (Devika, 2006: 54). It is from this group that the school found its professional but economic teaching staff.

Last, but not the least, overwhelming support for the private English-medium school gestures to the degree to which the local is integrated to the supra-regional. As Parayil and Sreekumar (2003: 478) note, Kerala's development experience was such that the region was integrated with the international and 'forces from without' were as crucial or perhaps even more definitive than those from within. Osella and Osella (2002: 20) clarify:

> Nor in our experience do Kerala villagers content themselves with literacy classes or local health dispensaries, but want to participate directly in and receive full benefits from *progress* as they define it, which would mean striving to bring their standards of living up to those enjoyed not only by the affluent Indian middle-classes but by those who set the international pace, particularly in consumption – notably Arabs, Europeans and North Americans. Theories of development which implicitly set acceptable standards of living for Malayali villagers different to those enjoyed in 'developed' regions deny coevalness and the reality of one complex world.

To summarize, the universalization of Malayalam-medium school education in the post-independence period was accompanied by elite anxieties about being left behind. However, the scale at which elites were able to respond differed. While Thiruvalla elites established a full-fledged ICSE school comprising primary, middle and high school grades, the next section explains how Edanadu elites were only able to manage an English-medium primary school that was not officially affiliated to any school board.

The Re-establishment of Private English-Medium Schooling in Edanadu

With regional elites in Thiruvalla circumventing the state's *Malayalikaranam* (making Malayali), richer families in Edanadu began patronizing private English-medium schools in Thiruvalla. The distance of 10 kilometers was prohibitive for primary grade children, unless the family was rich enough to own a car. Only three families in Edanadu owned cars in the 1970s. All three sent their children to the newly established Malankara School in Thiruvalla. Even for them, mishaps were common. Sanjay was one of the few students from Edanadu who attended the Malankara School in Thiruvalla along with his two siblings. He remembers that one day, his father's car didn't turn up after school. After a rather long wait, the three of them started walking. After about three to four kilometers, they hitched a ride from a bullock cart that was passing by.

After a few more kilometers, they saw their car approaching. It had broken down. They reached home late at night, tired and hungry but also excited about their adventure. With the lack of transportation facilities barring English-medium schooling for young children in Edanadu, families began agitating for an English-medium primary school in the village itself.

Eventually, the Edanadu church took action. It helped that the vicar had young children of his own. Unlike the private English school of the colonial period, St. Johns, which was set up by a group of cousins, the New English School is owned and managed by the Edanadu Evangelical Church. Like with the Malankara School in Thiruvalla, the school was temporarily housed in a church property, here, a chapel that catered to families who lived further away from the main parish church. Educated mothers joined as teachers on low wages. Three teachers who had joined the New English School in 1981 explained that the three of them, all pregnant at that time, had gone around the parish collecting building funds. The building itself was to be a Parish Hall, for weddings and other church activities, of which the ground floor would function as the English-medium lower primary school.

The New English School was established in 1979 as a 'feeder' school to the English-medium section of St. Johns School. Admission records from the New English School document a 21-student first cohort, exclusively upper caste, for the 1979–1980 academic year. In one year, enrollment doubled. The academic year 1980–1981 saw an intake of 49. During the 1980s, the school saw steady enrollment, ranging from 48 in 1984–1985 to 71 in 1989–1990. Regardless of the increase in enrollments, cash was still a scarce commodity, and only a few could afford fee-charging private English-medium schooling.

Universalization of Aspiration

By late 1980s, parent profile in the admission registers at the New English School saw a shift from professionals (bank officers, government servants, clerks, doctors, engineers) to drivers, welders and conductors. Lower status upper castes were also shifting to the New English School. Over the next two decades, this once elite school became firmly branded as a low-fee, low-status school that catered to non-elites, including former slave castes. The democratization of English-medium schooling in Edanadu was achieved by 'downgrading' exclusively elite institutions. The first upheaval for the New English School came in 1994, when a local elder who had made it big in the Middle East fell out with his family and decided to spend his assets on a philanthropic venture. The elderly gentleman decided to establish a residential K-12 English-medium private school affiliated to the Central Board of Secondary Education (CBSE) in Edanadu. From 1990 to 1995, five more private CBSE schools were established around Edanadu and Thiruvalla. Another four followed in the next five years. The pace intensified, and another eight were established between 2000 and 2005.

The proliferation of CBSE schools in Kerala requires an additional note. The CBSE was constituted in its present form in 1962 to serve the children of transferable central government employees, a key elite bloc. This English-medium federal-state-funded school board provided 'sponsored mobility' to the children of privileged educated Indians (Kumar, 1985). The CBSE also affiliates private schools and all government schools in Delhi, the union territories and states that do not have their own State Education Departments. In the initial decades, the largest sector of CBSE schools was this government school category (Table 2.1). In the post-economic reform period, the percentage of private schools increased exponentially. This growth has been uneven. Kerala recorded the fourth highest number of CBSE schools in the country in 2014 (Table 2.2).

For the New English School, a second upheaval followed. The Kerala state was waking up to the expansion of private schooling and the concomitant rise of uneconomic state-funded schools. As a feeder school to St. Johns English-medium section, the New English School had not sought affiliation with any state board. This meant that it was unrecognized. The arrangements between the state-funded and the private sections had ensured that students graduating from the New English School wrote their primary school exit exams under the aegis of St. Johns Lower Primary School (earlier Grant School). By the late 1990s, this arrangement ran into trouble. The Additional Education Officer supervising the Edanadu region strictly stated that 'under no circumstances' would St. Johns be allowed to conduct the New English School examinations. In dire straits, the New English School reached out to a parishioner, Mr Joseph, who had spent his

Table 2.1 CBSE schools: Growth in sectors[5]

Year	Total	Fed%	Pvt. %	Govt. %
1967–68	619	NA	10.99	70.3
1988–89	796	NA	14.95	54.65
1998–99	5391	21.78	52.25	25.97
2008–09	10,111	14.16	66.85	17.54
2015–16	17,300	9.83	74.95	15.14

Table 2.2 States/UTs with highest number of CBSE schools in 2014

Delhi	1933
Uttar Pradesh	1842
Haryana	1148
Kerala	1127
Punjab	933

professional career with elite boarding schools in the hill towns of North India. He recommended that the school shift to its own independent building and seek affiliation with the CBSE. Faced with the option of closing down the school or upgrading it, the Edanadu Evangelical Church decided to go ahead and apply for affiliation.

Having worked in the system all his professional life, Mr Joseph proved to be an invaluable asset. He supervised the affiliation process. He notes:

> It is a difficult process. You have to have all the infrastructure as the CBSE stipulates. They send two senior principals or one of their officers with a principal from the locality to come and inspect. So we arranged our infrastructure. I knew what they were looking for and what they want. Because I knew that, I specified on those things.

Land was bought on the outskirts of Edanadu. The church bought a paddy field that had become available for sale and filled it up. Paddy fields are cheaper real estate. Construction began. Donations were solicited from the parish, and about 20 lakhs was raised. Another 70 lakhs was raised through bank loans. During August 2014, when I interviewed Mr Joseph, the school trust had repaid all but 10 lakhs of the bank loan. Since the school was constructed on a paddy field, there was no approach road. Ever resourceful, Mr Joseph approached the Member of Parliament from the region, who advised the revenue minister to sanction some money from the flood relief funds. Five lakhs were sanctioned and a tarred approach road was constructed.

However, with the establishment of an unprecedented number of private English-medium schools in the 1990s and the 2000s, the geography of educational prestige in Edanadu and Thiruvalla was changing. Families began preferring urban schools to rural ones. Higher fee-charging schools had their fleets of buses to cater to the expanding geography. Even low-fee-charging schools began to arrange for private vans if they did not own a school bus of their own. The New English School now had its own school building. Its application for affiliation to the CBSE was successful. It bought its own school bus. However, the school now seemed modest in comparison to the competition that was coming up. The aesthetics of schooling had changed profoundly from functional PWD style block buildings to resort-style ethnic architecture. But the Edanadu church did not want any more financial liabilities. By the time it had come to fruition, the New English School had already become segmented in the educational market as non-elite. In the post-2000 decade, parental profile in the admission register further diversified, but now in terms of family background rather than parental occupation. Plumbing, driving, farming and so on continued to be represented. But the residents doing this work had changed. Families belonging to low-status upper castes, former untouchable castes and former slave castes began patronizing the New English School.

Meanwhile, Malayalam-medium schooling had completely come undone in state-funded schools, especially in primary grades. In 2013, about 90% of state-funded lower primary schools were listed as 'uneconomic' in Pathanamthitta. The Economic Review (1988: 78) defines 'an uneconomic school' as one 'which does not satisfy the para (1) of rule 22 A of Kerala Education Rules which warrants that the minimum strength per standard in LP|UP|HS shall be 25'. According to the state, which is responsible for teacher salaries, a class strength of 25 students made the salary of one teacher viable. Schools which met this requisite number in all grades and classes are termed 'economic', and others are called 'uneconomic'. It is important to clarify that unlike other Indian states, the Kerala state did not close down any uneconomic school in the fieldwork region unless gross student enroll-ment was zero. In 1987–1988, there were 650 uneconomic schools in Kerala of which the highest number at 118 were in Pathanamthitta. By 1999, the number of uneconomic schools had increased to 1950 with Kannur district now listing the highest number of uneconomic schools at 374. In terms of percentage of uneconomic schools, Pathanamthitta had the highest percent-age at 39.3% (GoK, 1999: 161). By 2013, the number of uneconomic schools in the state stood at 5573 and 378 of the 418 lower primary schools in Pathanamthitta were uneconomic (Appendix 16, GoK, 2014).

The student distribution in Edanadu village in 2013, according to state-complied statistics, is noted in Table 2.3. The largest percentage of the stu-dents were enrolled in two low-fee-charging private English-medium schools, both of which were K-12 and affiliated to the CBSE.[6] The New English School was one of these. The two low-fee private CBSE schools charged tuition fees of around Rs. 8000 annually in the primary section, while the medium-fee school charged around Rs. 15,000. Though Edanadu did not have any high-fee private schools, a few students from Edanadu attended them in Thiruvalla.[7] State-funded schools do not officially have kindergar-tens, so any unofficial kindergartens remained unenumerated.

Visiting all state-funded and private schools in Edanadu, I found that of the 13 state-funded primary schools, the 2 listed as economic in 2012 had opened English-medium sections in 1994 and 2003. According to state policy, an English-medium section can be *opened* in a primary

Table 2.3 State-compiled statistics of student distribution in Edanadu for 2013–2014

	State-funded Grades 1 through 4		Private English-medium Lower K through 4		Total
	Uneconomic	Economic (Eng.-medium)	Low-fee	Medium-fee	
Schools	11	2	2	1	16
Students	201	359	621	123	1304
Student %	15.41%	27.53%	47.62%	9.43%	

school only if it has sufficient enrollment in at least two Malayalam-medium sections, but a 2012 government order clarified that an English-medium section can be *retained* if student enrollment has gone down and only one Malayalam-medium section is presently operational. Schools that were economic in 2013 had prudently opened English-medium sections early on and retained them as the state revised and clarified its stand. Thus, though Malayalam-medium sections were uneconomic, the schools themselves were listed as economic on the strength of their English-medium students. Or to put it more bluntly, Malayalam-medium sections at all state-funded schools were uneconomic.

To summarize, for close to a hundred years, English-medium schooling was an integral aspect of local hierarchies in Edanadu. The privileged from the dominant castes found ways to access it during colonial and post-independence decades despite obstacles. Non-elites were disallowed access. The unsettling of this century-old educational relationship between different social groups precipitated radical educational change.

Development and its Afterlives

'Afterlife of development' captures the shift from modernization premised on state investment to a market-based system dependent on responsible, enterprising subjects (Rudnyckyj, 2010). Kerala's development experience raises the question about how aspiration under conditions of marketization is different from those of earlier periods. The rest of the book attempts to answer this question. Unlike in earlier periods, the massification of consumer culture afforded non-elites a much more expansive tapestry of gendered resources with which to craft new social selves. The *salwar kameez* instead of caste-specific apparel, cooking gas instead of firewood and packaged food alongside traditional culinary items allowed a wider range of women to perform aspects of middle-class, respectable femininity. This protracted training in gendered middle-class self-making automatically spills over into educational desire since respectable womanhood is defined around domestic responsibility and child rearing. The opening up of access to respectable femininity through consumer practices expanded and intensified educational aspiration. While education as a vehicle of aspiration is therefore not peculiar to the contemporary historical moment, what is different is its articulation with consumer citizenship.

The Research Design: The Ethnographic Encounter and Teaching as Research Method

Ethnographic research pays attention to the everyday, the ordinary and the mundane. It is characterized by historically informed, long-term fieldwork, which allows the researcher to form substantive, often strategic, relationships with respondents. One strength and weakness of this research method is its relative open-endedness, or what is called the ethnographic surprise. Unlike experimental-, survey- or questionnaire-based methods, the luxury of long-term, immersive fieldwork allows for iterative recalibrations of the research questions, focus and themes of inquiry. On the one hand, this allows the researcher to explore previously unexpected directions of inquiry. On the other hand, this constant revision can be taxing as newer areas of inquiry may require new theoretical frameworks, analytical themes and methods.

The primary ethnographic sites were St. Thomas and the New English School, where I conducted fieldwork from June 2013 to December 2014. Though anthropologists typically 'hang out' with their interlocutors, it would have been impossible to pursue this method at the two school sites, especially the uneconomic school, which functioned with three teachers teaching four grades. New teaching posts would not be sanctioned at the school given its declining numbers. Accordingly, I was enlisted to teach, first at St. Thomas and eventually at the New English School as well. My role as a teacher not only shaped the kinds of access I had to school families but also reshaped my research interests and the questions that drove the research project.

During 2013–2014, St. Thomas had 12 Dalit students enrolled in Grades 1–4. I was enlisted to teach English in second grade, and I taught the Kerala state English curriculum to two second grade cohorts, to three students during 2013–2014 and to four students in 2014–2015. At St. Thomas, mothers routinely rest and socialize inside the school building after their long walk to and from school to pick up and drop off children. The lunch corner – at the far end of the hall – with its single bench and desk was their hub as they chatted with each other and teachers, including me, about children's antics, lessons, trajectories of old students, academic performances of enrolled students, as well as the mundane details of everyday life that produce caste and gender differences. Only high-fee schools in Edanadu are gated spaces, in accordance with the recent rise in gated housing societies among the upper middle-classes (see Tripathy, 2015). Toward the end of my fieldwork, I also conducted more formal semi-structured interviews with mothers of all enrolled children. In addition, I participated in festival celebrations and village fairs, attended weddings and funerals with school families, conversed with mothers at bus stops, grocery shops, village offices and walked to and from school with mothers and grandmothers accompanying their children.

Meanwhile, the New English School had 307 enrolled students in 2013. Of these, 5.2% were listed as Scheduled Castes (former slave castes) and 15.6% as Ezhava, a former untouchable caste. I was at the New English School six hours per week when the school was in session, and after a few initial weeks, the school management enlisted my help in teaching 'Spoken English' – an ungraded English language class that had been piloted previously and was considered to have been popular with parents. Subsequently, I provided supplementary lessons in a weekly 'Spoken-English' class for the 153 students in Grades 3, 4, 5 and 6, in 45-minute classes scheduled with each grade. After about a year of teaching, I identified a random sample of fourth grade students who had received high, average and poor scores in the tri-monthly tests routinely conducted at school and approached their parents for more structured interviews to understand parental aspirations concerning English-medium schooling. Mothers typically handled all school-related work, so in the 22 families I interviewed, only two fathers obliged. Moreover, in 8 of the 22 families, fathers had emigrated for working class jobs in the Middle East and elsewhere and were away during my fieldwork period. Juggling the many responsibilities of parenting, mothers asked if I could interview them in their homes. When word got around that I was willing to travel to parents' homes to conduct interviews, other mothers too requested home interviews, which allowed me to converse with five grandmothers who lived in with the families.

Since mothers viewed me as their children's teacher, they were simultaneously guarded and intimate. On the one hand, they enquired regularly after their children's performance and updated me on their home efforts. On the other hand, the resource-deprived nature of schooling and its moralization of mothering constructed mothers, rather than teachers, as responsible for children's academic performance. This meant that mothers expected to be held accountable for children's work, and therefore, they were wary of teachers in general. As I explain in Chapter 4, some of the key insights about mothers' labors came from acquaintances and neighbors whose children I did not teach.

As fieldwork progressed, the frustrations of teaching drove me to examine the state and market structures that supported and directed English teaching and learning at the two participating schools. In her review of anthropology of policy, Tate (2020: 84) notes that policy is created by bureaucrats and administrators through institutional processes and enforced through administrative sanctions and individualized decisions. Anthropological study of this variegated terrain looks very different from the typical ethnography. For one, it is a 'studying up' that poses challenges in terms of access and legibility. While I have attempted to trace the multilayered, contradictory terrain of language policy that shaped pedagogy at the school sites, the registers of policy analysis were assembled through document and interview analysis. Transitions between registers of power are jerky. But they are attempted because 'partial studies of the oppressed are of limited use especially in the absence of even partial studies of the oppressors and the ways in which their institutions operate' (Tate, 2020: 93).

The inquiry into English pedagogy at the two school sites was similarly structured. At both schools, the textbook was the principal technology of teaching. At both, the textbook was such that it could not be taught. Discussions, interviews and ethnographic observation confirmed that this was not an isolated experience. The textbooks were designed with a set of assumptions that was grossly disconnected from the experiences of existing classrooms. But differences in the administrative location of the school – one state-funded and the other private but non-elite – resulted in differing data. Kerala state-funded schools are administratively governed by District and Additional Educational Officers, and pedagogically governed and supported by the Kerala State Council of Educational Research and Training, the Sarva Shiksha Abhiyan (Education for All program), the District Institute of Educational Training, the Block Resource Center and the Village Panchayat. Accordingly, I interviewed educators across the various agencies, participated in teacher development programs, and worked with the District Institute as a resource person. Since I taught the official curriculum, I was subject to the examination patterns and requirements of the Kerala state, which conducted three standardized tests in all grades during an academic year.

In comparison, the private school was isolated from teacher training and development networks, not because it was a private school but because it was a *non-elite* private school. Teacher training programs were conducted by the CBSE, typically at high-fee schools in Thiruvalla, and only for secondary grade teachers. Training was in general an expensive affair and teachers from the New English School only attended those that were mandatory, for instance, the orientation session for secondary grade English teachers after the Assessment of Speaking and Listening skills were mandated by the CBSE.

In general, research on English pedagogy began from the textbook. I analyzed textbooks as they were taught and learned, talking to teachers, mothers, after-school paid tuition teachers; examining student notebook work; and chronicling my own preparation and teaching work. In addition, I attempted to interview the textbook writers listed as authors of the textbooks. In the case of St. Thomas, the Kerala state textbooks were produced out of a long series of reforms initiated from as early as 1994. As for the New English School, the *Marigold* textbooks in use during 2013 were produced by the National Council of Educational Research and Training (NCERT), the nodal academic agency for school education in India. The *Marigold* English textbooks were the outcome of a parallel set of English reforms conducted at the national level.

What began as textbook analysis thus expanded into a longer inquiry into English reforms and pedagogic policy at the national and Kerala state levels and its key actors, including but not limited to textbook writers. This exercise took me to the NCERT, New Delhi, the English and Foreign Languages University at Hyderabad, which works closely with the NCERT on English pedagogy, the Kerala State Council of Educational

Research and Training, Thiruvananthapuram, and the homes and offices of policymakers and pedagogues in Delhi, Hyderabad, Pune and in towns and villages in north, central and south Kerala.

Lastly, since the textbooks were largely unteachable in non-elite classrooms, I procured all beginner-level teaching and reading materials available in the market, from both state and private publishers. These were used in classroom teaching and also used to set up libraries at the two schools. These materials provided a broader sense of the pedagogic market and were complimented with interviews and classroom observations in high-fee schools in Thiruvalla. In addition, privately published textbooks were also analyzed to understand the comparative framework of English pedagogy. Where possible, I also conducted interviews with textbook and picture book writers attached to private publishing houses.

Though the primary objective of this inquiry was an understanding of English pedagogy and policy, interviewees, especially those associated with the Kerala reforms, were keen to talk about the social contexts, controversies and debates surrounding English schooling, uneconomic schools and development in Kerala. Their pathologization of parental aspiration emerged as a formidable counter narrative to the desires and labors of non-elite mothers. This unexpected data compelled me to trace English as a relationship between the privileged middle-classes and non-elites. Consequently, the data chapters are organized around such relationships. The next chapter focuses on non-elite mothers' aspirations and educators' shaming of non-elite aspirations.

Notes

(1) All names of institutions and people in the fieldwork village are pseudonyms.

(2) According to PRDS Joint Secretary KK Vijayakumar, Yohannan established a lower primary school in 1912 in Madapally, Amarapuram, about 10 kilometers from Thiruvalla. But as late as 2012, they were still petitioning the Kerala State to upgrade what was then an upper primary school into a high school. The PRDS president pointed out that though the Kerala development narrative is built on community owned but state-funded schools (about 56% in 2018), the Dalit community in Kerala owned only one school. After over a century, in 2014, the Government of Kerala sanctioned an aided Arts and Science College at Amarapuram under the Mahatma Gandhi University for the PRDS College of Arts & Science. The Amarapuram PRDS School remains an upper primary school.

(3) While the preparatory class (Grade 4) had 80 students, Form 1 (Grade 5) had 77, Form 2 had 87, Form 3 had 65, Form 4 had 119 and Form 5 had 73 students.

(4) Acknowledged as the greatest modern Malayalam poet. He also wrote flawless petitions in English to the colonial government to support the Ezhava cause.

(5) Compiled from CBSE Annual Reports and MHRD Annual Reports.

(6) Two federal state-funded CBSE schools serve the 68 villages that constitute the district of Pathanamthitta, and the vast majority of CBSE students attend private CBSE schools.

(7) Malankara School was one popular high-fee school in Thiruvalla.

3 Temporal Migrations

'What do you remember about your childhood?' Holding out the tape-recorder, making sure the red light for recording was on, fifth grader Tutu asked his grandmother. Elsamma ignored his question. She was busy explaining to me that the unbecoming state of their house was temporary. A bright blue tarpaulin sheet had been draped over the wooden rafters of the compact house. The Mangalore tiles that typically covered the rafters were stacked in a corner. Elsamma explained that the roof had started leaking during the monsoon. The tiles needed repair. Tutu had decided to take over my interviewing role but was doing poorly. I repeated the question about her childhood and Elsamma responded:

> Childhood? We were there, in Alappuzha.
> We are ten children.
> So, that is how we were brought up.
> Our parents didn't care much about educating us.
> They were parenting in those times [*annathe mathapithakkal alle?*]
> Today, we motivate children, isn't it?
> We wake them up in the morning,
> See, make him [Tutu] brush his teeth
> Call him again and again and again, to get out of bed
> Will he get into trouble if I say all this? [laughs]
> Get him out of bed, make him brush his teeth, get him to go to the toilet
> I have to tell him a 100 times
> In those days, there was nobody to care for us like this.
> We were five, eight, ten children.
> Parents didn't have time to care.
> So, we grew up like that, our education was also like that.
> I learned only till eighth standard.
> After that, I decided I didn't want education [*paditham venda*]
> I only decided, not my parents.
> Today, we won't let our children off like that.
> If they don't study here, try some other school, isn't it?

How did Elsamma's family transform from one which 'did not care' about educating children to one which unconditionally embraced the labors of intensive mothering? This chapter describes how educational aspirations became obligatory, intense and urgent for non-elite carers like Elsamma.

Most of Elsamma's account is devoted to the affective work she undertakes to ensure that Tutu is schooled within a system that defines parental affection around gendered middle-class resources of time. Every school day, Elsamma ensures that Tutu wakes up on time, washes up, eats breakfast and reaches school in time for first bell. Their family is atypical for the New English School, where most mothers stay at home to meet the demands of primary schooling.

Unlike other mothers, Tutu's mother Bindu worked as an administrator at a large automobile showroom in the nearby town. Tutu's father had gone to the Gulf, yet again, but he had been unlucky, yet again. He was contracted out for hard jobs for short durations. With a full-time job, the mother–daughter duo had divvied up their care responsibilities. Bindu was the breadwinner, and Elsamma the homemaker. This arrangement also allowed Elsamma to retreat from a stigmatized labor market. She had worked most of her adult life as a domestic help for the landowning families of the village. Across from her house, bordering the paddy marsh, was one such prominent household. Their rubber plantations stretched as far as our eyes could see, and beyond. This household belonged to one of the three families [kudumbam] that had set up the English school in the village as early as 1910.

Literature on low-fee private schooling follows standard consumer theory to posit a 'sovereign individual consumer standing face to face with the market and behaving in a manner calculated to maximize his or her individual utility, independently of the decisions of others' (Vries, 2008: 7). Development researchers compare school infrastructure, teacher presence and teaching activity across private and state-funded schools to model the calculations the consumer *must* make to maximize utility.[1] While economic rationalizations are certainly part of Elsamma's household's pursuit of English-medium education, reducing their memories, desires and labor to rational calculation obscures more than it illuminates. What would it mean to situate the consumer in history, social relations and desire?

Departing from development education scholarship, which calculates the efficiency of private and state-funded schooling to explain consumer choice, and drawing on an anthropological understanding of value, which considers the ways 'in which actions become meaningful to the actor by being incorporated in some larger, social totality' (Graeber, 2001: xii), this chapter describes how radical changes in the social world have altered the ways in which schooling practices become meaningful to non-elite carers like Elsamma and Bindu. Rather than English education altering life trajectories, transformations in social life had made English education indispensable.

As Ravinder Kaur and Nandini Sundar (2016: 6–9) remind, in the absence of social security that protects citizens, like in Euro-America, 'minor upgrades' are experienced by the poor in India as relatively 'greater experiences of mobility'. Elsamma's household now has running water, a fridge and a gas stove. Bindu rides to work on a scooter, dressed in the latest fashions readily available in the village market. They have a Mangalore tiled, brick and mortar house. But mothers, more so grandmothers like Elsamma, remember a very different world where they spent the whole day collecting firewood and water, scrubbing soot blackened vessels and completing the everyday labors of a subsistence livelihood. Note Elsamma's discomfort with the dilapidated roof, an unsettling memory from a very recent past. Memories of deprivation, hunger and poverty thus co-mingled with a sensorium of ease and prosperity to be experienced as radical social mobility.

Building on situated experiences rather than absolute measures of social mobility, I suggest that non-elites in Edanadu experience the transformations accompanying market reforms as a large scale temporal migration, a sense of having 'emigrated without leaving [home]' (Berdahl, 1999: 202). Edanadu residents had emigrated from the hardships of an agrarian subsistence society to the relatively prosperous, aspirational worlds of a middle-classed consumer society, without leaving home. This experience of radical social mobility in one's own lifetime compelled them to aspire, intensely, for similar mobility for their children. Since English is 'fundamentally embedded in the history of modern Indian social stratification' (Chandra, 2012: 5), non-elite mothers thus found themselves obliged to patronize English-medium schools to become 'good mothers'.

Temporal Migrations

Annamma, a 62-year-old woman, vividly remembers a different time, a time when there was nothing and when life was difficult [budhimuttu]. 'There was nothing hereabouts', she reminisced about life only a decade ago without running water, motorable roads or a sturdy house that could weather the monsoons. As for her earlier everyday life, it seemed to her an odyssey of work: 'In those times I didn't even get to sit [annu kuththi irunnittilla]', she said of a lifetime spent cooking with firewood, scrubbing soot-blackened vessels with coconut fiber and ash, bringing up children, taking care of aging in-laws and tending a cow and a goat that provided the crucial extra income that helped them subsist. Unlike Annamma, who had cooked with firewood, 38-year-old Abhiya remembers her mother cooking with dried leaves [karila]. Firewood supply discursively indicates the extent of land ownership, for firewood had to be collected off somebody's land, and collecting dry leaves indexed destitution. For all the grandmothers and mothers I interviewed, the re-structuring of their material worlds through running water, cooking gas and refrigerators had configured migrations into a 'now' of comforts and ease [sukha-saukaryangal]. This temporal migration from a past dominated by physical labor and material deprivation obliged aspirational work: if mothers in earlier decades barely had time to 'sit down [kuthi irikkan]', now, mothers had to 'sit with [koode irrikkanum]' children when they studied.

Five households who could claim privileged family names [kudumbam] were among the few who had regular salaried incomes. The average monthly salary for the late 1990s was Rs. 2000. Within the interview sample, the highest income for this time was reported by Jintu's grandfather, who worked as a survey officer in the plantations of Peerimedu earning Rs. 6000 per month just before retirement in 1998. His son, Jintu's father, walked eight miles to go to school. Clothes, food and, most of all, money was in short supply. Annamma's husband worked as a turner in a company, and his income during the late 1990s, just before he retired, was Rs. 3500. That was hardly enough to build a durable house and living conditions were dismal, Annamma explained. In comparison, salaried employees like senior bank officers from Edanadu earned around Rs. 20,000 during the same period.

Unlike Annamma's husband who had a steady job, Abhiya's father did odd jobs, and Abhiya refused to give me an 'occupation' that would fit into a neat category. When I tried to supply her with alternatives I had become familiar with from school enrollment registers like 'farming', Abhiya clarified that only those who owned agricultural land could be farmers in Edanadu. 'We didn't own any land, what farming could we do?' she retorted. Lalamma remembered that during her school-going years, if she needed a pencil or a book for school, it might be bought after months, if and when cash became available.

Meanwhile, Elsamma was the only grandmother in the interview sample who had worked as a daily-wage laborer. For former slave caste women, wage labor was a necessity, and they rarely, if ever, talked about how they, as working women, cared for children. The presence of the mother is seen as fundamental to childcare in Edanadu. Though they may have arranged for supervision through family members or neighbors, talking about it would only highlight their 'lack'.

In sharp contrast to the earning capacities of the previous generation, average monthly income among the interviewed families in 2014 had increased around 900% to approximately Rs. 20,000 (Table 3.1). In comparison, senior high school teachers earned around Rs. 50,000 and bank employees around Rs. 75,000 in 2014. It is important to note that though policies of economic liberalization came into place in early 1990s, the most radical economic changes villagers narrate are for the post-2000 years. Eight fathers who worked as drivers, construction workers, electricians and plumbers in the Middle East earned between Rs. 20,000 and Rs. 25,000 per month, while others doing similar work in Kerala reported an income of around Rs. 10,000. One mother, Annamma's daughter, worked as a nurse in Saudi Arabia earning Rs. 80,000. As for other working mothers, all except Bindu and Jintu's mother did home-based work such as tailoring.

Table 3.1 Reported monthly income of 22 families in 2014

		Not presently employed	Less than 5000	Around 6000 to 10,000	Around 20,000 to 40,000	More than 75,000
Mothers		12	4	4	1	1
			4 Home-based			Gulf
Fathers		None	1	6	15	None
			8 in Gulf; 1 in North India 2 'good' jobs; 20 working-class jobs			

Additionally, the social value of particular kinds of work had also shifted. In earlier generations, when cash was in short supply, family name and land ownership mediated employment to define social worth. That is, young men from 'good families' could also work as plumbers, drivers, painters and electricians without losing face. But now, skilled labor had become the purview of non-elite men. Despite this rearrangement, the ascendance of a cash economy had increased the economic value of work, and those willing to do unskilled work could make money. Nine families had repaired or built new houses, a previously inconceivable expense. Four of these were non-emigrants like Abhiya, who had a new house, just finished, not yet painted. When I visited her at home for the interview, Abhiya offered me cold water from her refrigerator and remarked 'things are much better now [*ippam orupadu better aa*]'.

While the house indexed durable change for the entire household, the gendered fabric of public life had also transformed robustly. Eight women drove two wheelers, including Elsamma's daughter, who rode 10 kilometers to go to work. Two mothers were learning to drive. I often met them at the football field turned driving ground where the instructor, a self-assured woman in *salwar kameez*, barked instructions at wobbling drivers. All mothers wore *salwar kameez* to go out, the sartorial choice of the demurely modern (Lukose, 2009). Only grandmothers and the two mothers who worked as teachers felt the compulsion to attire themselves in the traditional *sari*. Long-standing material markers of distinction related to the body and the household – spatial mobility, attire, availability of food, a *pucca* house, English education – had now become available to almost all villagers. The resultant ambivalence of social value became a fertile ground for non-elite aspiration.

Continuity amidst Change

Even though marginalized mothers had migrated into new material worlds, the precarious economic positions of most families had not changed. Even as incomes had risen, costs of essential commodities had also increased, and one kilo of mackerel, a local staple, cost around Rs. 200 in 2014 as compared to Rs. 20 in late 1990s. Furthermore, the prices of essential household goods and services rose significantly during my fieldwork period: Railway freight rates rose by 6.5% in June 2014, leading to increased prices of all goods that arrived in the local market through railway transport, including rice, vegetables and fish. By July, vegetable prices had doubled. The wholesale rates of *payar* [long beans] went up from Rs. 40 to Rs. 80 per kilo, brinjal from Rs. 20 to Rs. 40 per kilo, and tomatoes from Rs. 20 to Rs. 50 per kilo. The price of coconut oil climbed to an all-time high of Rs. 180 per kilo a few months later. Green chili *kanthari* prices rose to Rs. 50 for 100 grams by August.

Likewise, domestic electricity rates went up by 24% in August 2014. But what most worried mothers and teachers was the state's move to gradually de-subsidize cooking gas. During 2014, the mode of payment changed from payment of a state-subsidized rate to the reimbursement of state subsidy through bank accounts. Subsidized cooking gas was priced at around Rs. 415 per 14.2 kg cylinder, while the unsubsidized rate was around Rs. 750. The number of subsidized cylinders available per year was capped at 12, one for every calendar month. Mothers carefully strategized cooking gas consumption by using firewood for items that required prolonged cooking time, especially the local staple, Kerala rice. Non-elite mothers felt increasingly trapped by the fickle, hostile market. If in their childhood, parents had struggled to make ends meet without money, mothers now struggled to make ends meet with money. The beginning of the school year was an exceptionally hard time with money having to be raised for tuition fees (about Rs. 5000 for first term), books (approximately Rs. 1500), uniforms (about Rs. 1500) and bus fees (typically around Rs. 500 per month). But mothers prioritized schooling expenses and sometimes even borrowed money from better-off neighbors. This simultaneity of change and continued precarity underscored the import of particular kinds of education, especially, English-medium schooling.

Shifting Aspirational Horizons

Mobility between dissimilar material worlds precipitates movement between regimes of value (Berdahl, 1999; Pine, 2014; Rofel, 2007), and parents' temporal migrations into new material worlds scaffolded the possibility of migrating to more valued, and valuable, social locations. This entailed the recalibration of aspirational horizons, but as Pine (2014) reminds, desired-for futures are built on memories of pasts that have to be eliminated. Present experiences of children's English-medium schooling were thus deeply entangled with memories of parents' Malayalam-medium schooling and simultaneously oriented toward aspirations for children's professional higher education.

The humiliations and foreclosed futures associated with Malayalam-medium schooling were most eloquently articulated by Raghu, an educational researcher and Dalit activist whose child attended the other low-fee CBSE English-medium school in Edanadu. Rejecting the shaming evoked through slave-caste naming in Kerala (Satyanarayana & Tharu, 2011), Raghu self-identified as Dalit. Literally crushed or broken, the term Dalit is an assertion of self-worth and a rejection of the norms of worth sanctified by caste. Like most fathers at the New English School, Raghu had completed schooling in Malayalam medium, and financial struggles had disallowed higher education. In one of our many discussions, Raghu reminisced about his high school years in Edanadu during the late 1990s and said:

> I was Malayalam-medium. Most of those who studied with me are still around here. Very few [*valare churukkam*] have government jobs. A few have been to the Gulf. English-medium students, I don't know where they are. We don't know them, do we? That school, my life at that school, was horrifying [*bhikaram ayirunnu*].

Raghu had completed schooling in Malayalam medium like most of the fathers, and distinctions within his high school, between the two sections and based on the official medium of instruction, had figured his world in horrifying ways, denying his claims of social value and dignity; so much so that he identified himself as that space rather than as belonging to that space. 'I was Malayalam medium [*njan Malayalam medium aiyurunnu*]' he said, rather than 'I was in Malayalam-medium [*njan Malayalam mediuthil aiyirunnu*]'. Raghu also explicitly articulates the very real economic implications that cohered along the English-Malayalam divide. Very few non-English literates get government jobs, and further, government jobs available for non-English literates are stigmatized menial jobs like cleaning work. A few of his Malayalam-medium cohort-mates had been to the Gulf, but working-class jobs in the Gulf offer hard labor and precarious lives. On the contrary, the social, economic and occupational privileges of his English-medium cohort-mates are duly noted as an unbridgeable divide: 'We don't know them, do we?' Raghu asks. He went on to describe his English-medium cohort-mates as 'primary citizens [*pradhana pauranmar*]' who believed they 'were born for this [*ithinu vendi janichavara*]'. For Raghu, citizenship claims, social belonging and economic security were indexed through medium of instruction, a point Kumar (1996) too notes in great detail. Crucially, Raghu was a fluent English speaker and an incisive educational researcher but did not have higher-educational certifications that adequately legitimized his English or academic research competencies. English-medium education is thus not just about learning a language but also about claiming legitimacies and profits, which are encoded institutionally.

Like with Raghu, my questions to New English School parents (Where did you study? Was your school English or Malayalam medium?) were most often met with 'there were no English-medium schools for people like us [njangale polullavarkke]', and only 'big people [valiyavar]' or 'people with money [kashullavar]' went to English-medium schools in those times. Of the 44 parents whose educational histories were collected, except for two, all had attended Malayalam-medium schools in Edanadu and in other parts of Pathanamthitta, Alappuzha and Kottayam districts. Interestingly, only seven women had grown up in Edanadu. Others had moved to their husband's house in Edanadu after marriage, and their memories covered a larger geographical area spread across Pathanamthitta as well as neighboring districts.

Though all except one mother had attended vernacular-medium schools, 17 of the 22 mothers had post-10th educational experiences. Post-10th grade, educational systems in Kerala were in English-medium and mothers' struggles with linguistic transitions and their own increased competencies in English drove their desires for children's English-medium schooling from the earliest grades. Mothers did not desire to reproduce precarity but hoped for the absence of such difficulties for their children. For instance, when wives of Gulf migrants said, 'wherever you go, you'll need English', rather than denying the robust trajectories of non-English-literate migration they gesture to the difficulties their husbands face. Gardner (2010) describes the precarious nature of construction labor that migrants from Kerala perform in the Middle East. Unlike in the case of dominant groups for whom assumptions of English proficiency and legitimacy coincide (Ramanathan, 2005), for all interviewed mothers, legitimate participation was yet uncertain and fraught with peril. 'It will be difficult [budhimuttu] if you don't have English', another mother remarked, using the same term budhimuttu that several mothers had used to describe their childhood years of privation as well as their contemporary economic precarity. Good futures are thus indexed by desires for absences as much as presences (Appadurai, 2013; Pine, 2014).

Meanwhile, possibilities of capital accumulation through English-literate professional work were also recognized as possible, enabling a fuller participation in economies of hope. All interviewed parents expected their children to complete schooling and also perhaps procure some professional certification. Older children of New English School parents I interviewed were enrolled in engineering, nursing and commerce courses. Other graduated students who returned to meet their old teachers were enrolled in engineering, pharmacy, nursing and physiotherapy courses. Professional courses in India use English as the medium of instruction. The normative aspirational orientation to professional courses (and English) silenced alternate aspirations as failures. Additionally, unlike in the times of parents, the completion of schooling itself now required two additional years of English-medium education. In accordance with the recommendations of the National Policy on Education, pre-degree courses, that is, 11th and 12th grades, were delinked from colleges and added to schools. Called 10 +2 or simply plus-two, these additional years were now necessary to complete schooling. The process was actualized by 2000–2001, but the Kerala state had not produced Malayalam textbooks for all plus-two subjects. State-funded schools also used federally produced English-medium textbooks. Though the temporally urgent need for English came from this plus-two requirement, as I explain in the next section, mothers 'needed' English-medium schooling in profoundly deeper ways.

Aspiring as a Practice of Ethics

'Don't you need English for everything nowadays? [*ippam ellathinum English vende?*]' a mother counterposed as I asked her why she had enrolled her children at the New English School. I nodded in agreement to this self-evident truth before I stopped to ponder where exactly English was 'needed' in the village. Unlike the mother's assertion, the headteacher at the non-elite school regularly lamented the *lack* of a need to speak English in the school and Malayalam rather than English was indispensable both in the school and the village. In this case, what was the mother asserting? Some mothers used the appendage of a 'good future [*nalla bhavi*]' to qualify this need for English, and one grandmother explained, 'times are different, to live in these times you need English'. While English oracy was superfluous in Edanadu, English literacy had always been the key marker of respectability and secure employment. As Ramanathan (2005) has described so eloquently, an orientation to good futures in India already assumes English literacy and prospective affects like aspiration and hope are always already entangled with English. It was when the possibility of this aspirational practice fell apart that its significance emerged in fuller measure.

Rebecca, who was 39 years old, was the only mother I interviewed who had to choose which of her children could attend the New English School. She had four children, and the oldest two studied at a state-funded school. Reni was Rebecca's third child. I taught Reni for two consecutive years at the New English School and knew her as one of the top scorers in her class. Her mother concurred, 'she [Reni] studies so well, she gets full marks for everything'. She continued, 'I couldn't study, but I want my children to reach a respectable level [*nalla nilayilavanam*]'. She knew that as an 'uneducated' person, she could hardly claim respectability in Edanadu. However, for Rebecca, the morality and ethics of mothering, of investing in and imagining the good futures of children, was not possible for all her children.

Her older children, Rebecca said, joked about the differential schooling arrangements in the family. She had recently enrolled her youngest child at the New English School in first grade even though they could not afford it because Rebecca could not rationalize expenses with such a young child. CBSE English-medium schooling thus opened up the ethical world of being a good mother, for both Rebecca and her children. 'But we don't have that much money (to send two children to a private English-medium school), what will I do?' Rebecca was crying profusely by now. Her husband worked as a fabricator in construction projects, and during 2014, their reported monthly income was around Rs. 5000. The average monthly income at the New English School was around Rs. 20,000. Discriminating between her children broke her heart, and the continuous struggle with schooling expenses wore her down. Aspiring as a practice of ethics became most painfully evident when that practice was fractured and the possibility of producing an ethical self became interrupted.

Limits of Temporal Migrations

Like Rebecca, those who did not fit the 'appropriate' profile of new English-medium parents crossed material, symbolic and social borders every day and bore the many costs of crossing. One of the few people at the New English School who lived in left-behind worlds was Menaka. She was divorced and Dalit. She lived with her natal family, conscious of her transgressive presence [adhikapatta]. The family itself lived in a dilapidated house, without running water or cooking gas. Menaka was employed as a 'non-teaching' staff at the school, a euphemism for cleaning staff. Along with the other non-teaching staff, she swept the classrooms, the school grounds and washed the toilets. We talked often in the library, while I prepared my lessons and she swept the room. Our conversations began out of her interest in one of the students in Class 4, Anand, whose answers I had appreciated in the staffroom. His mother was Menaka's friend. When Anand's family had newly moved to Menaka's area about two years ago and was looking for schooling options, Menaka had recommended the New English School. Menaka's son studied here, and she promised to keep an eye on Anand as well.

Menaka's movement out of traditional, feudal, caste occupations was not accompanied by the material transformations described in this chapter. The labor she performed (toilet cleaning) and the remuneration she received – a fraction of what she would have gotten for agricultural labor – had not accrued any symbolic or economic value. Menaka's salary was around Rs. 3000 per month, and she often did not have enough to pay the school's tuition fees. She routinely participated in the *Kudumbashree* chit fund, a microcredit program, to accumulate enough credit to pay her son's tuition fees. Her everyday life did not bear the comforts or ease narrated by school mothers. In fact, her life world was similar to those of Dalit mothers at the uneconomic school, described in Chapter 6. But what offered her the possibility of change was the English-medium schooling she pursued for her son. She explained to me that she had taken up the job at the school because it allowed her to send her son to an English-medium school; the school offered tuition discounts to the children of teaching and non-teaching staff.

The following section shifts registers to move to policy analysis. It moves from the embodied experience of social relations to geographically distant but consequential discourses. While the terrain is varied and uneven, including village-, district-, regional state- and national-level discourses as documented through interviews and in texts, what unifies them is their shaming of non-elite aspirations.

Aspiration Shaming and the Bad Consumer

During September 2013, the then Director of Public Instruction (DPI) for Kerala released a statement titled *Where is Our School Education Headed?* [*nammude school vidyabhyasam engotte?*]. In his text about what ails the state-funded schooling system in Kerala, DPI Prabhakar (2013: 7) had this to say about new English-medium parents:

> A few days ago, I had the opportunity to participate in a program orga-
> nized at a CBSE school as the Chief Guest. There, amongst the people
> who received and welcomed me [*varavettavaril*] was my peon [*ente* peon],
> from when I used to work at the Corporation.[2] He gets Rs. 9000 per
> month in daily wages. Both his children study at the CBSE school.
> Though the government promises to educate his children for free; though
> state schools have highly qualified, well trained teachers, who have passed
> the PSC exam; though state schools are competently resourced with com-
> puters, multi-media rooms,[3] free lunches, and everything else[4]; why
> doesn't an ordinary Keralite [*sadharanakaran*] enroll his children in
> state-owned or comparable state-funded schools? Why does he pay such
> hefty fees [*valiya fees*] to send his two children to a school that has none
> of these facilities [*aparyapthamaya*]?

The son of former Finance Minister Thachadi Prabhakaran, Biju Prabhakar is an officer in the permanent bureaucracy of the Government of India, the Indian Administrative Services, with educational certifica-tions in engineering (B.Tech), law (LLB) and business (MBA). Meanwhile, the CBSE parent, known to the world as Prabhakar's peon and an ordinary Keralite [*sadharanakaran*], earns Rs. 9000 per month in daily wages. He spends his meagre salary on the hefty fees of a private CBSE school that has limited facilities even though government schools have computers, multimedia rooms, free lunches and highly qualified, well-trained teachers. According to Prabhakar, the peon fails to make the astute choices that will uphold rational markets and, in doing so, erodes the democratic possibili-ties of state-funded education. At the core of the malaise is his aspiration, which makes him an irrational consumer. Prabhakar constructs a bad consumer, who by extension becomes a bad citizen.

The following sections examine how critical pedagogues, headteachers, textbook writers and policy documents respond to non-elite English-medium schooling. Since these unanimously deride non-elite parental aspirations as engendering depraved forms of consumer citizenship, I use the term 'aspiration shaming' to draw attention to both non-elite aspirational mobilities and educators' scrutiny of non-elite aspirations. What drives the peon's irrational consumer decisions is his aspiration, which mistakenly values symbols of present social mobility (CBSE schooling) more than substantive pedagogic processes which defer social mobility to the future (trained teachers).

One key technique within these formulations is the separation of the pedagogic domain from its economic basis and the ascription of differential moral value to these. This separation is recent. Dominant caste residents with economic resources could access fee-paying English-medium schooling from 1910 till the 1990s without being morally suspect (Chapter 2). In fact, only those who had exceptional economic resources could access English-medium schooling. With the deepening of a cash economy and consumer practices, vehicles, readymade clothes, durable houses and English-medium schooling have both massified and hypersegmented in the post-1990s. Thus, if economic resources accorded one moral value till the 1990s, these are being recalibrated in the contemporary. When those with a 'little money' can also access English-medium schooling, what happens to the value of this sociopedagogic practice?

Unlike the houses of school families, which barely had a yard, headteacher Thomas' house was nestled in the middle of a two acre cocoa garden in one of the better-off neighborhoods in Edanadu. My visit was a courtesy call. Anybody researching anything in Edanadu had to meet Thomas, the local historian; he was the author of 13 books, including one about the histories of football in Edanadu. Thomas met me in a *lungi* paired with a more formal striped shirt, and as we sat down in the living room, he immediately drew my attention to a newly framed photograph – a lanky teenager shaking hands with President Obama. A citizen of the United States, Thomas' granddaughter had won the President's award and 'President Obama himself handed over the prize to her' he emphasized, gently. Thomas' two sons were professionals who had settled down in the US and the UK.

Thomas did not have much to say about English learning or uneconomic schools. However, as we meandered to the topic of low-fee English-medium schools, Thomas waxed eloquent:

Those who have at least a little money now send their children to English-medium [private primary schools]. It is a spectacle [*kamyamaya sambhavam*]. It is their blundered notion [*abadha dharana*]. It is a wrong perspective [*tettaya kazchapadu*] on life and society. They do it for social recognition. It's a misunderstanding [*thetti dharana*].

I was taken aback by the tirade. But soon it became clear that Thomas was talking about a particular parent, his domestic servant, who had enrolled her daughter at the New English School. Only Dalit women work as domestic maids in Edanadu, and their comprehensive withdrawal from stigmatized work had engendered a crisis in wealthier households. Thomas was one of the lucky few who still had a servant, but they were 'unreliable [*vishwasikkan pattukela*]' and 'only wanted to leave work'. Conducting fieldwork near Thiruvalla in late 1980s, Kurien (2002: 157) records propertied Syrian Christians remarking that Dalits 'would not be willing to be servants after getting educated'.

Thomas marks out his subjects as those with 'a little money now', delineating parents historically (now) and economically (little money). Capturing the radical economic changes of liberalization concisely and drawing attention to shifting aspirational terrains, he denigrates parents' aspirations. Another headteacher, who I will call John, had a PhD in Education and intermittently participated in curricular and policy production. Speaking explicitly to my interest in the economic, social and educational changes engendered by liberalization, he offered:

> Their economic levels have gone up, that is the main reason, and for status they now send their children to English-medium. They say 'I didn't study, at least let my kids study.' The state syllabus is good, but parents don't understand that, they want Western style education, shoes and socks, tie and pants.

John too identifies low-fee CBSE parents accurately even as he belittles them. He even ventriloquizes parents like Rebecca but unlike her claim, 'I couldn't study [*padikkan pattiyilla*]', for John, parents 'didn't study [*padichilla*]'. Furthermore, he models the decision-making of bad consumers like Rebecca, who allegedly value peripheral utility like the status that accrues from wearing shoes and socks (associated with private schools) rather than the central utility offered by schools (teaching and learning). Like Biju Prabhakar, John overlooks how this easy access to 'Western style education' has unsettled enduring local hierarchies, generated hope for non-elites and advanced deep anxieties among privileged families. He further elides the actual pedagogic practices of non-elite mothers.

I met Mary, another headteacher, several times since she was passionate about Freirean pedagogies that had been institutionalized in the state system. Though Freirean pedagogy insists on privileging the knowledge learners bring with them, in Mary's narratives, new-CBSE parents' aspirational mobilities are a central concern. According to Mary:

Fathers labor at loading jobs and then give away their hard-earned money to English-medium schools. Ordinary people don't understand the meaning of education. Their desires are for what they do not have – a palatial house, jewelry and gold, a new fridge. They think education is also like that.

Mary identifies the aspirational parent as a subsistence consumer (daily-wage laborer) but also gives him the responsibility of ordinariness. Instead of peripheral commodities such as shoes and socks, Mary introduces aspirational commodities that are not directly linked to the educational market: houses, jewelry, gold and fridge. By imagining education as an aspirational commodity, bad consumers delink educational processes from its core pedagogic value and spend money to accrue spectacular social value. Thomas offered the same logic when he said: 'It is a spectacle. It is their blundered notion. It is a wrong perspective on life and society. They do it for social recognition. It's a misunderstanding'. Mary transitions seamlessly from low-income and un-educated (loading jobs) to covetous and greedy (desiring palatial house); in her cultural world, the aspirations of 'ordinary' people are 'intellectually and even morally inferior' (Bartlett & Holland, 2002: 15).

Unsatisfied with the tenuousness of 'ordinariness', Mary eventually fragmented the fluid *sadharanakar* [ordinary] into *pavapettavar* [poor] and *sadharanakar* [ordinary Keralites]. In her clarified terminology, ordinary Keralites patronize English-medium schools and the poorest remain dependent on free state-funded Malayalam-medium schools. Interestingly, the headteacher at the New English School offered a similar but different distinction. According to her, the New English School served the 'most ordinary of ordinary Keralites [*sadharanakarilum sadharanakar*]'. If for Mary all ordinary Keralites now attended English-medium schools, the headteacher at the New English School asserted that some were more ordinary than others.

As explained in Chapter 2, Kerala's development trajectory was in part constituted by a translation of 'relations of domination into the language of legitimation' (Baviskar & Ray, 2011: 7). The ordinary Keralite [*sadharanakar*] was a key technique in this translation – it was the figure that could collapse landless lower castes and landowning dominant castes into a progressive citizen.[5] For instance, Prabhakar had equalized the peon and himself through the figure of the ordinary Keralite even as he accentuated the rational and moral differences between them. However, since the frame of the consumer highlights differences, both economic and rational-moral, it fragments the lie of the *sadharanakar*. The next section explains how the fragmentation of the ordinary Keralite is repaired by the frame of the good human, who shifts the focus from the irrational consumer parent in the present to the humanized child in the future. This shift was morally amplified by juxtaposing the humanized child with the child who is animalized through subjection to rote.

As alluded to in the previous sections, the limits of the ordinary Keralite are encountered at the caste line. Those who denigrated non-elites they were intimately familiar with specified them as Dalit (Thomas). If personal, specific references to non-elite English schooling highlighted caste as the immediate indicator of difference, general comments fore-grounded class even as caste was discursively indicated; loading work and paid domestic work are normalized as Dalit occupations in Edanadu. Meanwhile, the most explicit articulation of emergent Dalit educational desires as 'inappropriate' was made by a local philanthropist. In the 1970s, when even public transportation was limited, this philanthropist was one of the very few Edanadu residents who traveled by a private car to the nearby town of Thiruvalla to attend an (elite) English-medium school (Chapter 2). I met him every other day during my walk to school, and he repeatedly said to me, 'Even children from [the Dalit colony Raghu lived in] now go to English-medium. How times have changed! [*kalam poya poke*] What else will I have to see in this life time!' His apocalyptic descrip-tion of the annihilation of old social worlds reveals deep-seated anxieties about the new social relationships that non-elite English-medium school-ing symbolizes. English-medium schooling used to accrue spectacular social value, similar to that of a palatial house or gold. But what is its value when non-elites begin to access it?

If discourses of non-elite parents as bad consumers portray them as ignorant of the core value of schooling, policy perspectives affirm that non-elite parents are ignorant of the fundamental processes entailed in language learning. The national position paper (NCERT, 2006: 1) states:

> The opening up of the Indian economy in the 1990s has coincided with an explosion in the demand for English in our schools because English is perceived to open up opportunities. The visible impact of this presence of English is that it is today being demanded by *everyone* at the very *initial* stage of schooling. ... The popular response to systemic failure has been to extend downwards the very system that has failed to deliver. The level of introduction of English has now become a matter of political response to people's aspirations, rendering almost irrelevant an academic debate on the merits of a very early introduction. There are problems of systemic feasibility and preparedness, for example, finding the required number of competent teachers.[6] But there is an expectation that the system should respond to popular needs rather than the other way around.

From a position of disciplinary expertise, the national position paper pro-nounces non-elite parental aspiration as 'extending downward the very system that has failed to deliver'. Interestingly, the position paper's con-cern is that 'English is being demanded by *everyone* at the very *initial* stage of schooling'. Meaning, while *everyone* can and should demand English at *secondary* levels, only *some* should demand English at the *pri-mary* stage of schooling. In effect, according to the position paper, those who have historically had access to English-medium schooling are the *few* who can legitimately demand English at primary school levels. The privileged, by virtue of their privilege, make rational choices. But non-elites, by virtue of their deprivation, do not have the linguistic resources practically necessary to aspire for English-education for their children.

The position paper contends that non-elite aspiration, and political responses to such aspirations, should be based on, or at the very least subject to, expert knowledge.[7] This concern dovetails with discourses about bad consumers to construct non-elite parent aspirations as misplaced and faulty. As bad consumers, parents fail to provide quality education at comparable prices. As ignorant pedagogues, parents will fail their children in their efforts to learn English. Ultimately, there is nothing redeeming or redeemable about non-elite educational aspirations. Though aspiration shaming disrupts celebratory discourses about the ordinary, progressive, Keralite, it simultaneously produces a powerful moral geography that disassembles the ethical claims parents make by aspiring. As the next section details, the rupturing of the ordinary Keralite [*sadharanakaran*] is repaired by the production of the natural human [*manushyan*]. If the bad consumer described the irrational choice of aspirational non-elite parents, the good human shifts the focus to the child to reconstruct the rich–poor dichotomy into a human–animal difference.

From Ordinary to Human

Authoritatively explaining the lives and desires of new CBSE parents, the headteacher at an uneconomic state-funded school advised the Dalit mothers in attendance at a school function thus: 'These English-medium schools don't teach kids anything, education is not about speaking English, it is about becoming human'. Like the headteacher, textbook writers and curriculum committee members explicitly differentiate state and CBSE pedagogy along human and non-human lines, referring to CBSE pedagogies in primary grades as 'animal training', 'dog house', 'raising broiler chickens' and the like. Instead, the promise of education should lay in crafting a 'good human' who values humanism [*manushathvam*] and friendship [*sakhitwam*]. Aspirational bad consumer-parenting is thus aligned with a pedagogy that animalizes children.

'Becoming human' is a key Freirean concept wherein the oppressed, whose humanity has been stolen from them by traditional forms of education, become more fully human through critical, dialogical, education. At the heart of the Freirean project is the notion that becoming human is an awareness of unfinishedness and a commitment to change (Freire, 1998: 21). The oppressed can liberate themselves, and oppressors, by understanding that existing arrangements of oppression can be otherwise: we may be conditioned but are not determined (1998: 26). The critical pedagogy institutionalized by the state of Kerala builds on Freire's contributions to education and urges for pedagogy to be respectful to learners, especially non-elite learners, and for learning to be sensitive to the knowledge non-elites bring with them.

However, the Kerala state also predefines 'critical' such that the moral human is located outside the market. To become human, non-elites are urged to be critical of their desires for private English-medium schooling as well as the rote pedagogy characteristic of postcolonial second language contexts. The Kerala state thus urged marginalized mothers to become human by subscribing to norms that diminished their dignity and exacerbated their experiences of inequality. Writing about her work with a Freirean literacy program in Brazil, Bartlett (2010: 171) cautions that the Freirean teleology of learners moving from false to true (critical) consciousness can produce fervent convictions that some forms of literacy liberate oppressed people. On the contrary, she contends,

> No literacy or literacy pedagogy is inherently liberating ... instead, literacies provide certain affordances that people take hold of and use in various and somewhat capricious ways depending on their literacy ideologies, cultural resources, and social networks, as well as the larger social and economic relations in which they are situated. (2010: 169)

The idea that consumer practice, privatization or marketization can be liberating is unthinkable within a Marxist-communist framework. But in the context of liberalization, the unsettling of an agrarian subsistence society through marketization had profound affordances for non-elites to actively reconstruct their identities and aspirations in ways that challenged existing hierarchies. But these strategies – of understanding that existing arrangements of oppression can be otherwise – are delegitimized by the state. Freirean critical pedagogy became yet another deficiency theory defined around non-elites' (un)willingness to be critical of low-fee private English-medium schooling. The moral human would thus be critical but in ways that consolidated the interests of dominant groups.

Elaborating, the Kerala Curricular Framework (SCERT, 2007: 18) lists 'critical approach' as one of the aims of education and writes:

> The education we envision should have the space for learners to engage in critical dialogue. The practice of passive listening has to be discarded and in its place, learners need to become active participants in the process of constructing knowledge. ... Learners must be able to analyse the ideas in vogue at social, political and cultural levels, discern errors and take positions by responding to them.

It goes on to state:

> There is a general tendency to portray certain knowledge as noble and certain others as of less value in our textbooks. Culture, language and

situations in life are pictured from a hegemonic point of view. The negative impact that such treatment of knowledge makes on learners from disadvantaged background is immeasurable. Therefore the content, language and presentation of knowledge in a textbook should be organized from a critical point of view. (2007: 25)

For the Kerala state and Freire, the purpose of education is humanization for the building of a more authentic democracy.

The state however follows 'a general tendency' to portray certain practices (consumer activities and rote) as negative without considering the historic context (transition) or power relations (unsettling hierarchy) that situate them. The Kerala state is explicitly against privatization and consumerist agency and the Kerala Curricular Framework (SCERT, 2007: 16) states:

In the context of globalisation, Kerala is facing serious issues in the field of education arising from privatisation of education, mushrooming of self-finance institutions and the craze for market-oriented courses.

This generalized anti-privatization stance is clarified for school education by linking private English education with cognitive and moral degradation (SCERT, 2007: 44):

Privatization and the growing competition that take place in the field of education promote English-medium schools. This tendency can be seen in the middle and upper strata of the society. The National Curriculum Framework points out that there is a deterioration of values among learners of such elite schools. This can be attributed to the medium of instruction followed in these schools. A language that does not assimilate the thoughts and ideas of learners of Kerala society cannot facilitate well their cognitive development.

While the framework isolates 'elite schools' as morally corrupt, its ascription of causality to the medium of instruction and privatization extends moral degradation beyond the elites. In fact, the linkages between English, privatization and low learning levels (lack of cognitive development) evoke non-elite rather than privileged groups.

Interestingly, even as the state derided marketization, pedagogues in the state system proposed diverse ways to become human through more efficient participation in markets. Even as he affirmed the state's denigration of private school students, the headteacher at an uneconomic school claimed that state-funded, Malayalam-medium education humanized learners through its affordances for market differentiation.

I invite you to compare our students with private school students. Our students are in the forefront. They can survive in the face of adversity [*prathikula sahacharyangal*]. They are humane [*manushathvam ulla*]. They are not like broiler chicken, they are *nadan* [indigenous chickens]. Take courage, send your children to state-funded schools.

Pitiable white chickens in broiler cages are a common sight in Edanadu meat shops. But, *nadan* is available only on request. Colorful and strong-willed to the point of arrogance, *nadan kozhi* have tougher meat, live longer and more robustly, are free of hormonal injections and are higher priced in the market. Broiler chicken is standardized and commodified in the extreme. While *nadan* seems to suggest a disregard for the market, it actually indexes an entrepreneurial engagement with the market. Differentiation, not standardization, is the key. State-funded curriculum nurtures difference and creativity, but private CBSE schools standardize to the point of animalization.

Like the headteacher, who combined humaneness with strategic commodification in the figure of the *nadan* (chicken), the panchayat president Rajiv too advanced an entrepreneurial orientation to parenting:

> The mother sits with the child to teach everything. This spoon feeding shapes how the child will arrange his life. This is a world where children are at the center [*pillare chutti ulla lokam*]. If a pant loses its buttons, he will throw away the pant itself. There is no effort towards anything. English is not the issue. Children from earlier times knew how to survive.

For Rajiv, non-elite mothers' care work is 'spoon feeding' that propels passive learning and wasteful consumerism. Building on the notion of *jugaad* or frugal innovation, which celebrates adversity, deprivation, poverty and the lack of state support as a necessary condition for capitalist innovation and market expansion (Kaur, 2016), Rajiv re-signifies the literacy pedagogies of mothers in deprived circumstances (sitting with the child to teach) as regressive. Chapter 4 describes the labors and proficiencies of 'sitting-with' pedagogies and the ways in which such labors, and its resistances, are ameliorated through greater market participation. But for Rajiv, mothers' sitting-with work interferes with children's ability to survive, innovate and thrive. While the headteacher's account seems (but is not) oppositional to privatization, Rajiv urges for planned deprivation, which is what is required for the child to become entrepreneurial.

If the risks of dehumanizing educational practices, so far, have been animalizing or standardizing pedagogy, the stakes escalate when the social reproduction of privilege is threatened. In such contexts, becoming human is literally a matter of life and death. The National Focus Group on Curriculum, Syllabus and Textbooks (NCERT, 2005: 1) begins with such a scenario:

> *I have decided to end my life because the pressure of exams is getting to me. I can't take it anymore,* wrote Sudhanshu in his suicide note on

March 4, 2005. The education that should give hope, teach the worth of life, develop capabilities to shape it, is often taking life and enabling very few. The majority of even those who pass exams with flying colours are capable only of seeing life as a deadly competitive race in which they have to win to survive. The principal, to whose school the unfortunate child belonged, seems to be utterly bewildered. *We have conducted several workshops involving students on the need to combat stress. One just doesn't know what goes on in the minds of students these days,* she says. ... Children are being mercilessly overschooled in this misdirected educational system. That is one alarming aspect of Indian school education today. The other equally alarming aspect is millions of children grow up without entering a school, and many of those who enter drop out of unconcerned schools without learning anything. A very brief survey of the present-day classrooms would be enough to convince a keen observer that the most marked features of most of our educational practices in schools are a dull routine, bored teachers and students, and rote learning.

The twin concerns of Indian school education – hypercompetition among elites and resource deprivation among the 'masses' – are collapsed into one malaise, rote. Exam toppers see life as a deadly competitive race in which they have to win to survive, and in Sudhanshu's case, it led to suicide. Education should give hope, teach the worth of life and develop the capabilities to shape life. Education should teach one to become human. Instead, education takes life. While privileged groups negotiate the uncertainties engendered by economic liberalization through regimented childhoods and 'over schooling', national policy extends their encounters with precarity to eclipse the hopes of non-elite parents. As the following chapters explain, all children are to be saved through 'natural', oracy-focused pedagogies even if literacy rather than oracy is the more readily available resource in non-elite contexts. If value is the 'way in which actions become meaningful to the actor by being incorporated into some larger social totality' (Graeber, 2001: xii), the larger social totality against which all actions are evaluated is defined from the perspective of privileged elites.

Conclusion

Literature on low-fee private schooling imagines non-elite parents as ahistoric, sovereign individual consumers maximizing the utility available in the educational market. In contrast, this chapter argued that non-elite women migrating from the labors of a subsistence life to the relative ease of a consumer economy turn to English-medium schooling to substantiate and extend the radical social mobilities they have already experienced. Their ethical obligation to produce a similar experience of social mobility for their children drives the business of low-fee private English-medium schooling. Meanwhile, radical alterations of the social world provoke elite anxieties. Critical educators, textbook writers and policymakers manage this anxiety through aspiration shaming narratives. Non-elite parents are portrayed as bad subsistence consumers whose irrational aspirations jeopardize the democratic possibilities of education. This moral code strips non-elite action of meaning and value. If ethical obligations drive economic action in the case of non-elites, privileged groups reorder recently unsettled hierarchies by subordinating non-elite economic action to the moralities and life worlds of privileged actors. The following chapter shifts focus from aspiration to labor, specifically the labor-full contours of rote pedagogy. It details the pedagogic labors and English proficiencies of non-elites, and the ways in which these are delegitimized by an allegedly humanizing pedagogy.

Notes

(1) For example, see Tooley *et al.* (2007).

(2) Prabhakar was Chief Executive of the Kerala Medical Services Corporation from 2010 to 2013. The Medical Services Corporation is the central procurement agency for the 1200 government hospitals in Kerala.

(3) State-owned schools, as beneficiaries of the Sarva Shiksha Abhiyan (SSA) (Education for All) program, have benefited infrastructurally. SSA infrastructural funds are not extended to state-funded, community-owned schools such as St. Thomas. But both state-owned and state-funded Malayalam-medium schools in Edanadu were uneconomic (Chapter 2).

(4) As explained in Chapter 2, English-medium sections in state-funded schools did not have enrollment issues. But narratives like Prabhakar's typically use state schools as a synonym for Malayalam-medium schools. Further, differences between primary and secondary schools are also elided even though uneconomic schooling is largely a primary school phenomenon. Secondary schools almost invariably had English-medium sections.

(5) As Thiranagama (2019) points out, this collapsing is possible because of the social mobility experiences of Ezhavas, a former untouchable caste.

(6) As explained in later chapters, English users are not recognized as competent teachers. Only English speakers are accorded this status.

(7) As the book explains, disciplinary expertise is also historically situated and further, often works to legitimize the agendas and resources of privileged groups.

4 Social Lives of Rote

Located about a kilometer from the main road, The New English School is a non-descript, three-storied building situated on one corner of a one-acre plot. As noted in Chapter 2, it was designed and built according to the CBSE's affiliation requirements. A yellow mini-bus stands along the narrow driveway during school hours, near a smallish, tin-roofed hall that adjoins a boundary wall. The mandatory playground, earlier a paddy field, is usable only during the month of sports competitions. At other times, a variety of grasses and shrubs grow over the uneven, often slushy ground. The main building housed classrooms for Grades 1–12 as well as the administrative office and the staff room, and the tin-roofed hall, with its semi-partitioned rooms, housed the kindergarten classes. A couple of animal-shaped seesaws with fading and chipped paint bounded the kindergarten, which opened out into a makeshift playground. The tin roof kept the kindergarten rooms hot during the tropical summers, but there was no expectation for classrooms to be added to the main building. In fact, teachers routinely hoped that their meagre salaries, which for primary school teachers amounted to a little less than Rs. 5000 per month, would be paid, on time. Chandrika was one of the star teachers in the kindergarten section, with over 10 years of experience, most of it at a mid-fee-charging school.

Chandrika was initially uneasy with my request to observe the upper kindergarten (UKG) class she taught at the New English School. 'Observation' within a pedagogic context is by default evaluative, and she disliked the idea of being assessed by a Mallu PhD student from Ameerika. It took some convincing to assuage Chandrika's worries. I shared my difficulties with teaching Spoken English. Teaching is difficult work, making sure that students learn, even more so. This shared experience of legitimate interest and frustration mellowed the inspection-like character of my request. Furthermore, it was February. The academic year was drawing to a close. Chandrika was confident of what the students had learned over the year.

Tall and well built, Chandrika is an imposing presence in the classroom. She began the pedagogic display by facing away from the blackboard that organized most of the teaching activity.

She asked her class of 32 upper kindergarten students: '*What is today?*'
A chorus replied '*Tuesday*'.
She continued: '*What is the date?*'

The chorus replied '12-2'.
'*Year?*' she prompted.
'2014' pat came the chorus.
She turned to me to ask what subject she should teach.
When I suggested English, she turned to the blackboard.
She drew a pen, picked out a student, and asked '*What is this?*'
A shy boy stood up and answered: '*This is a pen*'.
She continued, to another girl now: '*Is this a pencil?*'
I realized that Chandrika had drawn a cap on her blackboard-pen to ensure that it would not be mistaken for a pencil.
'*No, this is not a pencil. This is a pen*'. The girl responded.

This was the English lesson the class had just completed. Translated from the textbook to the blackboard, and further onto student notebooks, re-drawn, re-written, asked, answered, the lesson had been taught and learned.

Curious, I asked Chandrika if she could try out a picture book I had with me. Titled *Big People*, this was a beginner-level picture book with a one-line sentence per page of illustration. One of the critiques against low-fee private schooling is that student proficiency is limited to class-taught material and oriented toward tests that require rote memorization. *Big People* was 'unseen' reading material. Since I had only one copy of the book, Chandrika wrote out the words on the blackboard and displayed the picture. She wrote it one line at a time, in sync with the display format of the picture book.

Brother is bigger than me.
She turned to her class and spelled it out: B-r-o-t-h-e-r and asked '*can you read?*'
A girl stood up and read '*Brother*'.
Chandrika pointed to the next word.
A chorus replied '*is*'.
The next word brought a pause.
Chandrika hid the *ger* from the '*bigger*' with her palm.
The chorus came back '*big*'.
Chandrika took her palm off and read for the class, '*bigger*'.
The chorus came back strong and sure, '*bigger*'.
Another girl read the rest of the line, '*than me*'.
Delighted, Chandrika told her class, '*Aparnakke oru clap [A clap for Aparna]*'.

The reading proceeded, and in no time they had finished the four-page, four-line book.

Though the school library did not have any picture books, and the practice was foreign to them, Chandrika demonstrated the reading readiness of her UKG class.

Later in the day, Chandrika qualified the impromptu pedagogic spectacle she had assembled for me: 'I had good students this year [*Ee varsham nalla pillara*]'. Though she was committed to her teaching work, she also recognized that her pedagogic success was contingent and fragile. She explained that she had difficulties with one particular child but immediately shifted the focus from the classroom to the home. The child's mother had three young children and could not 'pay attention at home [*vitti shradikkan pattilla*]'. Chandrika's consternation at having a student who could not be taught reveals the conditions necessary for her to be able to teach.

This chapter illuminates what is entailed in teaching English to young non-elite learners, in a postcolonial, second language context. I traverse between the classroom and home, using the narratives and practices of teachers, mothers and out-of-school paid tuition teachers to map out the density, scope and outcomes 'of non-elite sociopedagogic practices. I begin with an overview of the general organization of English pedagogy in kindergarten and primary schools in the region to orient readers to the literacy-focused nature of English pedagogy in academically oriented, second language contexts. Since this pedagogy is organized around copy writing in primary grades, I then present mothers' narratives about the intense labors they perform to ensure meaning-full, repetitive copy writing. Mothers delicately monitored home rote schedules and ensuing student resistance with motivational talks and after-school private tuition. Regular testing schedules further ensured consistent rote work. Much of this was possible only because mothers themselves were English literate, having completed their pre-degree courses (11*th* and 12*th* grades) in English-medium. This dense network of affective and pedagogic labors is what manifested as 'school readiness' in Chandrika's class, with its ready stock of beginner-level vocabulary. Teaching English for academic purposes in deprived circumstances is primarily undertaken at the home, and it is an exhausting job.

In stark contrast to the enormous efforts expended by mothers and other carers, national language policy and federally produced materials demanded labor-less, 'natural', oracy-focused pedagogy. As the postcolonial context transitioned into a new consumer society, on the one hand, critical educators maligned the aspirations of non-elite parents who had recently become consumers of private English-medium schools. On the other hand, they sought to reform literacy practices into oracy pedagogies on the pretext that conventional literacy practices animalize children. However, a comparative analysis of textbooks and pedagogic materials available from state and private providers shows that humanizing reform pedagogies actually demand resource plentitude, which has to be procured by parents through market participation.

English Literacy Pedagogies: Notebooks and Ezhuthi Padikkuka

The teaching of English in India has focused primarily on literacy proficiency. In fact, Fraser Gupta (1997) characterized India as a 'scholastic country' as far as learning English was concerned because English was principally encountered in and used in scholastic domains. English was the language of academic success in a postcolonial context. Indian English has largely been a 'modulect' used in specific modules or compartments primarily to do with professional work (Krishnaswamy & Burde, 1998: 154). Regional languages, not English, dominated social life, and for the most part, English pedagogy did not consider socializing in English, or oracy skills, a realistic or desirable pedagogic objective in India (Tickoo, 1986: 54). The hierarchies of English, as Ramanathan (2005) so incisively points out, were distributed around the production of different kinds of *literate*-in-English students.

Curiously enough, theoretical perspectives on learning English as a second language tend to prioritize oracy over literacy. This orality bias is traced to the disciplinary affinities of second language acquisition with linguistics. Kern and Schultz (2005) and Harklau (2002) clarify that linguists in general assume the primacy of oracy, while spoken language is considered natural and biological, writing is conceived of as a derivative of speech. Likewise, Pennycook (1994: 122) explains that linguists propose numerous arguments in favor of the primacy of speech: historical priority (in the course of human development speech developed before writing), structural priority (writing is a visual representation of speech) and biological priority (spoken language emerges before the written in children). This orality bias is so significant as to make literacy 'invisible'. Harklau (2002: 335) notes that two of the most influential overviews of second language acquisition by Larsen-Freeman and Long (1991) and Ellis (1994) contain no explicit references to literacy, reading or writing.

Critiquing the orality bias of linguists, Davies (2013: 36) distinguishes second language acquisition from second language learning, where the former refers to theoretical investigations of informally acquired language competencies and the latter pertains to institutionally structured, organized learning of language(s) geared toward particular expected proficiencies. Second language acquisition is primarily concerned about acquisition of speaking proficiencies, while second language learning tends to focus on reading and writing abilities.

Except in a miniscule set of elite schools, English classrooms in India were thus, by default, 'acquisition-poor' but learning-rich contexts (Tickoo, 1990). Tickoo (1995: 261) elaborates:

(a) ...the main source of the language is a prescribed textbook taught by the teacher. ...

(b) The teacher of English is a native speaker of one or two other languages which she shares with her pupils.

(c) The primary goal of learning the language is to gain access to it for what it has to offer as our world's most powerful source of scientific knowledge; it is primarily needed as the most important 'library language'.

While this context has its own entrenched internal hierarchies, what I elaborate below are the broad outlines of English pedagogy in primary grades in a literacy-focused pedagogic context.

Except for one high-fee-charging school in the nearby town of Thiruvalla, which followed a phonic approach scaffolded by the international *Letterland* curriculum, kindergarten English teaching in high- and low-fee schools focused on literacy learning. Lessons taught letter recognition and formation, adapted from *ashan-ashatti* teaching methods.[1] The teacher holds the pencil along with the child and traces out the letter form on paper and repeats the exercise about four to five times so that the child can mimic the pencil movements to read and write the letter independently. The first three to four months of lower kindergarten teaching is typically spent in this kinesthetic training, and complemented by a soundscape of rhymes, songs, stock greetings and story reading with extensive translation. During my month of apprenticeship-observation in the lower kindergarten class, the teacher traced out English capital letters from A–Z, one letter a day, with each of the 30 students. My job was to draw a bigger and bolder version of the capital letter in each of the student copybooks and draw out four columns for them to repeat the alphabet training activity at home. From individual letters, students graduate to words and upper kindergarten assumes students who can recognize and form Malayalam and English letters and can copy words from the textbook or the blackboard. In this context, the student notebooks, or comparable workbooks, were key conduits between the classroom and the home.

Primary grade teaching moved on to the reading and writing of words and sentences organized and managed around a textbook lesson, typically a story or a poem, which was read, translated and explained in class. As Tickoo (1986: 47) reminds, an exciting story line hid and clothed the language items, anchoring them in culture and affect. Classroom notes were structured by the questions supplied in the textbook, typically at the end of each lesson. In primary grades, notes inevitably began with individual words and ended with 'comprehension' question answers, and variably included opposites, plurals, and a variety of grammar exercises based on the lesson text but without a grammar definition that students had to memorize. Homework in early grades required the mastering of these notes, accomplished by the repeated writing of each item. Called *ezhuthi padikkuka* or writing-learning, each spelling word, plural, opposite and question-answer had to be copied out three to five times for it to be learned. Interestingly, the bright/weak student dichotomy ubiquitous in educational discourse in India becomes a bright/lazy [*midukkan – ozhappan/madiyan*] dichotomy in Malayalam. Children are not 'weak' learners; it is their capacity to do 'hard work' that matters.

There was surprising similarity across private schools, regardless of fee-type, when it came to student notebook content in primary grades. A class one notebook from the highest-fee-charging English school in Thiruvalla had almost the same content as the New English School, except for the fact that the notebook from the high-fee school was especially printed for the school and carried the school logo on its cover. But inside the 200-page, four-lined notebook, English lessons were constituted by individual words (say, good, walk, back); fill in the blanks (Tom is Suma's cat, Balu has a red kite); young ones of animals (tiger-cub, cat-kitten, dog-puppy); rhyming words (men, ten, pen, hen); question answers (Where's the mouse? The mouse is in the house. Where's the lion? The lion is in the den.); past tense (live-lived, walk-walked, open-opened); opposites (late x early, come x go, before x after) and so on.

In Edanadu, the differences between seemingly comparable notebooks became explicit only at the end of primary school, through testing transitions, from notebook-based to textbook-based testing. Reputed, high-fee-charging schools in Thiruvalla followed a notebook-based testing approach till fourth grade. Only what was recorded in the notebook would be tested, through oral and written tests. From fifth grade, these schools shifted to textbook-based testing. This meant that relying on notebook content was insufficient, and students had to identify textbook material as answers and reproduce the content without much deviation in form. The testing transition assumed that students could, and would, read and comprehend all the material contained in the textbook. The transition was rough and fifth grade was known for mass student failures and those who didn't make the cut transferred to other schools, both state-funded and private. The two low-fee-charging schools in Edanadu did not make the shift to textbook-based testing though attempts were made occasionally. The costs of communal student failure were far greater for low-fee schools, which did not have the linguistic or symbolic resources required to override the staged failures necessary to transition to new academic standards.

The broad pedagogic organization described above gives us a glimpse of the different kinds of interactions that transpire in the classroom. In his influential book on post-method English pedagogies, Kumaravadivelu (2006: 8, 71) differentiates between (1) textual interaction or the work required to negotiate the relationship between form and meaning at the sentence level, (2) interpersonal interaction or the roles and relationships that become available in the pedagogic encounter and (3) ideational interaction or the meaning potential of language in specific sociocultural, political and historic contexts. It is this relationship between textual, interpersonal and ideational interactions that I describe as the social lives of rote.

Teaching at the textual level of interaction made the modified input recorded in the notebook accessible to individual learners through translation, explanation, comprehension checks and simplification of input. English classrooms in India are marked by an abundance of translation and biliteracy practices, but only recently have these been seen as decolonizing and culturally relevant (Vaish, 2005). The roles and relation-ships available in this context have typically been seen from a deficiency perspective, which assumes monolingualism as the desirable norm. In contrast, interpersonal interactional activity is characterized by student resistance even as it was propelled by carers' ethical impulses. Within the literacy-focused English pedagogies pursued at the New English School, cumulative encounters with language input were guaranteed through forceful, fatiguing, but meaningful pedagogic labor. The responsibility and burden of labor-full, meaning-full rote, in primary grades, was largely shouldered by mothers. Mothers struggled to ensure a teachable student in the classroom to be recognized as good mothers.

At the ideational level, against the communist backdrop of Kerala, social relations and discourses tend to be dominated by an ethics of labor and resistance.[2] But in a consumer society driven by desire and aspiration, the exploited laborer morphs into the aspirational consumer who demands the pleasures of self-exploitation. As the next chapter explains, reformed pedagogies devalue labor and ascribe new values to expressive communi-cation, thereby aligning pedagogy with the new political economy.

The Responsible Home: Regimenting Rote

Children at the New English School wholeheartedly resisted the labor-full notebook-directed home pedagogy that required them to write, re-write and write again every bit of English they had to learn. In 20 of the 22 families interviewed from the New English School fourth grade class, mothers and grandmothers complained that children 'would not sit to study [irikkathilla]'; children's sitting was contingent on somebody, usually the mother, 'sitting with [kude irikkanam]' them. Annamma, a 62-year-old woman, described the labors she had to expend to get her grandson to 'sit' to do this fatiguing work:

He is very bright [bahu midukkana], but he needs attention [shradhik-kamenkil]. He'll get marks if someone will force him to sit and study [kuthi iruthi padippikamenkil]. He will not sit on his own [irikkathilla]. If I give him some work and go away, he will do everything else but study. Appachan [grandfather] will teach him, but he gets impatient and will hit him. So I don't ask him to.

She went on to describe how Bobby had, in the past few days, sat down to study and broken all his pencil points meticulously. She also reveals the gender dynamics of pedagogic labor: men could become impatient and vio-lent; women could and did get impatient and violent, and managing their own affective selves was part of the work involved in labor-full pedagogies.

Annamma was the only grandmother interviewed who was responsible for regimenting rote, since her daughter worked as a nurse in the Middle

East. In all other homes, the mother was responsible for this 'sitting-with' work and grandmothers supported or commented on the regimes. While grandmothers were typically ambivalent about the work required of young children, mothers were matter of fact about school expectations and the regimentation required to generate class-ready students. Especially in the case of the two working mothers, whose daily schedules were stretched to the limit with a six-day working week and its accompanying office work, house work, elder care and children's lessons, home teaching required a firm hand. Bindhu worked six days a week and was too fatigued to do any pedagogic work after she got home. Bindhu's mother Elsamma explained that 'she comes home and first thing she does is she pops a tablet [for body/head ache]'. But when class tests were around the corner, Bindhu made sure to sit with her son to get the required work done. Her teaching sessions were sharp, no-nonsense sittings, and her son knew not to fool around with his mother [*avade aduthu kali nadakkukela*]. Daisy too worked six days a week but made sure that she sat with her daughter on Sundays to go over the week's work. She also distributed her pedagogic work with others in the family, sending Jintu to older relatives for assistance. Jintu's great aunt was an English instructor who had spent considerable time abroad and considered English her first language alongside Malayalam. The ready availability of competent substitute instructors marked out the more privileged families at the New English School.

In comparison to working mothers, stay-at-home mothers were in-part appreciative of the fertile and furious imaginative work children produced to inhabit a world sans labor, right in the middle of 'sitting to study [*padikkan irikkumbam*]'. Gayatri described her daughter's tomfoolery during study time sarcastically as 'creative pursuits [*kala paripadikal*]' but went on to describe these with much laughter. But eventually, she still had to sit down with her daughter to get the pedagogic work done. 'Play' [*kali*] was a word that emerged frequently in mothers' accounts of what children did during their expected study time, particularly in the case of boys. Girls were expected to have a greater acceptance of anticipated servility. Meanwhile, mothers' descriptions also gave clues to the pedagogic basis of their work. Annakutty noted that her daughter 'brings notes [note *konduvarum*]', and she explains the notes [*paranju kotuthu*] to teach it. Abhiya clarified the difference between the earlier generation and her own – her mother would often *tell* her to study [*padhi padhi ennu parayum*] but Abhiya actually *taught* her daughter.

This difference between *telling* and *teaching* was crucial, and it was Ponamma, a much respected after-schoolteacher, who provided insights into the work entailed in home-teaching. Ponamma was a Dalit elder with a Bachelor's degree, who found salaried employment unattainable due to endemic caste discrimination. She was a skilled English user and a deeply reflective pedagogue with over 23 years of teaching experience. She explained that someone had to 'sit with' children during labor-intensive sessions and accomplish 'sense making [*senseilekku konduvaranam*]' for the lesson to be fruitful. Without adequate exposure to English, learners at the New English School needed help in extracting sound and meaning information from graphic symbols (Koda, 2005).

For instance, sitting-with work ensures that students repeatedly writing 'snail' understand it as a small animal with a shell. 'Snail' could as easily disintegrate and disappear into the constitutive letters of the word s-n-a-i-l. In my teaching work at the Malayalam-medium school, St. Thomas School, I often saw words copied out in this disintegrated manner. The child wrote 's' five times, then repeated 'n' five times, and so on. It was imperative that somebody sit with the child and insist on s-n-a-i-l, all together, written, read and repeated in this fashion. If the meaning got lost during this exercise, it had to be retrieved through a comprehension check at the end of the repetition. Ponamma noted:

Question answer	I explain all the words in the
Athinde words *muzhuvan*	question-answer
paranju koduthathinu	Only then do I give the answer
sheshame	
answer *kodukathollu*	
athu paranju answer *enne*	If the answer is not told back to me
kepichilengi	(after repeated writing) I'll hit
njan adikkum	I won't allow even one mistake
oru word *polum thettan*	You (learn to) study without mistakes
sammathikathila	If we start giving them concessions
ni perfect *ayitte padikku*	they will only repeat these mistakes
nammale oru concession	Steve (a student) hated
koduthu poyale ee thettukale	repeated-writing
avarthikkathe ullu	[He's in UKG], four opposites
Steve *ezhuthathe illayirunnu*	Big x small
[He's in UKG], four opposites	Happy x sad
Big x small	Day x night
Happy x sad	Left x right
Day x night	He would take up the use of each
Left x right	word
ee kunge oro use *edukkuva*	"I like small"
"*enikke* small *aa ishtam,*"	it has become meaningful to him
sense-*ilayi*	"Day is day"
day *pakala*	"I do not like right at all"
enikke right *eshtame alla*	He wrote very slowly, he did not
ezhuthan speed *illa*	have speed
enikke satisfied *aa*	But I was satisfied.

Ponamma's textual interactional activity includes bilingual explanations; diverse kinds of comprehension checks including observation of student work and oral questioning; and permission for some but not other deviations. With Steve, the non-classroom context allows Ponamma to not only dismiss his writing speed as inconsequential but also be attentive to individual student attempts at comprehension. What she insists on is cumulative, accurate, meaningful reading and writing in a pedagogic context with limited resources. As Amritavalli (2007: 12), explains:

> Acquiring language is very much like acquiring spatial familiarity with new territories; the exploration of our neighborhoods is for each of us a matter of personal choice, and our intake of new spaces proceeds at our own pace. In language acquisition as in spatial familiarization, many landmarks emerge from our repeated encounters with them, although a few are "given" to us by those who have gone before. And familiar features in new territories—a chain store in a new city, a known face in a crowd—stand out of the landscape to greet us and urge us on.

For Steve, his encounters with small, day and right have triggered associations and meanings, but he must encounter these terms repeatedly, meaningfully, for them to stay with him. Meaningful encounters too can fade away if they do not reappear frequently.

Lastly, accuracy and corporeal punishment surface time and again as integral to the pedagogic economy of rote for mothers, carers and competent substitutes like Ponamma. As the following section explains, to ensure learning in an acquisition-poor environment, carers mobilize a range of affective resources to coax children and themselves to endure and learn. To briefly summarize, mothers and carers regiment a forceful [*nirbandhichu*], meaningful and exhausting literacy pedagogy to ensure cumulative exposure to linguistic items. Mothers referred to the literacy skills accrued through rote as a 'foundation [*adisthanam*]' and candidly admitted that they planned to transfer children to English-medium sections in state-funded high schools after the foundation was well laid.

Managing Rote

While mothers regimented children's meaning-full rote schedules, they also strived to orient children toward self-management of resistance. Interestingly, such narratives drew on the deprivations of the past to motivate children to work hard toward better futures. However, secondhand memories of precarity were inadequate to allay student resistance. In its stead, what worked was the geographical distribution of rote through after-school tuition and the temporal resurgence of rote through regular class tests. While language learning theories traditionally isolate motivation into 'individual variables facilitating or hindering the cognitive activity of language learning' and organize a '"cause-effect" bearing between affect and learning', I follow recent sociolinguistic trends that consider the sociohistoric situatedness of motivation (Liyanage & Canagarajah, 2019: 2). Rather than children, it is mothers who were motivated, and their motivation was a sociohistoric emergence.

Mothers often expressed surprise at children's lack of responsiveness to rote requirements and mobilized personal histories of deprivation to urge students to study. As Lali explained:

Nowadays kids don't lack for anything [*onninum kuravilla*]. We give them everything they need, but they don't utilize it. He doesn't study hard enough, doesn't do well in school [*padithathille pora*]. He just wants to play.

Like Lali, Sonia too lamented her daughter's disinclination to study despite all the comforts parents made available. 'These days, kids grow up in such comfort [*sukha saukaryam*]. We grew up in difficult circumstances [*ellam budhimuttayirunnu*]'. Sonia deplored, 'all she has to do is study, but that is the one thing she will not do'. Spoken in front of and often to children as much as to me, these exhortations attempted to responsibilize students for their rote work. The relative comforts of the present were contrasted against the destitutions of the past in order to instill in them a sense of accountability. Mothers often drew on their own experiences of hardship, privation and poverty to produce aspirational children who would subject themselves to hard work. As Anju explained:

Our growing up years were times of deprivation and suffering [*kashtathayil-lula jivitham*]. We grew up in poverty [*daridryam*]. My father was a laborer [*kulipanikkaran*]. These days there is no suffering [*innu kashtatha illa*]. Everything you want is there for the taking [*kaiyille kittum*]. We should tell our children about the old days. We should tell them of how we used to live.

This mandate to teach children about the privations of the past in order to deter privations in the future meandered to educational labors.

In the two relatively privileged families that had experienced downward mobility, grandmothers were especially caustic. Jintu's grandmother had spent much of her married life at an estate in Peerimedu where her husband worked as a survey officer. Though everyday life without basic amenities was fatiguing, she had sat with her three children, making test papers at home to compensate for the uncompetitive school in the remote estate location and insisting on study time even during holidays. But her son, Jintu's father, had barely passed his 10*th* and had not attended pre-degree college. He now had a make-shift job administering a petrol pump, which paid him only about Rs. 5000 per month. She openly called him a fool [*mandan*] and cautioned that those who did not study would 'get nowhere [*engum ethathilla*]'. Similarly, Leni's grandmother, whose husband had worked as a CRPF officer in Bilai Steel, insisted that 'if men did not study', they would 'end up in trouble [*anungale padichile prash-nama*]'. Her son worked as a foreman in Abu Dhabi, but they had better-off cousins whose children studied in Kendriya Vidyalayas. Leni's English had 'no standard' compared to theirs and this familial competition pressed her regimentation of rote. The message was reiterated that doing well in life and becoming respectable was dependent on children's capacity for hard work. Responsibility mingled with shame became an everyday affect that could *potentially* interrupt play and precipitate work.

However, the only two cases where children discarded play for hard work were those of Reni and Ruby, both girls. Unlike their classmates, Reni and Ruby confronted multiple forms of embodied precarity. Ruby's father had died unexpectedly in an accident; he had worked as a driver in the Gulf. Following his death, her father's siblings contested his inheritance, the house they lived in. They lived frugally, and the mother noted how 'Ruby never asked for anything', knowing how difficult it was to make ends meet. Similarly, Reni too made no demands of her parents. She had three siblings, and the oldest two had studied at state-funded schools because the family could not afford English-medium schooling for all children. The sacrifices of the family funded her schooling and made Reni a 'responsible' child who 'sat to study on her own [*thane irunnolum*]'. Both Reni and Ruby were toppers in their class, alternating in some subjects with Leni. Motivations came from embodied affects rather than from (remembered) proxies of precarity.

Mindful of the limitations of their responsibility lessons, mothers complemented their management of resistance with the distribution and routinization of repetition. Of the 22 families, 16 sent children to an after-school teacher. Except for one mother who referred to herself as 'uneducated', all the other mothers supervised children's work, especially before tests, but also patronized after-school paid instruction. Particularly in the case of boys, mothers felt that 'tuition' was a method to accomplish more sitting-with work. As Preethi explained: 'if I don't send him for tuition, he will play that much longer [*athrem samayam kude kalikkum*]'. Regardless of relative docility, girls too were sent to after-school teachers. The time spent sitting-writing-learning was thus extended geographically.

Meanwhile, periodical class tests were a crucial institutional scaffolding that reinvigorated both mothers and children. When students, mothers and even teachers became fatigued and lax, the test shocked them back into labor. Preetha explained that the teaching at the New English School was 'good [*nallatha*]' because teachers conducted periodical tests and by extension, timely revisions and notebook corrections. A common refrain among mothers was '*pariksha verumbam padikkum* [child will study when exams are round the corner]'. Competitive comparison with friends, the possibility of failure and its accompanying punishments and potential intensification of rote in the case of low scores all spurred furious study during test weeks. Teachers' note-checking and mothers' note completion were also stimulated by tests, since the basic prerequisite for study was the completed notebook. In case of incomplete notes, either due to absence or student negligence, mothers or carers typically borrowed notebooks from neighboring students or took time out to come to school and copy notes. Bobby's notes, for instance, were often incomplete, and his grandmother and tuition teacher managed by copying notes from a classmate who lived close by.

Testing disciplined all involved and though most mothers appreciated regular testing, they also disproportionately shouldered the responsibilities of teaching to the test. Sheeja, a teacher at the Malayalam-medium school and whose child was enrolled at the New English School UKG, provided regular updates during the test weeks: she had to teach multiplication tables from 1 to 10 and a range of tenses over the course of a unit-test schedule (two months). 'They just send all the work home', she routinely remarked. Beena provided a more intimate record of what this involved. Beena was a Dalit mother I became acquainted with at church. Beena's son was enrolled in UKG and the quantum of rote she imposed on her son frequently upset her carefully crafted balance of affection and punishment, with the routine class tests generating much anguish. After one particularly harrowing episode, Beena confided:

> There is so much to teach, 'this, that, those, these;' '1-100.' And there is 'fox and the stork.' The entire story. His marks are zero, one, five, like that. How am I supposed to teach all this [engane padippikana]? I teach a little, what he can learn, but when he comes back with marks like that, won't we feel sad? [mark medichondu verumbam namukke sangatam verathille?] He studies so much [avanayita ethrem padikkunathu], I feel bad for him. I taught him everything in the morning, but when I asked him in the evening, he had forgotten everything. Sometimes when we ask out of context, they might forget? Maybe that is what happened. But I was furious and miserable [enikkangu deshyavum sangatavum vannu], I hit him.

Beena describes work, resistance and punishment, and the affective registers that inflect these. She acknowledges her son's labors (he studies so much) but also notes its inadequacy. Her careful rationalizations – teaching only as much as her son can learn and repetitive revisions to ensure learning – fall apart, but she continues to arrange her affective and pedagogic responses. Perhaps he forgot because she had asked out of context. Though she had hit him in the moment, her own analysis of the pedagogic moment continues well past the event. Beena concluded by saying: 'I am thinking that we should send him somewhere else next year'. However, her ability to manage pedagogic responsibility remained unbreached that year for her son scored well (86%) in the exams. Her son seemed to have crossed a learning threshold for Beena herself seemed startled at his improvement.

> He had written everything, grammatically correct also [grammar anussarichu], 'we see with our eyes,' 'between,' everything, I was so surprised [njanathishayichu poyi].

On the one hand, testing stretched her to the very limits, pushing her to corporeal punishment so that her young son would reliably produce the academic performances required of him. In the event he did not, they would even have to change schools. On the other hand, it is this intensification of rote pedagogy that pushed young Pratyash over a learning threshold. Schooling entailed the crossing of such thresholds, and even a small miscalculation could upset the careful balance of learning and requisite academic performance.

Conditions of Possibility: Mothers' Education and English Teaching

In Edanadu, non-elite mothers mined their affective resources, familial connections and scarce economic funds to shape motivated, resilient students who could follow literacy directives with adequate fluency. However, the most crucial resource at the New English School, in addition to the affective labors described earlier, is mothers' and carers' linguistic resources. As Table 4.1 shows, of the 22 mothers interviewed at the New English School, 17 had post-10*th* grade education, which during their school going years was available only in English-medium. All parents except for one father and one mother in different families had attended Malayalam-medium schools till 10*th* grade. To put it bluntly, mothers' linguistic resources and pedagogic work was crucial to the existence and success of English-medium schooling.

Table 4.1 Educational levels of 22 families at the New English School

Educational Level	10th grade or less	Pre-degree/Voc.	Degree/Diploma	Profess.
Mothers	5	10 Pre-degree	3 Deg./1 Dip.	3
Fathers	15	2 Pre-deg./2 Voc.	2 Degree	1

The gendered work that allows for English-medium schooling in non-English-speaking life worlds is neither recent nor peculiar to private schools. The first English-medium section in Edanadu during the post-independence years opened in 1964 in the only state-funded high school that served the region. A retired headteacher from this school, Cherian, who in 1964 was a senior teacher, noted that admission to the English-medium section was subject to a student 'interview' by the headmaster. Cherian had sat in on some of the interviews. He said:

The interview wasn't a big deal. The headmaster was just conversing [*chumma varthamanam parayum ennullathe ollu*]. So I asked him: 'Sir, what is this interview that you are conducting?' –He was just conversing– 'You are admitting everyone, then why are you doing this?' He said: 'I did not interview the children. I interviewed their mothers.' So I asked, 'you interviewed mothers?' If the mother knows some English [*ammakku vallom English ariyamengi*] she will teach the child. What are we going to teach here? [*Evidenna padippikana?*] So very prudently [*budhiyayittu*] he admitted only those students whose parents already knew English.

The headteacher was practical enough to recruit to his English-medium section only those children whose parents, or rather mothers, could teach their children (English) at home. At the same time, he was strategic enough to conceal his expectations. The idea of the school as the *proper* location of learning could not be compromised even though the home had to be a *central* location for learning. Such surreptitious sorting, or what Ponamma calls 'selection', has long been institutionalized within the formal school system, earlier between English and Malayalam-medium sections within the same school and now separated out across private English-medium and state-funded Malayalam-medium schools, especially in primary grades.

Unsurprisingly, rote pedagogy disciplined mothers as much as students and defined what they could and couldn't do. As Table 3.1 showed (p. 42), 12 of the 22 mothers interviewed at the New English School were stay-at-home mothers, and another 6 worked in professions 'suitable' for women, whereby they would be available for their children, after school and during vacations. One such acceptable full-time work was school teaching, an extension of their familial roles. Teaching at low-fee schools paid significantly less than domestic work or female agricultural labor, but it was not uncommon for mothers to take up low-paid teaching work since low-fee schools offered tuition discounts to children of staff. The social norms around mothering were so strong that a nurse who worked in the Middle East earning Rs. 80,000 per month had to resign and return home during my fieldwork period because her son was doing poorly at school. Among the mothers I interviewed, the only one who disregarded expectations of the regimented home, without encountering heavy sanction at the school, was Anila, whose only son Abel was enrolled in fourth grade. Anila had lost two children in miscarriages, and Abel was a 'child born of many prayers [*prarthichu kittiya kuttiya*]'. Having experienced the pain of losing two children, Anila's perspective on success and future living was different from normative imaginings in Edanadu. Abel went to Ponamma teacher for after-school tuition but was not harried at home. Though he was seen as a 'below-average' student, the school community accepted the mother's exceptional valuing of life, after encountering death, to let her child be.

Between the Market and the State

My staffroom desk at the New English School was sandwiched between those of two regular English teachers. Jessy taught Grade 1 and Suja taught Grades 3, 4 and 5. Mini, who taught Grade 2, sat across from us behind a heap of student notebooks that regularly came in for correction. Recess, lunch breaks and the odd free periods were cacophonous, with teachers discussing students, sari fashions, the rising costs of fish and bananas, and their mothers-in-law. Every now and then Jessy would lament the impossibility of teaching the English textbook. She could not get students to read the textbook. Suja was quieter by nature, but she too wondered 'how she was supposed to teach this kind of textbook'. Mini plodded on, providing us with brief descriptions every now and then of how she persisted to get students to read the textbook. For all three teachers, students reading their textbooks – accurately, fluently, individually – was an indicator of learning proficiency that eluded them.

This section explains how the state fractured opportunities for reading fluency even as private publishers amplified it. To do so, I compare two federal state subsidized textbooks with a non-subsidized, privately published textbook popular in Edanadu and Thiruvalla. Both the federal-state textbooks are designed and published by the National Council of Educational Research and Training (NCERT), the apex body in India entrusted with framing school educational policy. The NCERT *Marigold* series were developed to exemplify the stance of the National Curricular Framework (2005) and the Position Paper of the National Focus Group on Teaching of English (2006). Recognizing the incompatibility of the *Marigold* series for non-elite contexts, the NCERT started work on a second series, *Raindrops*, explicitly for 'first-generation school goers as well as children whose only exposure to English is in school (and even within school, usually, with limited time duration and constraints in quality)' (NCERT, 2011a, About the Book). But the series was suspended after the completion of books for Grades 1 and 2 since it seemed to reinforce existing inequalities. The reliance on a singular, simplified textbook inadvertently relegated *Raindrops* to the 'survival English' variety. As Ramanathan (2005: 59) explains, English teaching in India has historically been organized around two kinds of 'literate-in-English' users: one expected to reason and express opinions and another limited to survival English and the minutiae of writing, like capital letters, punctuation, neat writing and so on. *Marigold* and *Raindrops* would have continued this legacy, the former for advantaged literary users and the latter for the 'masses'. In primary grades, the New English School prescribed the *Marigold* textbook. This is the text that Jessy, Suja and Mini struggled to teach in their classrooms.

The privately published textbook analyzed here is the glossy *New Broadway* published by Oxford University Press, priced at Rs. 146 in 2013. It was the revised version of the *Broadway* series, first published in 2003 under the editorship of Paul Gunashekar, a senior professor in the Materials Development department at the English and Foreign Languages University (EFLU), Hyderabad. Of the 10 authors listed in the *New Broadway*, five are affiliated to the EFLU, and the others work at elite schools such as the Mother's International School, Delhi, the Hyderabad Public School, Hyderabad, and the Lawrence School, Sanawar. In textbook writing circles, the *Broadway* series was considered a runaway success like the earlier *Gulmohur* series edited by another EFLU professor, V.

Shasikumar, who was the Head of the Materials Production department at EFLU. The first edition of the *Gulmohur* was published in 1975, and in 2013, the seventh edition was available in the market.

Mindful of students' need to revisit linguistic items meaningfully, textbooks for primary grades (1) are heavily illustrated and (2) they build various kinds of repetition into the lesson text as well as the exercises. These meaningful encounters are then supposed to be copied into the notebook, repeatedly. I analyze one lesson from each of the textbooks, focusing specifically on its appropriateness for primary grades.

To briefly introduce the three lessons, the NCERT *Marigold* lesson *Storm in the Garden* tells the young snail Sunu Sunu's account of his first big storm. It is sourced from a picture book published by Tulika. The original picture book is a 24-page, full-color, illustrated book. According to the publisher's description of the picture book:

> Sunu Sunu the snail is playing in the garden with his friends, the ants. Suddenly there is a storm. He hurries home to his mother and tells her all he saw and heard. This delightful picture book has simple text, with sound words capturing the mood. Eloquent illustrations evoke a snail's-eye view of the storm in his world – the garden.

The second lesson, from the NCERT *Raindrops,* titled 'What's Going On?' is based on a single-page description of two culturally familiar activities: playing carom and preparing dinner. Unlike the *Marigold* and the *New Broadway,* which organize language teaching around stories and poems, *Raindrops* uses much more simplified text like the picture description genre.

The third and last lesson analyzed here is *A Clean Street*, from the Oxford *New Broadway* textbook. This lesson is an event-based moral lesson written by the textbook author. Classmates Neela and Shakeela chance upon a cow eating a plastic bag, a common enough sight on urban streets. The agitated girls confront, albeit 'politely', the roadside vegetable seller, Kumar, whose plastic bags are the cause of the trouble. The girls' reformist entrepreneurism prompts the vegetable seller's wife to start making cloth bags. The problem of dirty streets is solved by 'polite' middle-class schoolgirls who say 'please'. As Janaki Nair (2015: 2) points out, the institutionalized arrangements that underpin 'cleaning' in India are so embroiled in the caste order that middle-classed cleaning campaigns find it 'safer to take refuge behind a strategy of psychologizing and individualizing such habits and ways of thinking'.

Table 4.2 briefly summarizes the pedagogic analysis to show how the NCERT *Marigold* textbook design with its minimal illustrations, patterning and repetition atrophied literacy pedagogy. First, only 3 of the 13 scenes in *Marigold's Storm in the Garden* are illustrated. The original picture book published by Tulika illustrates each and every aspect of how

Table 4.2 Textbooks, comparative analysis

Publisher Textbook Price	Oxford *New Broadway* Rs. 146	NCERT *Raindrops* Rs. 30	NCERT *Marigold* Rs. 45
Grade	1	2	2
Prose Lesson	*A Clean Street*	*What's going on?*	*Storm in the Garden*
Pages	2	1	3
Words	55 + 73	72	46 + 103 + 68
Illustrations	All scenes illustrated; 4 of 6 scenes alongside; remaining 2 on same page	Every activity is illustrated	Only 3 of 13 scenes illustrated
Formatting and textual design	Each action/location is in one easily recognizable block. Dialogues are separated out from running text.	*ing*-form in bold; 4 examples of plural-*ing* in 1*st* paragraph (*are playing*); 5 of singular-*ing* in 2*nd* (*is getting*)	Sounds in italic but built into running text *Hee, Hee, Hee Kaa, Kaa, Kaa, Kaa Shay, Shay, Shay, Shay*
Exercises	13	6	5
Revisiting lesson	All 13 revisit lesson content: 3 revisit *please*; 5 revisit illustrated vegetable/s & colors; 4 revisit illustrated story title/main theme	Ex. 1 & 2: Picture description using *ing* form (Illustrated)	Ex. 1 & 2: Listing of new words; Comprehension questions

the garden experiences or expresses the storm, for instance, the swaying trees, the falling rain drops, the booming thunder, the zapping lightning and so on. Unlike the *Marigold*, the *New Broadway* and *Raindrops* offer illustrations for every aspect of the lesson text. In *A Clean Street*, all the main characters and events – the two schoolgirls, the cow eating the plastic bag, the girls confronting the vegetable seller and his wife making cloth bags – are illustrated, and the theme of dirty/clean is carried forward in the exercise illustrations. The pedagogic activities that follow are also thoroughly illustrated. *Raindrops* is similarly designed, though without the glossy finish of the *New Broadway*. The actors and activities (playing carom and preparing dinner) are minutely illustrated and the lesson text is effectively a picture description.

The significance of illustrations, especially for beginner readers, is underscored by Amritavalli (2007: 41–45), who records that every learner *chosen* text inevitably has at least one picture to go with it. As Krashen and Terrell (1983: 55) clarify, illustrations and visual aids 'supply the extra-linguistic context' that helps learners understand the message encoded in alphabetic symbols, similar to the context-embeddedness Cummins (1979) describes for face-to-face interactions. In Kumaravadivelu's (2006) terminology, illustrations perform crucial textual interactional work that make the form meaning relationship accessible for beginner learners.

Second, both *Raindrops* and *New Broadway* chunk the lesson text and use formatting to break up reading length and to highlight patterns. In *Raindrops*, syntactical repetitions are set in bold to draw attention to the repeated tense form: present progressive tense, first in plural and then in singular, but grammatical labels are avoided. *New Broadway* had short sentences and dialogues that were chunked and took up only a quarter of the page. In contrast, the second page of *Marigold*'s *Storm in the Garden* has around 70% running text. Short, complete blocks of reading material are crucial for beginner readers. Amritavalli (2007: 26) explains that 'a satisfactory reading experience' requires 'closure in terms of reading a complete and coherent text'. 'Focus on forms' integrate form with meaning, increase noticing capacity, and promote intake processing (Kumaravadivelu, 2006: 64–65).

Last, *Raindrops* and *New Broadway* revisit lesson chunks at word, sentence, structure and thematic levels through exercises. Koda (2005) explains that the cumulative exposure afforded by repetitive encounters with visual-sound input engenders 'fluency' while the inverse precipitates difficulties in print-information extraction (comprehension) with readers eventually giving up trying to read (Koda, 2005: 30, 58–59). Similarly, Jangid (2004: 34) describes how patterns, refrains and predictable sequences help children catch on to meaningful chunks of language, and even 'children with very little English' are enabled to 'use and practice vocabulary and language patterns in an interesting and meaningful way'.

Raindrops continues the picture description pattern of the lesson into the first exercise and asks students to describe a similar but different picture. The activities to be described are the same as those previously encountered (a number of persons sitting and standing). The lesson text therefore provides the lexical (word level) and syntactic (structure level) scaffolding required for students to complete the activity. The second exercise follows the same logic but is designed as a written activity, and again, learners are invited to revisit the lesson text. The third, fourth and fifth exercises are vocabulary exercises that overlap with but do not entail a return to the lesson text. The last is a counting activity where the actors are new (animals not introduced in lesson text), but the concept remains the same: singular and plural. The repeated revisiting of the lesson text through similar but different activities, detailed illustrations and coherence across the text and activities are design elements geared toward meaningful encounters with English.

New Broadway offers an even greater range of exercises that substantively revisit the lesson at word, sentence, structure and thematic levels. A before-the-lesson activity asks students to match words (plastic, cloth, paper) to images of different kinds of bags. Plastic versus cloth bags is central to the story and is repeated in two more exercises. Two reading exercises, one true or false, and another, question answer based, prompt students to revisit the lesson at the sentence level. The four exercises that follow illustrate the colors and vegetables noted in the lesson. The next two on indefinite articles (a, an) and present tense verbs (is, are) revisit nouns and sentences from the lesson. Two writing exercises revisit the lesson heading and main theme through a poster-making activity, and three listening-speaking exercises pick up on the dialogues in the lesson and the central theme respectively. In short, a student who has completed the exercises in the *New Broadway* and *Raindrops* would have had multiple opportunities to both understand the lesson text and to repeatedly encounter English words, sentences and structures meaningfully.

In contrast, *Marigold*'s *Storm in the Garden* exercises provide minimal occasions to revisit the text. The first is a list of 'new words', which includes the 'snail' that we saw earlier as a dictation word. The second is a set of comprehension questions which transfer one-sentence answers from the lesson text into the notebook. The revisiting of the text stops here for the two following questions are general questions which do not revisit the lesson content at word, sentence or thematic level.

Toward the end of my fieldwork, Jessy came from the principal's office with a variety of grammar workbooks, produced by private publishers, to complement the *Marigold* textbook. It had been a long-fought battle, and Jessy had enlisted my status as an 'expert' to insist that the *Marigold* be supplemented with other materials. If students could not learn to read their textbook, Jessy felt her literacy-centered English pedagogy was stuck. The textbook design – minimal illustrations, patterning or repetition – atrophied her efforts. Mindful of the economic implications, the principal decided to prescribe one grammar workbook instead of changing over to a course pack that included a textbook, activity cum workbook and a grammar book.

As a federally subsidized textbook, the *Marigold* was the most reasonably priced textbook in the market, and the principal was hesitant to put additional burdens on parents. Jessy chose *The Grammar Tree* from the several offerings at hand. Table 4.3 lists the kinds of materials available and the economic and peripheral costs at which these were available.

While picture books encourage creative revisiting of the text and offer a welcome substitute to the trials of rote pedagogy, the glossy pictures made them expensive; consequently, private publishers did not target small towns let alone villages. The nearest location for many of the subsidized books was the state capital Thiruvananthapuram, about 120 kilometers away. Furthermore, though state-subsidized publishing houses such as the National Book Trust and Children's Book Trust have an online presence, the cataloging and web-design did not provide book previews, making it difficult to choose the appropriate level. Ultimately, the peripheral costs of subsidized English picture books made them extremely challenging to procure.

Table 4.3 English markets: Materials with price and availability during 2013–14

English textbooks (Grade 1)	Publisher	Rs.	Grades
Marigold	NCERT (State)	45	
Raindrops	NCERT (State)	30	1–2 only
Broadway	Oxford (Pvt)	146	
New Generation (English, Maths, Science, Social Studies) Per Semester × 2	Holy Faith/MBD (Pvt)	180 × 2	
Workbooks (Grade 1)			
Workbook for *Marigold*	Holy Faith/MBD (Pvt)	40	
New Generation Activity book Per Semester × 2	Holy Faith/MBD (Pvt)	65 × 2	
The New Grammar Tree	Oxford (Pvt)	136	
Picture books			**Market**
I Can Read (series)	Harper Collins (Pvt)	113 each	Town
Tulika books, limited titles	Balasahitya Institute (State)	35–40	
Various	National Book Trust (State)	25–40	Metros, internet
	Children's Book Trust (State)	25–40	
	Pratham Books (NGO)	30–40	
	Tulika Books (Pvt)	95–150	
Storybooks (Primary school)			
The Three Little Pigs Chicken Licken, etc.	Ladybird (Pvt)	99	Town
Storybooks (Middle school)			
Alice in Wonderland Beauty and the Beast Panchatantra Tales, etc.	H&C Publishers (Pvt)	20	Village
Weekly Children's Magazine			
Magic Pot	Malayala Manorama (Pvt)	15	Village

Textbooks and workbooks were thus the most readily available materials, and private publishers aggressively marketed their offerings through agents who made regular school visits, regardless of remoteness of location. The growing popularity of workbooks that stand in for or supplement notebooks attest to parental and teachers' desires for institutionalized repetition. Private textbook publishers offered discounts to schools, anywhere between 20% and 70% off the marked price, which, however, are not passed on to students but form a key source of revenue for private schools (CABE, 2005). The NCERT offers a flat 15% discount to all schools. Toward the end of the school year, the principal confided that she wanted to shift from the NCERT to a private publisher, MBD. The MBD agent had offered one 'free' smart classroom, a digitally enabled white board with attached classroom content worth Rs. 160,000, if the school agreed to purchase 'books worth net value of Rs. 300,000 for three consecutive years', which meant textbooks from MBD for all subjects and all grades from kindergarten to 12th grade.

The rote pedagogy that allowed non-elite mothers to access and make-do with private English-medium schooling for their children was thus located at the intersection of an inattentive state and a hyper-segmenting market. Pedagogic materials especially picture books have proliferated in the post-market reform period but remained inaccessible for non-elites. As the next section explains, though the state's pedagogic policy fully supports diverse kinds of repetition, both oral and literacy-based, its deep-seated assumptions about oracy as the natural domain of language dominated the *Marigold*'s textbook design. Therefore, though the state claims that all children are teachable, not just those who are made teachable at home through rote pedagogies, it effectively delegates proper English teaching to English *speakers*. English *users* like Ponamma, mothers, and teachers like Jessy, Suja and Mini became illegitimate teachers.

The English Speaker: Transforming Bad Pedagogy into Good Teaching

The pedagogic design of the *Marigold* – with its lack of illustrations or repetitive encounters with linguistic items – was imagined as good pedagogy through the figure of the English *speaker*, an entity who did not exist in the context of non-elite schools. The input-rich communicational environment that the *Marigold* sought to generate in the classroom was dependent not so much on the textbook as it was on a teacher who could bring the diverse elements of the textbook into coherence through oracy.

In my interviews at the NCERT and EFLU (Chapter 8), the chairperson of the position paper, Prof. Amritavalli, who also drew up the blueprint for the textbooks, explained how the *Marigold* was to be taught: through questions about the illustrations and through activities that delivered a constant flow of teacher talk, at least part of which was in English. Elaborating, NCERT English faculty Prof. Keerti Kapur assembled an impromptu lesson plan for the first lesson from the *Marigold* textbook for Grade 1, a poem titled *A Happy Child*. The poem began with the line 'My house is red' and Kapur suggested that the teacher spend a week on the color red: on vegetables, fruits and such like. She continued:

Then move on to shapes, sizes (big, small).
Do a worksheet on the house.
Let children color it.
Student can say 'I live in a green house'.
Text is just one resource, you have to generate your own resources.
My lessons do not come to an end.
Ek lesson *de do* [give me one lesson], I can teach for one year.

Amritavalli concurred:

> You need input, where is the input going to come from?
> Day one, talk about poem.
> Talk about the picture (of a smiling girl on a swing) in mother tongue.
> Children have very good memories, they will learn to listen.
> Do activities.
> English comes with activity.
> Activity is an excuse to do English.

Interestingly, both the *Raindrops* and the *New Broadway* adopt a similar strategy but by scripting activities into the textbook, which emphasize repetition and literacy. In textbook writers' parlance, this is called 'exploiting' the (authentic) text. *Marigold* on the other hand assembled an array of activities which are disconnected to the lesson text. For instance, the *Storm in the Garden* is preceded by a poem titled *Rain* with its own set of dictation words and comprehension questions, a story completion exercise called *Counting Clouds* followed by a crossword puzzle about clouds, a riddle on water, a drawing and picture description of a fish tank, a four-line song about rain, a rhyming exercise with none of the words encountered so far and a fill-in-the-blanks exercise that introduces four new water bodies (river, pond, sea and lake). This atrophied repetition and further laid expectations of oracy on the teacher to generate the connections and coherence lacking in the textbook.

Amritavalli acknowledged that the activities in the *Marigold* were 'trivial' but expected teachers to generate sufficient meaningful repetition through oral interaction. For her, the triviality of the exercises, the disconnected jumble of activities and the lack of exercises which revisited the lesson text were not particularly significant because the primary input was meant to be spontaneous teacher-talk. She insisted, as did Keerti Kapur, that the lesson was not meant to be read, and definitely not meant to be written and re-written and mastered for tests. Ultimately, what the NCERT presented non-elites with was a single textbook that was designed for an English-speaking teacher. Neither mothers nor teachers at the New English School had the oral resources necessary to teach the *Marigold* or the textbook design skills necessary to transform the *Marigold* into a teachable textbook.

The *Marigold* attempts to provide a diverse and rich spectrum of inputs within a single textbook, or what national policy calls an 'input-rich curriculum'. But by substituting meaningful repetition of literacy activities with an oracy-focused pedagogy, it ended up providing a sociopedagogically alien curriculum. On the one hand, the *Marigold* is composed of 'authentic texts' including poems, stories, rhymes, jokes and so on, which are supplemented by a range of disconnected activities and tasks including origami, drawing, dot connecting, completing the maze, crossword puzzles and the like to stimulate an 'input-rich' environment through a single textbook. On the other hand, the teaching of the textbook, both lessons and the various unconnected tasks, assumes an English *speaker*. Though the *Marigold* includes a version of input-rich curriculum, it falls apart when oracy cannot be assumed.

The Position Paper of the National Focus Group on Teaching of English (NCERT, 2006: 5) emphasizes that 'input rich communicational environments are a prerequisite for language learning', and inputs can include:

> textbooks, other print materials such as Big Books, class libraries, parallel materials in more than one language, and media support (learner magazines, newspaper columns, radio/audio cassettes, etc.) and the use of 'authentic' or 'available' materials. (2006: 6)

It also notes that 'a single textbook presented over a year is inadequate. *The emphasis should shift from mastery learning of this limited input to regular exposure to a variety of meaningful language inputs*' (emphasis in original). However, the position paper (NCERT, 2006: 4) also notes that successful second language pedagogy should result in 'the spontaneous and appropriate use of language for at least everyday purposes' and exhorts that the English-language classroom should 'replicate the universal success in the acquisition of basic spoken language proficiency that a child spontaneously acquires outside the classroom for the languages in its environment'. The objective of English language learning is noted as 'the acquisition of basic spoken language proficiency' and the input-rich curriculum is the desirable, allegedly ethical, pedagogic technique to arrive at this objective. Table 4.4 summarizes the kinds of pedagogies discussed so far, the resources required for each, and the expected outcomes.

To summarize, 'input-rich' pedagogies allegedly provide meaningful, creative linguistic experiences to generate confident, expressive learners who can produce spontaneous speech in English and further, entrepreneurial solutions for societal problems (Chapter 8). This chapter disrupts

Table 4.4 Pedagogies, comparative analysis

	Method	Resources required	Learning outcomes
Rote-based	Repetitive writing and reading; fatiguing but meaning-full	English *users* and textbook	Word recognition and basic vocabulary
Oracy-based	Exposure to spontaneous interaction/talk	English *speakers*, activities and tasks	Basic conversational proficiency
Market-intensive	Utilization of diverse, well-designed materials	Families and schools with economic capital and IT capabilities	Literacy and oracy learning

the assumptions underpinning national policy to argue that the bundle of mothering practices glossed as rote is a culturally relevant pedagogy. As Table 4.4 summarizes, English users with minimal resources mobilize rote to achieve emergent literacies. However, national policy asks that the fatiguing labor of rote be substituted with embodied (English speaker) and objectified resources (picture books) that are expensive and locally unavailable. Without the intervention of the market, this promotes first language acquisition in a second language 'acquisition-poor' context.

Conclusion: The Social Lives of Rote

Rather than examining whether rote is 'good' or 'bad' pedagogy, this chapter traced what specific people did with rote pedagogy. The social life of rote runs in many directions. Historically, it has been a quintessential middle-class practice, nurtured within the cultural and pedagogic life of the home with the educated mother crafting the child into a teachable student. In the contemporary moment, several non-necessary connections converge to produce an old practice in a new idiom. Non-elite mothers had gained access to post-10th grade English-medium education but stay at home to teach their children since there are few, if any, respectable employment opportunities for women with young children. A new genera-tion of young, educated, unmarried women yearns to taste independence even if on a meagre schoolteacher salary before they too will have to return to the duties of homemaking and child-rearing. Expanding mar-kets bolstered the cash economy leading to increased non-elite wages even as a new set of English-medium schools targeted this specific segment. The ready availability of young teachers willing to work for a meagre salary, increasing wages for non-elites and educated mothers come together to prop up the business of non-elite English-medium schooling.

The intersection of these socioeconomic and aspirational formations engenders a set of pedagogic labors that we commonly gloss as rote. The textbook is translated onto the blackboard and then the notebook before it is worked upon, laboriously, into cumulative sense-making encounters with linguistic items. Mothers sit-with young children to coax and threaten them into sense-making. Their morality tales of past deprivation and present ease rarely work, and children's labor is managed through after-school tuition and regular school tests. Disciplining mothers, chil-dren and teachers, rote takes on a life of its own that is unrelenting except in the rarest of cases.

Even as earlier pedagogic practices of the established middle-classes escape beyond its borders, a new set of borders are put into place by the market and the state. Professionally designed privately published text-books maximize repetition and amplify rote and are supplemented by a whole array of picture books that encourage repetition without the exi-gencies of labor and boredom. But this market does not target non-elites.

Meanwhile, in its zeal to humanize English pedagogy, the state eroded the pedagogic possibilities of the moment. The denigration of labor-full rote and the valorization of resource plentitude and oracy allow only the privileged to become pedagogically human. The chapter attempted the recovery of a pedagogy that is robust but devalued, as English was made 'universal' and 'natural' in liberalizing India.

Notes

(1)   Literally, male/female teacher. Traditionally, the letters of the alphabet were taught by such teachers at homes. The *ashan/ashatti* taught the child by tracing letter forms in fine sand. After a few assisted writings, the child was expected to recognize and write the letter independently. Errors could result in painful punishments where the teacher ground the young learner's writing finger into the sand during assisted remedial writing sessions. The school was never the site for instruction in the letters.

(2)   Critical theory in the Marxist tradition follows a similar valorization of resistance.

5 Scripted Lives of Communication

The 2014 super hit Malayalam film *Bangalore Days* begins with a job interview. Actor and latest heartthrob Nivin Pauly, who plays Krishnan PP in the film, faces four men in suits in a seminar-style office. Krishnan PP is styled to evoke a contemporary version of the *nattinpurathe payyan* or countryside boy: oiled hair neatly parted and brushed down, not quite at ease in his interview shirt and tie, with an IT-related degree and an endearing lack of English-speaking skills. An older interviewer asks Krishnan: *Your father is a farmer. But you opted for the software industry. Why?* His face tense, Krishnan momentarily lifts his hand as if volunteering an answer in a classroom and then delivers a memorable concoction of an answer:

> That is because
> after a great consideration, consultation
> I came to the conclusion
> that the socialist illusion was a great botheration
> to the Indian nation
> whose basic occupation was cultivation and irrigation.
> But with further contemplation and deliberation
> I discovered that without globalization, exploration
> there cannot be optimization
> to make India's transformation
> into a super-power nation
> sooo

Rather than an IT-related question that is answered with relevant disciplinary jargon, Krishnan is asked a social question that he answers with a *tion*-jargon. Note that he has a professional degree but cannot fluently socialize in English. The cleverly crafted, comic, rote-inflected answer, and tongue-in-cheek dismissal of socialism, is scripted twice: by an educated Malayali *payyan* answering an interview question for a job in the private sector and by director and screenplay writer Anjali Menon with an educational footprint spanning Dubai, Calicut, Pune and London. The answer impresses both audiences. The company offers Krishnan aka

Kuttan a coveted posting in the software capital and dream city, Bangalore. Film audiences love the homage to rote-based academic success enough to repost it as 'interview comedy' on YouTube channels. Meanwhile, *Bangalore Days* goes on to educate Kuttan and uninitiated Malayalis in the aesthetics, morals and practices of urban, transnational, cosmopolitan culture with its world-class offices, gated communities, international but ethnic home décor, malls, fashion, bike racing, graffiti, assistive technology for managing disability, companionate marriage and, of course, 'Spoken English'.

Scholars of liberalizing India point out that fluency in the vocabularies and civilities of global technocratic English cultures is increasingly necessary to participate in middle-class life in India (Fuller & Narasimhan, 2006; Irani, 2019; Jayadeva, 2018; McGuire, 2011; Sancho, 2017). As Krishnan PP finds out, literacy in professional English is necessary but no longer sufficient. Moving out of the cinematic script of Krishnan's success, non-elite families find that the goalposts are shifting after they gained entry to the field. The previous chapter documented the fragile English literacies and the possibilities of a professional education that non-elites are assembling 60 odd years after independence. This chapter explores what happens when standards of English proficiency begin to include transnational socialization skills in addition to scholastic proficiency.

Rather than a straightforward elite/non-elite binary around proficiency/lack of communication skills, the chapter reveals a more complicated landscape. In the case of privileged groups, the requirement for expression in English has emerged in a context where regimented coaching has intensified, especially in crucial school-leaving grades (Mathew, 2022; Sancho, 2017). This test-prep orientation overdetermines all learning in secondary grades, including communicative English. Thus, the transition from one dominant formation (English academic literacy) to another (English communication skills) is fraught, even for elites. This difficulty in transition refracts on to non-elite classrooms such that neither rote nor communication can emerge in its acceptable formats. The resources and exposure required for English speech that is free of 'mother-tongue influences' are beyond the purview of non-elites.

To present a landscape where privilege *feels* like marginalization but *functions* as domination, the chapter moves between multiple spaces and registers of power. An initial overview of the false binary of rote and communication sets up the context, focusing on the implications of coaching for learning. The next section presents the scripted nature of testing, which standardizes English speaking to such an extent that communication is no longer possible, even for elites who may be proficient in this performance. The following sections elaborate the resources and practices required to teach cosmopolitan English cultures to non-elite learners at the New English School, who learn to attempt personalized, expressive speech in a foreign language but come across as rude due to vernacular distances from positive politeness. While my teaching taught cosmopoli-tan English cultures in the classroom rather than outside of it, albeit fal-teringly, the last section explains how this is forbidden in the contemporary. Ultimately, the space where non-elites should be able to access cosmopoli-tan cultures – the English classroom – was forbidden to teach it.

The (False) Binary of Rote and Communication: Spatial Segregations

To begin with, the continued salience of rote across school types, from elite British-style public schools to non-elite schools such as the New English School, suggests that the conditions under which rote can be erased have not yet emerged. Rather, rote and communicative pedagogies have been spa-tially segregated. Classrooms and coaching centers are sites of regimented rote and extra-curricular activities are the assigned sites for learning cosmo-politan English cultures. This is especially true for secondary grades.

Secondary schooling in India is overwhelmingly skewed toward pro-fessional undergraduate education, mostly in engineering, medicine and allied fields. Entry into these courses is decided by competitive exams that test students in the sciences, typically in the multiple choice questions (MCQ) format. An elaborate and extensive coaching industry trains high school students to prepare for these tests. Chidsey's (2017: 236, 269) eth-nography at four elite high schools in north India notes that high school students must learn *ratification*, or rote memorization to 'achieve success in the immediate'. Students have to be fluent in the double task of under-standing and memorizing in order to score the marks that will get them into a reputed institution. Time management and task orientation, skills typically learned through regimented coaching are crucial. Efficient, effec-tive and productive use of concentrated periods of time toward a particu-lar activity or goal, punctuality and task-oriented disciplined action are indispensable. At the top level, the smallest of margins have life-altering consequences, and the fatiguing, laborious, drill and practice that charac-terizes rote can only be ignored at one's own peril.

Secondary schools in Pathanamthitta tied up with coaching institutes that trained students in test preparation to provide such services on campus. If ideological differences regarding teaching and coaching did not permit such business collaborations, the implications were severe. In 2014–2015, the Malankara School in Thiruvalla lost 30 of their best 10th standard students to a competitor who had tied up with the popular *Brilliant Tutorials* for on-campus coaching for medical and engineering entrance exams. For the New English School, a non-elite school with no possibility of coaching facilities in the near future, the percentage decrease of students from 10th to 12th grades was drastic at 80%. Table 5.1 gives an indicative list of how profoundly coaching defines school enrollments in higher secondary grades.

Table 5.1 Student enrollment in Grades 10 and 12 in relation to school provision of coaching

CBSE schools	Total	Std 10	Std 12	% change
New English School[1]	366	25	5	−80.00
Popular high-fee schools in:				
Thiruvalla school 1, no coaching	1775	142	85	−40.14
Thiruvalla school 2, no coaching	1409	119	89	−25.21
Ranny school, with coaching	1872	105	203	+93.33
Changanassery school, with coaching	3249	242	340	+40.50

While rote acts as a powerful gatekeeper to middle-class aspirations, cosmopolitan cultural capital offers crucial affordances for distinction *within* the diversifying middle-classes. Writing about campus placements at engineering colleges in Chennai, Fuller and Narasimhan (2006) point out that students are not allowed to sit a company aptitude test unless they have high marks in 10th and 12th exams and in all their engineering college courses. Companies recruiting final-year engineering students sort *this* population on the basis of their 'communication skills', which include a lack of deference, the ability to verbalize one's opinions, and that elusive element of 'confidence' (2006: 259).

For the professional middle classes, English proficiency is described as polite, unhesitant but not-too-fast speech in a 'neutral' or pan-Indian educated accent that is free of 'mother-tongue influence' (Jayadeva, 2018). This speech has to be assertive. An educated or professional vocabulary helps. Handshakes and eye contact are necessary. Politeness has to be positively expressed, for example, with a please and a thank you. Silence or deference is no longer a virtue. Additionally, assertive, polite speech must span a variety of spaces, not just offices, board rooms and video conferences, but also cafes and malls which mutate sites of world-class consumption into places of work.

Elite schools thus pursue rote pedagogies *inside* classrooms and coaching centers, and cosmopolitan cultures *outside* the classroom – in school assemblies, intra- and inter-school competitions and activities, interactions with school guests, field trips, excursions and study abroad trips. As I explain later in the chapter, the spatial segregation of rote and communicative pedagogy is strictly upheld in secondary grades. In fact, the CBSE English reforms that shifted secondary school pedagogy from scholastic to communicative English 'failed' because it challenged this segregation. But this also means that while transnational communication skills are necessary to become middle class in India, they can only be acquired by those who have the resources to assemble it in parallel to the formal curriculum.

While the spatial segregation of rote and communicative pedagogy might suggest that one is regimented and the other is liberatory, communicative pedagogy and testing is more often than not, scripted. As the previous chapter explained, English pedagogy in India has historically been literacy focused and the emphasis on spontaneous English speech is very recent. This chapter explains that English communication-as-talk may be hyper-scripted but still provides avenues for distinction by virtue of its distance from the vernacular. To summarize, the binary of rote and communication is a false binary. Elites pursue both rote and cosmopolitan English cultures even though they claim that one is opposed to the other. Assumptions about rote as poor pedagogy and poor people's pedagogy (Vaish, 2005) and beliefs about communication as spontaneous expression and liberatory pedagogy do not hold up empirically.

Scripted Form: Standardizing Communication

The Assessment of Speaking and Listening Skills in English (ASL) was mandated for CBSE-affiliated schools from 2012. It is in response to this new requirement that the New English School attempted to initiate Spoken English classes in middle school grades. The ASL is a structured, timed test that equates communication with a strict list of turn-taking, task completion and positive politeness. The test is organized as an 'interaction' between an examiner and a student-pair (a 'natural' conversation pair) and is structured as follows:

(1) Introduction (1 min)
(2) Topic presentation and follow-up questions (1 min presentation and 1 min of questions for each student = 4 mins)
(3) Problem-solving task with follow-up questions (3 min)
(4) Conclusion (1 min)

This structured 'interaction' is rendered measurable through a rubric comprising (1) interactive competence, (2) fluency, (3) pronunciation and (4) language range and accuracy to be scored between one and five with five signaling equivalence with the Common European Framework of Reference of B1 (CBSE ASL Descriptors; Specifications, n.d.). Interactive competence is defined around initiation, repair and continuation of conversation as well as the extra-linguistic outcome of 'task fulfillment'. Language is to be evaluated on students' range and accuracy of vocabulary and grammatical structures; pronunciation on a transregional notion of 'clear, natural pronunciation' and 'intelligibility'; and fluency on the basis of organization and coherence of the speech content and 'speed' of delivery. The CBSE ASL Assessment Guidelines outline speaking skills as constituted by 'unhesitant', not-too-fast, confident speech with an 'expressive and appropriate range' of vocabulary, complex grammatical structures, a range of cohesive devices and clear progression. Any performative 'lacks' are coded as individual student lacks that should be 'remedied' with drills, prepared scripts and listening exercises.

To support ASL, orientation materials and testing guidelines were produced by Trinity College, London, and were made available on the CBSE website. In a sample video uploaded by the CBSE (n.d.), a sari-clad examiner typifying the educated, respectable woman-teacher assesses the communicative competence of two uniform-clad high school girls named Bhavya Upadhyay and Uma Pillai by the video. The room evokes a conference or meeting room in a well-to-do institution, with understated but comfortable office chairs, well-designed office desks, a white board and an air conditioner. The surnames of the students index dominant caste names. Both the room and the social location of the persons are similar to the *Bangalore Days* interview scene, but the alienation of the ASL interaction reveals how much effort and training go into scripting engaging interactions.

The assessment begins with the mandatory introduction, liberally garnished with 'please', 'thank you' and similar polite speech (Would you like to begin please?). Since the format prescribes one minute for the introduction, 51 seconds into the interaction, the introduction is terminated and Bhavya is invited to present her topic. Bhavya names her topic as 'glossophobia' and explains it as 'fear of public speaking'. Bhavya both personalizes her fear (palms gone sweaty, body was trembling, words just weren't coming out) and abstracts it out with scientific terminology, 'glossophobia', balancing the emotional with the rational. As the allotted time runs out for each sub-section, the examiner abruptly terminates conversation.

Midway through her presentation, the examiner cut Bhavya off, instructing, 'stop', ironically enough with a 'thank you'. The structured format now requires Uma to 'ask Bhavya a question'. Uma's question (So Bhavya, how did you get over glossophobia?) is altered by the examiner into 'Uma, can you ask Bhavya a question about the reason for this particular fear of hers?' which Uma repeats in the form of a question to Bhavya. By the time they came to the problem-solving task, the girls had given up the pretense of interaction and the evaluator has to gesture to them to face each other and talk. The 'task' asked the 'conversation pair' how they will go about setting up a story reading club at their school. With no time to collect their thoughts or prepare points, Bhavya and Uma hesitantly present a point each (there should be clear guidelines; students' interests should be taken into account) and repeat them during the question answer segment.

The sentence-level interaction in the clip is clearly insignificant. The evaluator is too preoccupied with the clock and the formalities of assessment to actually take interest in what Bhavya and Uma are saying. Ironically, genuine interaction can only happen when and if participants break out of the straitjacket of evaluation. The conversation is grammatically accurate and communicatively fluent, but the roles (examiner, examinee) have overridden the persons. What is undesirable as clarified in the grading rubric are: lack of initiative, purpose and effort, recitation from memory, lack of progression in thought, unintelligible speech and fragmented speech. I turn to these in later sections.

Curiously, the ASL transmutes presentation skills into communication skills, shrinking the audience to one evaluator and one peer. While communication skills are understood to involve specific communicative functions, for instance, asking for advice (Jang, 2017: 158–161), presentation skills entail greater engagement with a specific topic and organization of talk, as well as explicit attention to bodily comportment (2017: 169–171). Prepared presentations on a chosen or given topic are popular both in and out of school in the region, under the aegis of elocution. However, with the CBSE ASL, topic organization, delivery and bodily comportment have to be scaled to the level of an individual rather than a group, making it much more personal, individualized and potentially interactive.

The failure of ASL lies in its hyper-standardization. There is very little if any space for language-as-identity. But the English-vernacular divide is so entrenched that even this hyper-standardized format has its affordances. Literature on call center communication, one exemplary site of standardized communication, provides additional insights. As Aneesh (2015) describes, Indian call center communication is scripted to mime American norms of attention to strangers, cheerfulness and enthusiasm in order to neutralize the dissonances of intercultural communication. In these telemarketing calls, Indians who have never been to the US make up for their lack of cultural familiarity with American clients through cheerful, upbeat speech. While call centers teach how to perform familiarity across distance and difference, the ASL interaction introduces distance between persons who are physically, culturally and linguistically proximate. The appeal of ASL, despite its hyper-standardization, lies in the platform it provides to neutralize vernacular cultures and thus perform distinction. Call center work and luxury retail work are seductive even though these are regimented because they allow scope for aspirational identity work. The seductions of English as a language of power allow ASL participants to perform personal projects of distinction regardless of its standardized format.

But what happens when non-elite learners are asked to neutralize their vernacular communicative fluencies and mimic the politeness and enthusiasm of Anglophone cultures? The next section moves to the New English School, far away from the air-conditioned schools in metro cities that serve as the CBSE's model schools. We have seen the English literacies assembled with much labor and heartache at the New English School, in the previous chapter. The CBSE now also asks these students and their teachers and carers to speak English fluently but in a straitjacket format that can be measured strictly. I was charged with teaching a Spoken English class at the New English School to prepare middle school students for the ASL test. There was no other speaking instruction in any other grade, including secondary grades which actually had to take the ASL.

Explaining the acquisition of embodied cultural capital, specifically desirable forms of language use, Bourdieu (1977: 647) writes that 'practical competence is learned *in situations,* in practice: What is learnt is inextricably, the practical mastery of language and the practical mastery of situations which enable one to produce the adequate speech in a given situation'. How was practical mastery of accurate, polite, measurable English speech to be achieved at the New English School? And what kinds of (dis)fluencies and subjectivities resulted out of this requirement?

Scripted Content: Reciting from Memory

Every morning at the New English School started with a school assembly. Since the school did not have an auditorium on campus,[2] the 300-odd students congregated in the courtyard in the middle of the C-shaped building.[3] Prefects and teachers disciplined unruly lines of students and glowered at stragglers who walked in late, dragging their school bags. Mothers dropping off their children crowded the entry path on their scooters, glancing back to make sure that their wards were allowed to line up for the assembly. The principal, a teacher and a small group of students led the assembly. The usual routine consisted of a prayer song, the reading of a short passage from the Bible, followed by a read-out prayer, and a short speech delivered by a student. The assembly typically ended with announcements about upcoming competitions, exams or felicitations of winners. This 15 to 20 minute performance was the only time of the day when all interactions were conducted in English. This literacy-inflected performance of interactional English was the preferred model for almost all English-speaking activity at the school. What had to be spoken was first written out. It was then recited, or read out, with adequate expression. However, the scripting of speech was communal rather than individual, and in many cases, students or their carers copied already-scripted speech off guidebooks.

During my initial month of teaching 'Spoken English', every English exercise I formulated was met with scripted answers. The first exercise asked students to narrate a memorable event or describe an object they liked. In response, several of the students memorized or read out short texts that were modeled after school assembly 'speeches' given by senior students, which were themselves versions of compositions learned for school examinations. One such response repeated by several students was 'books':

Good morning everybody.
I am going to say a few words about books.
Books are a store of knowledge.
One can find a wide variety of books in all subjects and in different languages.

We have books on arts and science.
Books on religion can be found in great number.
We have children books.
Books are our best friends and valuable guide.
Though the modern age is proceeding towards TV, radio, and other media, there is no match for the books.
We can read books at all times and in all ages.
Men can never feel alone in the company of books.
Thank you.

As soon as the presenter finished reading, her friend borrowed the notebook and read out the same readymade composition.

The scripted nature of the ASL and recitation were similar but different. The similarity lay in personalization, which could potentially liberate the interaction from its scripted nature.

For instance, describing a recitation at a Sunday School elocution competition, Vlad Naumescu (2019) notes that participant Aleesha's speech on *Jesus as the Bread of Life* included several biblical quotes as well as the entire Eucharistic liturgical song *The Lord Said: I am the Bread of Life*. But Aleesha drew on these memorized texts to profess her personal faith. In fact, the alleged depth of her faith was put on display precisely through her familiarity with the key referential texts of her faith. Like Thorkelson's (2008) description of a graduate school theory classroom, the skilled presenter here is the reflective individual, who can perform the claims of sacred and canonical texts passionately in one's own voice. Bhavya from the ASL clip was also able to manage this task of personalization and individualization of a topic. But students at the New English School had not been trained in this yet.

Vernacular Scripts 1: Personalized but Disfluent

When asked to perform more individualized presentations, students in the Spoken English class turned to the obviously personal script of the *Myself* composition. Students at the New English School start learning *Myself* from kindergarten. In the tin-roofed kindergarten classes taught by Chandrika and her colleagues, students finishing kindergarten copy down four to five sentences from the blackboard, personalize it individually (name) and communally (number of boys, girls, benches, desks), and learn it by-heart through the usual writing-learning method.

My name is _____.
I am studying in UKG.
There are ____ boys and ____ girls in my class.
There are _____ benches and desks in my class.
My class is big and clean.

The *Myself* composition becomes more elaborate as students move through beginner grades, and by fourth grade, it becomes a detailed report about the self and the school, documenting the number of classes, students, teachers and all sorts of sundry details including names of 'best friends', and personal likes and dislikes.

When the Spoken English class demanded personalized expression in class, students immediately turned to this composition. In the fourth grade class, of the 30-odd students, around a dozen extended the standard *Myself* linguistically and sartorially. For instance, a group of three boys, Eldo, Aditya and Richu, attempted to re-write *Myself* to reflect their current enthusiasm for football. When it was their turn to speak, they took out football jerseys, long football socks and sports shoes, bought cheaply at the village fair, wore them and came up to the front of the classroom to present themselves in English. In addition to the standard format, they included their favorite players, Ronaldo and Messi, and emphasized how much they liked the sport. Not to be left out, girls brought in 'color dresses', allowed in school only on birthdays and wore it over their uniforms as they came up to speak about themselves. Latest fashions including *anarkali* and net *kammez* made their way into the presentation of the 'my-self'.

Though students in the class were clearly invested, this personalized version of a standardized script could be easily read as 'disfluency'. Beginning from the classic 'Indianism' of the bobble head to anxious folding and unfolding of arms, the students displayed their lack of familiarity and practice with 'English cultures'.

Eldo: My name is Eldo K.
Aditya: (bobbles head) My name is Aditya Shankar.
Eldo: My, my, I am, I am nine years old.
Aditya: My (folds and unfolds arms) I am studying in class, uh, 4 A.
Eldo: I am same class.
Aditya: (folds and unfolds arms, pursed lips): My best friends are Eldo, Richu, uh
Eldo: My school name is ____ Central School.
Aditya: Uh (purses lips) It's, it's (folds, unfolds arms) standard, 3 are in my school.
Aditya: 28 teachers (uh) and 500 students in my school.
Eldo: (whispers) Miss (barely shakes head to indicate that they have finished).

Moving away from the secure reference point of the memorized composition to that of a vernacular self proved too taxing for many, and around half the class flatly refused to participate. Thus, while the largest section of my class displayed what ASL criteria calls 'lack of initiative', the few who were brave or rash enough to initiate speech in English fit into all the other 'lacks'.

Picture Books and Readymade Leaders: Teaching and Translating English Cultures

Building on the reading readiness and the rote pedagogies documented in the previous chapter, I tried to, one, assemble situations in which non-elite students would want to rehearse interactions with English speakers, and two, rearrange the value of the vernacular and its relation to English. In hindsight, this became possible when the presentation of the individual self was re-anchored in another set of referential texts: picture books that already always translated vernacular experiences into English. I had assembled a class library during my fieldwork period. In addition to a set of reading cards (pack of 100) from the English and Foreign Languages University, Hyderabad, the class library included picture books published by Pratham, Tulika, the National Book Trust, the Children's Book Trust, and Katha. A total of 262 picture books costing Rs. 8662, distributed across Levels 1–4, were available to students. The illustrations recorded vernacular life worlds. The sentences translated these into English words, sentences and narratives. This readymade translation elicited responses in diverse registers in Malayalam and English.

Additionally, one girl who had spent extensive time outside Kerala, in Mumbai, and another who had some transnational travel experience, modeled 'boldness', a readiness to attempt translingual speech in English, sacrificing accuracy for fluency when needed. In addition, toward the latter half of my fieldwork period, our class got a transfer student from a high-fee school in Ranny, Kaveri. She was responsive and expressive (in English) during classroom discussions and further used please and thank you incessantly while speaking to her classmates, for instance, 'please move' while trying to get to the teacher's table from her crowded student bench. She volunteered for any and all activities, regardless of training or expectation, including a 1500-meter walking competition. The class watched her carefully for the first week, assessing her. Soon, two enamored girls hung out with her, while others, especially boys, maintained a safe distance. As Sancho's (2015) ethnography suggests, Kaveri had all the makings of a mascot student: her cultural capital would be put on display during special functions such as the annual day in order to advertise and promote the school. In the classroom, she modeled new ways of being even as it taught students what they lacked.

Meanwhile, I was the most explicit example of readymade leadership (Chacko, 2020) as it related to pedagogic enterprise and linguistic fluency at the New English School. My graduate training in anthropology and education in the US had accrued as both naturalized English proficiency and an appreciation for diverse, culturally situated English pedagogies. Further, my fellowship stipend provided the crucial economic resources required to assemble the 'input-rich' classroom that could move between rote and interaction, albeit with some difficulty. These conditions allowed for the teaching of diverse kinds of cultural capital to non-elite learners.

Vernacular Scripts 2: Reflective but Rude

Student speech in English, when it emerged, suggests that what I taught students was the performance of an expressive self, who could verbalize sociocultural difference in the form of novel, creative, personalized commentaries on self and society. This entailed a shift away from participation in social life to reflection on and articulation of experience. The production of a reflective self that can distinguish itself through expressive acts (Kipnis, 2001: 482) is a necessary precondition for consumer economies and enterprise cultures (Irani, 2019). In the context of the non-elite classroom, socioeconomic differences generated innovative perspectives but also marked student speech and bodies as 'local'. Meanwhile, my failure in integrating the New English School into commodification networks undermined any potential productivity. Unlike the international school described by Irani (2019), which could plug itself into multiple nodes of cultural and knowledge production such as design studios, premier universities in India and the US, and global entertainment corporations such as Disney, The New English School was not integrated into production chains that could extract economic value from the performance of difference.

Before I detail student presentations, a note about the exam format and the grading rubric is necessary. After several weeks of classroom reading and response sessions, I introduced an element of competition, promising a grand prize to students who came first, second and third in a 'final exam'. The format of the exam was as follows. A group of two to three students presented a summary cum commentary of a picture book of their choosing. After the presentation, other students had a chance to critique the presentation or add novel commentaries. Each student would thus get one opportunity to present and several to respond to other presentations. Student performances were graded liberally, with marks foregrounding content generation rather than grammatical accuracy; all contributions secured marks, but more inventive contributions secured more marks. One key limitation was that attendance and quantity of contribution could skew cumulative marks. However, the method also generated readiness to speak in English. Since it had taken about a year to get students to *want* to talk in English, it was a trade-off I was willing to make. Spread out over 11 sessions, the exam elicited presentation skills explicitly; it also generated conversations in English, but these were not graded.

In what follows, I discuss student conversations and presentations of two picture books *Cheenu's Gift*[4] and *Rooster Raga*.[5] *Cheenu's Gift* tells the story of Cheenu, a primary school boy, whose father works as a scrap dealer. Unlike other children in his class, who are picked up by mothers or other female family members, Cheenu's father picks him up from school, and Cheenu accompanies him on his rounds to middle-class homes. The book middle-classes Cheenu by teaching him to value hand-me-down *books* more than other kinds of scrap. As the group of three students presented, another 32 waited impatiently for their turn to comment. The 35-minute class allowed barely a minute to each student, and I was perpetually hassled trying to ensure participation for all students. The tone of the presentation hovered around 'a little boy helping his father', but before they could finish, Reni interjected:

Reni: Turn [the page back]. What is the picture? Home or?
Ansu: It is a lift [elevator].
Reni: (pointing to picture of several children) Who is Cheenu?
(In answer, student presenter points to Cheenu in the picture.)
Eldo: (interrupting) What is the duty [employment] of Cheenu's father?
Ansu: Junk dealer
Eldo: Bakery items?
Ansu: *Pathram vangikkunathu* [Buys old newspapers]

Throughout, both presenters and students used the picture book as a crucial resource. Ansu pointed to the picture of Cheenu in response to Reni's question that sought to identify which of the children in the picture was Cheenu. To answer Eldo's question, Ansu borrowed 'junk dealer' from the book. Cheenu's father self-describes himself as *paperwala* and *kabadiwala*, and the book glosses *kabadiwala* as 'junk dealer in Hindi'. Junk dealer turned out to be an unfamiliar term and was further translated as a person who buys old newspapers, a familiar activity.

Reni's and Eldo's clarification exercise was not oriented toward grades, since they were not critiquing the student presentation or providing new commentaries. Though the sentence-level interaction to negotiate meaning through speech, gestures and pictures is successful, Reni came across as rude due to her lack of positive politeness. Unlike negative politeness strategies such as silence (Nakane, 2007), positive politeness requires expressive speech to mark friendliness, shared values and respect (Holmes, 2012). Alongside, Reni censored herself to monolingual English usage. Reni's expressive, confident but rude presentation of the self illustrates the communicative interactions that emerged in the form of conversations around the picture books.

Moving on to graded commentaries and critiques, Kaveri's responses were as follows:

Kaveri: Clouds cute, like a ball
Coconut tree, stem is also green
Cart is cute; everything is there in cart
[Illustration of] Flat,[6] like toys
Grass, creative grasses
Cheenu's cheek, color pink, cute
Dog is cute
I like [how] Cheenu [is] sitting.

As I walked closer to hear Kaveri above the ever-present hum of student talk, I saw that she had scribbled notes onto the inside flap of the brown paper that covered her copybook. Written hurriedly, in patches where the cello tape did not cover the brown paper, the notes read:

> Tree has different colors
> Feels like hilly area
> The bush is looking like a book
> A tree stem is white
> A ball like picture on front cover
> The front page, the flat is like toys.
> The cart feels like every *sadanam* is there
> Cute

Between her notes and speech, Kaveri's account of the illustrations was comprehensive. The clouds looked like balls, coconut trees did not *really* have green stems, the apartments had been drawn like lego blocks, the various grasses looked nothing like grass and Cheenu's and Cheenu's father's cheeks had blobs of pink reminiscent of clown/joker makeup. Kaveri read these as 'creative' and 'cute', personalizing but upholding the referential authority of the book.

In contradistinction, Reni explicitly critiqued the graphics as unrealistic:

> Lift [looks like] jail
> Cheenu put make-up, red color
> *pani vanna* [fever stricken] tree
> grass [looks] like water
> flower look like land
> Page 11, grandmother teacher
> cart, like cycle with three wheels

The book named the cart a '*bandi*', which was glossed as 'cart in Telugu'. While one version of the book did have a four-wheel push cart illustration, the book we had purchased had pictures of a three-wheel cycle with a make-shift cart attachment. Students consistently used the English vocabulary provided by the book, 'cart', and Reni pointed out the mismatch between the named object and its illustration. Similarly, she pointed out that the tree looked like it was fever stricken, the flower like land, the lift like a jail and Cheenu looked like he had put on circus makeup! What is more, a *kadabiwala*'s mother was drawn in ways that indexed a middle-classed schoolteacher. Unlike Kaveri, Reni did not pronounce these deviations as cute, but retained and elaborated a critical perspective. She called out the incongruity between experiences of poverty, like those of a *kabadiwala*, and the 'cute' middle-classed world portrayed by the book. In comparison to Reni's critique of and Kaveri's affirmation of middle-classed aesthetics, several students had minimal engagement with the picture book.

Anu: Home [is] very beautiful
Jintu: [I] like picture
Aby: Cheenu's house, home looks beautiful.

Student responses for the most part varied between these three kinds of responses: (1) common and inadequately personalized, (2) personalized response elaborating or upholding the referential authority of the book and (3) personalized and critical. Most students varied between the three depending on their bench mates during that class session, the cumulative interest of the group in the book and depending on what preceded or followed the lesson. For example, tests or mark distribution in the class immediately prior to the Spoken English class muted student participation as did the excitement of football matches and dance practice. Only a few students, including Kaveri and Reni, were consistent.

I labeled Kaveri's perspective middle-classed and Reni's critical, and personally favored Reni's responses. My disciplinary orientation, including those upheld by academic publication criteria, trained me to recognize 'critical' as the highest point of the global value chain of knowledge production. I was excited to find examples of similar practice in the classroom, especially by female students. In comparison, I intuitively judged Kaveri's responses, and her, as upholding arbitrary referential authorities. Since my marking scheme was designed to appreciate quantity and detail of response rather than my evaluation of student subjectivity, the marks I gave Reni and Kaveri did not clearly indicate my preference. Both scored well, and together, they set up an expectation of attention to textual and graphic detail and a commentary that was informed by cultural location.

Moving on, *Rooster Raga* is the story of an adolescent rooster Ruru, who is learning to crow the rooster's call. Roosters and hens were commonly grown in student households and a young rooster's un-rooster-like attempts to crow was a familiar anomaly. When the two female student presenters termed the story 'funny', boys in the class called them out saying they had not summarized the story adequately [*katha enthava? manasilayilla,* What is the story? We didn't understand]. Kaveri presented another aspect of what I called a middle-classed orientation: a morally prescriptive standpoint.

The cock is doing everything that the others are doing.
We need not try to copy others.

Reni was critical as usual: Rooster singing like it has [is] mental.

Anu and Jintu however had moved from their earlier unengaged performative stance to present more absorbed and elaborate versions.

Anu: Hen's color was different color.
One page, shadow look like flower
Hen's neck was look like horse hair
It was very beautiful
Jintu: Hen looks like *puda illatha* [without feathers]
The moral of the story
Hen is very laughing
Chirikkan pattum [it makes us laugh]
Koprayam kanumbam [when we see the antics]

Following up on Kaveri's interjection, Jintu recognized the obligation to provide a 'moral of the story' but diverged from the prescriptive 'don't copy others' to the experiential 'the book made her laugh'. Her word choice [*koprayam*] bordered on working-class repertoires. Meanwhile, students varied in their degree of engagement, picking out details that appealed to them personally when they did attempt speech.

Aditya: last illustration, the hen don't see
Only seeing [looking at] donkey and cow.
Milan: The pig was very happy because it play [in] mud
I like the hen because it was very colorful
Ajay: So many hens are fancy dress
One hen was crying
So many hens and *muttayum kunjungalum undu* [eggs and baby chicks as well]

While the exercise explicitly foregrounded speech in English, it also required students to face a crowd (here, 30 odd classmates), be interested and interesting, and perform an expressive self who could verbalize individualized feelings, opinions and preferences. Exploring the differences between American and Asian (Chinese and Japanese) schooling systems, Tobin *et al.* (2009) write that American cultural beliefs about choice, individualism and self-expression define classroom practices in schools there. Directed choice, or choice within a pre-defined menu of options, choice at the individual rather than the collective level and a belief in the power of words (say it with words) are foundational building blocks (2009: 195–198).

The teaching of Spoken English at the New English School was a very partial, distant and vernacular rendering of reflective self-making, individualization and positive politeness. Students were required to have an opinion, provide personalized responses to text and images and verbalize the translations they made between their village life and the middle-classed worlds they encountered in picture books. My lessons trained students to 'distinguish oneself through expressive acts' (Kipnis, 2001: 482). However, the Spoken English classroom at the New English School allowed for an expressive self to emerge only to re-embed it in the particularities of difference.

To summarize, my teaching was marked by an abundance of resources, student choice, iterative curricular revisions and diverse kinds of translations. The class trained students to recognize cultural difference as valuable and to articulate its value in transnational registers. However, the limitations of schooling based on entrepreneurial projects rather than sustained practice was evident. The 18-month experimental program, available only to some grades, could hardly stand in for the rich and diverse extra-curricular programs and activities that high-fee schools used to teach English cultures. It is important to note that the Spoken English class was introduced in middle school and not in secondary classes that would actually take the ASL tests and that it was ungraded. The affiliating school board, the CBSE, had already attempted to reform the regimented English pedagogy of secondary grades into more personalized and interactive sessions, and failed. I turn to these in the next section.

Failed Communication: Conflicting Scripts

Till now, we have followed the normative notion of communication that equates it with talk. As Cameron (2000: 2) writes, 'in its unmarked case, communication means talk'. This section shifts away from talk to look at a *literacy* pedagogy organized around communication, that too for high-stakes secondary grades. The New English School prescribed the CBSE produced *Interact in English* textbook series in Grades 9–10, which explicitly invokes a communicative approach to language teaching. The reforms that produced these textbooks will be described in greater detail in Chapter 8. The *Interact in English* series consisted of a *Literature Reader*, a *Grammar Book* and the *Main Course Book* (MCB). But the reforms expected the MCB to be the primary agent of communicative pedagogy.

If the NCERT *Marigold* modeled the authoritative national version of English pedagogy for primary grades, the CBSE MCB did the same for secondary grades. National models are split up between the NCERT and the CBSE which have distributed primary and secondary schooling between them. While the NCERT *Marigold* assumed the universal availability of English-speaking teachers in primary grades, the CBSE MCB did the same for secondary grades. That this pedagogy failed among its elite clientele gestures to how relevant rote pedagogies are regardless of class differences.

To bridge talk-as-communication with academic-literacy-as-communication, a historic detour is necessary. The assemblages that go by the name Communicative Language Teaching (CLT) are historically rooted in European transnationalism. CLT emerged in the 1970s in the context of increasing numbers of immigrant workers in Europe and UK. To help these foreign workers conduct the 'business of everyday life' with a 'relative degree of independence', the Council of Europe set out in 'systematic detail' the situations that learners might have to deal with as well as what learners should be able to do linguistically in those situations (van Ek & Trim, 1991: 1). This *Threshold Level* (van Ek, 1975) compiled a list of situations, activities, functions, topics, notions and degrees of skill. Wilkins' (1976: 18) *Notional Syllabuses*, also written for the Council of Europe, further argued that the existing method of teaching grammatically graded syllabi, through literary texts, should be replaced by syllabi that takes the 'desired communicative capacity as the starting point'. As Savignon (1991: 263) summarizes, the 'term communicative was used to describe programs that used a functional-notional syllabus based on needs assessment, and the language for specific purposes movement was launched'.

The institutional reach of the British Council (BC) went a long way in making this situated European pedagogy stand in for 'communicative language teaching'. English Language Teaching and overseas aid for development converged since the teaching and testing activities of the BC, undertaken and funded in the name of development, spanned the erstwhile British colonial map including India. British Council Manager for sub-Saharan Africa, Woods (2009) explains that by the 1960s, English language teaching had become a core element of the British Council's work. Woods notes that the British Council actively promoted communicative methods of language teaching, especially after British Council officer John Munby's (1978) *Communicative Syllabus Design* was published. The impact of Munby's more explicit integration of need-based, functional-notional syllabus with English for Special Purposes on the British Council's work was substantive, and the British Council's English Language tests were revised in order to align with Munby's specifications, in particular, reforming the academic content of the tests (Taylor & Weir, 2012). As explained in Chapter 8, the CBSE English reforms were funded by the UK Overseas Development Agency and routed through the British Council. Furthermore, as explained later in the chapter, the reformed MCB was modeled almost completely on the British Council administered IELTS exams (International English Language Testing System).

The transformation of European language policy and its marketized testing accompaniment into an Indian literacy pedagogy was aided by theoretical developments that emerged around the same time. Savignon (1991) explains that the field of sociolinguistics also developed in the early 1970s, articulating its theoretical dissatisfaction with Chomskyan grammatical competence and proposing a socially situated 'communicative competence' instead. Kumaravadivelu (2006) recounts that Halliday (1973) rejected Chomsky's emphasis on grammar to define language as 'meaning potential' and viewed language as a means of functioning in society. Around the same time, in 1972, Hymes expanded Chomskyan grammatical competence into communicative competence to account for socially situated competences. Concomitantly, pedagogic dissatisfaction with structural behaviorist methods of teaching grammatically graded syllabi was emerging.

The earlier grammar translation method was oriented toward translating literary texts, while the structural method was built on graded grammatical structures and vocabulary lists. The rejection of translation and drills, glossed as rote, for 'meaning' thus allowed the communicative method to lay claim over literacy pedagogy. Savignon (1991: 264) reports that 'communicative competence' came to characterize 'the ability of language learners to interact with other speakers, to make meaning, as distinct from their ability to perform on discrete-point tests of grammatical knowledge'. Alongside, the Munby-ian fetish with needs analysis, albeit metaphorical rather than empirical (Davies, 1981), registered a claim on 'learner centeredness' long before that term became a global buzzword. Chapter 8 describes how the CBSE reforms operationalized meaning and learner-centeredness as oppositional to rote, bulldozing over context as well as resource discrepancies. But the reforms 'failed' during implementation. The defining of communication in opposition to rote went against the basic assumptions of the CBSE's English-medium, technoscience-directed framework.

Historically, the CBSE had institutionalized rote *par excellence* in English pedagogy by crafting a peculiar entanglement between math and science education and English. On the one hand, English-as-subject retained an exclusive focus on literature but made these amenable to rote. On the other hand, techno-science subjects (in English-medium) were pursued rigorously through extensive drill and practice. The emphasis on science and math made CBSE the primary pipeline for professional aspirants in the country, especially in medicine and engineering (Chapter 8). Since the colonial government had promoted English studies rather than science and technology as appropriate civilizational pedagogy, nationalist struggles had argued for a correction of this approach to reclaim technoscience as the proper agent of modernization (Sarukkai, 2014). Therefore, for the CBSE, English was significant as the *medium* of instruction for science and math rather than for its literary or humanistic values.

This nationalistic de-emphasis of English literature meant that the CBSE assessed students on 'seen' comprehension and composition texts, that is, texts that had already been studied and revised in school curricula. The institutionalization of rote within the CBSE English curriculum is commented on by the national position paper (NCERT, 2006: 17), which laments that the nature of 'reading comprehension' in Indian contexts is such that 'scores on comprehension of unseen passages are conflated with scores on the recall of passages already studied'. Thus, for the 'national' school board, rote learning in English-as-a-subject along with English as the medium of science and math was culturally and pedagogically appropriate. It is this that the CBSE English reforms sought to reform along the lines of the IELTS exam.

The following sections analyze the pedagogic format, content and design of the MCB. The MCB follows the format of the Cambridge certificate exams and the IELTS exams, the former administered for residents of English-speaking countries and the latter for non-native speakers. These exams judge the preparedness of the test taker for tertiary education and professional or service sector work. While the MCB format is transnational, its content is middle-classed and Indian. In keeping with the alignment of secondary schooling with aspirations for undergraduate professional education in medicine and engineering, the MCB (CBSE,1994; CBSE, 2009) has specific units on Health and Medicine and Science. While these units introduced professional English in related fields, other units such as education and travel are also technical rather than literary, introducing students to statistical information, graphs and a predictive approach to social and economic life.

Elaborating, the format of the MCB follows the source variety, task range and response formats of the Cambridge certificate exams and IELTS tests closely. The IELTS and Cambridge certificate exams have reading, writing, listening and speaking sections. The reading texts are obtained from various sources including literary books, journals, newspapers and magazines, and tasks require learners to interact with the text to identify main points, detail, text structure, recognize an attitude, make an inference and so on, and response types are typically limited to multiple choice, multiple matching and sequence completion (Chalhoub-Deville & Turner, 2000; Vidakovic *et al.*, 2015).[7] The writing tasks include an essay and other genres such as summary of information presented in a table, graph or diagram; writing a report; an information leaflet and so on. Listening tasks involve listening to various inputs such as radio interviews, debates and discussions, and response types include multiple-choice items, short answers, labeling diagrams, summarizing information, matching lists and so on. The speaking tasks are largely of the hortatory kind, that is, tasks which require students to make a judgment about the desirability of a given entity of phenomenon (Moore & Morton, 2005: 55).

To illustrate the MCB's Cambridge/IELTS format with an example, the second unit in the MCB, *Education,* comprises two poems, one recorded speech, 10 prose texts and two graphic informational texts. The prose texts include an excerpt from *Up from Slavery* by Booker T Washington; four short stories; a bio sketch; two news items, one on the Right to Education and the other a story about the youngest headmaster in the world; a policy brief on the *Education for All* program and an article on vocational education. The recorded speech is by Steve Jobs, and the graphic texts include a map and statistics about girls' enrollment in primary and upper primary schools. The reading and writing tasks require learners to identify main points, detail, text structure and organization, categorize, recognize an attitude, make an inference and so on, and response types include multiple choice, multiple matching, and sequence completion, summarization, tabulation, graphic organization, illustration, poster-making, and the writing of articles, bio sketches, notices and letters.

Listening tasks include taped interviews, discussions, instructions, directions and so on and require responses such as matching, tabulating and making an itinerary or map. As for speaking, the *Handbook for Teachers* claims that the MCB 'provides ample opportunity for students to develop their oral skills', especially to develop fluency and accuracy (CBSE, n.d.: 26). It notes that 'all units contain a major oral activity' including role play, group discussion, debate and simulation. Unit 2, for instance, includes a role play, five discussion prompts, two debates, a speech competition and a presentation. Speaking prompts include topics such as 'The Right to Education Act is a realistic and achievable goal that will change the face of education in India' (CBSE: 50), 'Empowering the girl child is the best way to empower the nation' (CBSE: 57), and 'Education should be skill based rather than knowledge based' (CBSE: 78). Task guidelines provide possible aspects that could be considered and instruct students to maintain eye contact, pause occasionally, not to speak too fast (CBSE: 57) and use appropriate expressions such as 'In my opinion', 'I'd like to raise a question', 'I feel very strongly that' and so on (CBSE: 50). The positive politeness of Anglo-Saxon speech communities (Nakane, 2007) is followed closely. Conversation skills are assumed to develop through pair and small group work since 'students will need to converse in English' to complete the tasks listed in the MCB (CBSE, n.d.: 27). The MCB assumes that students would prefer to converse in English even if they share another language.

Coming to pedagogy, the MCB emphasizes a 'communicative orientation' comprised of student oracy, minimal teacher talk and disregard for explicit grammar instruction and test-preparation (CIEFL, 1997: 118A). In fact, the MCB tries to be 'teacher-proof' so as to promote a 'skill based communicative class' (CIEFL, 1997: 116). Teachers are explicitly discouraged from explaining and talking (CBSE, n.d.:18–19). The accompanying teachers' book (CBSE, n.d.) further asks teachers to replace 'traditional' classrooms (teacher lectures, translation and whole-class work) with individual work, pair work and small group work (CBSE: 10–13). Again and again, teachers are asked to 'resist the temptation to interfere too much' with individual, pair and small group work (CBSE: 10–14). The handbook writes: 'Be careful, of course, not to "take over" the activity by intervening too strongly. (*Students* need the English practice, not you!)' (CBSE: 14). Instead, the MCB builds in explicit reading instruction into the textbook, asking students to identify topic sentences, approach text comprehension through graphic organizers, semantic maps, outline grids and discourse organization through tasks that require matching of paragraphs to subheadings (see Grabe, 2004).

The reforms failed. The three key recommendations – the testing of oral skills, an entirely skills-based approach to teaching and testing and continuous evaluation instead of one final standardized test at the end of

Class 10 (CIEFL, 1997: 1; Rama Mathew, 2012: 196–197) – were systematically undermined by the CBSE during the materials preparation phase as well as during implementation. Mathur (1995: 308–309) explains that the MCB was originally designed to integrate grammar work and literary interpretation, but the Committee of Courses insisted on separate books for literature and grammar. Though the project team found this 'pedagogically unacceptable' since the revisions 'went contrary to the needs of learners and even to the broad objectives of the course', the Committee of Courses prevailed. But most devastatingly for the project team, its proposition that assessment 'be of skills of communication and literary interpretation rather than that of the subject matter of prescribed texts' was also rejected. The first post-reform standardized CBSE Board exams retained a 45% weightage for 'rehearsed tasks' of the kind derided by the reform (Rama Mathew, 2012: 196). Ten years after this first exam of 1995, in 2005, the test became 'more memory based' and 'regressive' with the weightage for rehearsed tasks increasing to 50% (CBSE, n.d.: 2012: 200). Neither oral testing nor continuous evaluation was adopted during this phase and the curriculum remained content/memory based.

The reforms sought to liberate English-proficient, urban, middle-class students like Bhavya and Uma in the model ASL clip from the regimented, 'traditional' classroom with its authoritative, explanatory teacher. It imagined expressive and enterprising students in pairs and small groups, directed by the MCB, interacting with each other and managing their own learning. But such a conceptualization is grossly at odds with the high-stakes regimentations of the crucial school-leaving years. The spatial segregation of rote and expression that overdetermines secondary schooling did not allow for the emergence of the MCB's expressive student and facilitator teacher. Only an *über* elite transnational, professional middle class who can plan for undergraduate education outside India can meet these expectations (Sriprakash *et al.*, 2014).

Though the MCB failed within its core clientele (privileged, proficient middle classes), its articulation of failure was directed at the CBSE's marginal clientele. The implementation report (CIEFL, 1997: 12) states:

> There seems to be a general feeling and this is corroborated by classroom observation data, that the new curriculum has not addressed the issues of weak students. This is widespread in remote areas, e.g., Arunachal Pradesh and under resourced schools. ... In order to cope with the problem, parents and teachers seem to be adopting ways that are not useful or effective in the long run, e.g., teaching and revising and rehearsing question answers.

The articulation of students from 'remote areas' and 'underresourced schools' as 'weak students' changes the terms of educational discourse from rich-poor and urban-rural dichotomies to the bright-weak

dichotomy (Viswanathan, 1992: 33). It defines rote not only as poor pedagogy but also as poor people's pedagogy (Vaish, 2005).

High school English teachers at the New English School as well as at
the other low-fee charging school in Edanadu did not teach the MCB. In
fact, the school principal requested me to teach the MCB since it had not
been taught at all that year, but I had respectfully declined. Teachers
focused on the *Literature Reader* and the *Grammar Workbook*, which
could be taught and learned through conventional literacy-based rote
pedagogies. I was curious if this rejection of the MCB was a specifically
non-elite rejection. It was not. As I scoured CBSE schools in Thiruvalla to
procure a copy of the first edition of the MCB, teachers at high-fee schools
told me that they spent the least amount of time, if any, on the MCB. Not
because students were not proficient, but because the make-or-break years
of exit exam grades had to comply with the pedagogic script of regimented
rote.

Conclusion

This chapter described how rote and communicative pedagogies inter-
sected in the context of liberalization. Within the pedagogic economy of
secondary schooling in India, regimented rote and expressive pedagogies
have been spatially segregated to manage the demands of high-stakes
competitive exams. Further, I have shown that the standardized expressive pedagogies of the national school board are also scripted. But what
distinguishes it from rote is the possibility of personal expression. For
non-elite students at the New English School, personalized expression was
learned through the accumulation of scarce resources, both books and
persons, which modeled translations from the vernacular to English. They
learned the value of difference for performing distinction, but the ease and
fluency of positive politeness eluded them. But the Spoken English class
was an ungraded, middle school course. A similar exercise undertaken by
the MCB, but for privileged, already proficient students in secondary
grades failed despite its privileging of medicine and engineering content
and transnational formats.

The following chapters move away from the New English School and
non-elite English-medium schooling to the abjections of uneconomic
Malayalam-medium schooling. If at the English-medium school, radical
experiences of mobility had prompted mothers to pursue English education for their children, Dalit mothers at the Malayalam-medium school
turned to education to manage despair. Left out of the temporal migrations of Edanadu, the only resource available for them to climb out of
poverty was education. Meanwhile, state responses to uneconomic
schooling offered moral solutions to resource deprivation. Mothers were
offered symbolic managerial positions. But with no resources to manage,
they were called on to manage their own unpaid domestic labor to run

the uneconomic school. Meanwhile, students were mandated to resist rote and pursue oracy-based pedagogies to become properly ethical, expressive citizens in a socialist democratic state.

Notes

(1) From DISE data for 2014–2015.

(2) The church parish hall more than a kilometer away, where the school had begun functioning in 1978, was used for special functions such as the Annual Day and Christmas celebrations.

(3) During the rainy season, the students stayed in their classrooms and participated in the corporeal singing and prayer under the supervision of the class teacher. Those leading the assembly congregated at the usual spot, to conduct this dispersed assembly over loudspeakers.

(4) *Cheenu's Gift* can be read here: https://storyweaver.org.in/stories/633-cheenu-s-gift, but the illustrations students were responding to in class were from a different version. The cover page of this version can be seen here: https://2.bp.blogspot.com/_EciA6JO4mAs/TJ7Nlg9_xyI/AAAAAAAAALk/7hsYQE285AY/s1600/kabadiwalla+hihg+res.JPG

(5) A read aloud of *Rooster Raga* can be found here: https://www.youtube.com/watch?v=b07OepRTRA4

(6) Apartment.

(7) The revisions in 2013 (CPE) and 2015 (FCE and CAE) introduced a cross-text multiple matching where test takers read four texts on the same subject to identify similarities and differences. This task tests language skills assumed to be crucial for undergraduate studies.

6 Obsessive Hope

'I've thought about ending my life many times [*ithellam avasanipichalo ennu palapravashyam vicharichittunde*]. I'm fatigued, teacher [*maduthu, teachere*]. What a hellish life I live [*entho narakicha jivithama*]. Why should I suffer like this? But when I think of my two children, who will they have if I'm not there? Will anybody else take care of them? You tell me', Jessy confided, watching her pot of water slowly filling up at the roadside water tap. I had taught Jessy's daughter Jaisy during the 2013–2014 school year, and Jessy continued to give me updates about Jaisy's progress every time she saw me, both at school and outside. Like most other mothers at St. Thomas, the uneconomic Malayalam-medium state-funded school, Jessy loved talking about her children Jaisy, and Jaisy's younger brother, Jesson. Our conversations outside school typically took place at the entrance to Jessy's colony, which I passed on my way to church. But that day, Jessy stopped me at a different place, across from her colony, and next to a nondescript water tap. I had never noticed taps by the roadside in Edanadu before. I didn't need to. I had running water at home. But for Jessy, this tap was her lifeline, from where she collected water in pots and buckets for all the needs of her family of four. Her colony, like most other colonies in Edanadu, did not yet have running water and to live in a colony is to live through the sufferings of structural precarity that Jessy calls 'life in hell [*narakicha jivitham*]'.

The student community at St. Thomas was exclusively Dalit and lived, like Jessy's family, in segregated Dalit colonies. Furthermore, of the seven students I taught over two years, four were from landless families, the single most intelligible criterion for destitution [*daridryam*] in contemporary Kerala and officially acknowledged as such [*bhu rahithar*]. They too lived near a Dalit colony, renting out half-finished or abandoned single-room houses for minimal rent. Visiting seven-year-old Jisna's house the first time, I was surprised to see her favorite play spot – an unfinished staircase that led into the open sky. The construction of this single-room house had been abandoned halfway, and the staircase led to a non-existent roof terrace through a gaping hole. I wondered what happened during the monsoon months but did not ask. Nearby, little Ajin lived with her family of five in an even smaller room, the single bed in the house stacked close to the wooden fire over which her mother cooked all their meals.

The door to their room opened out to a pit that had once been a red-rock [vettu kallu] quarry. I had to suspend my middle-classed notions of safety and risk when I visited my students; material impoverishment did not interrupt their fun, laughter, friendship and play. But the very real struggles of poverty were also simultaneously articulated, especially by mothers.

Jessy lived in another colony about a kilometer from St. Thomas; her colony was a strip of land wedged between wetlands and a pool that had over the years become a dumping ground. Land close to wetlands flood easily during the monsoons, but the conversion of a major chunk of the wetlands near Jessy's colony into dry land by a local liquor and real estate baron had exacerbated the periodical flooding into an everyday life in slush and mud. After every downpour, which in monsoon drenched Kerala is half the year round, Jessy's colony turned into a mud pool. Visiting Jessy's house through the slushy, smelly mud that slid and slithered underfoot, I was surprised when Jessy asked me if I had any cream. She pointed to the eczema on her children's feet and cursed the muck that was devouring their bodies and the flood waters that seemed bent on consuming their already dilapidated, bare house. Flooding had become severe with the reclamation of the wetlands and muddy, smelly, floodwaters entered her house regularly.

This chapter describes the social worlds of mothers attached to St. Thomas. At the New English School and in much of Edanadu, non-elite families had migrated into new material and social worlds without leaving home. St. Thomas introduced me to a small collective who lived outside this migration experience. That all were Dalit pointed to the profound significance of caste in Edanadu. Given the magnitude of deprivation and segregation, I expected anger and despair. Instead, I found obsessive hope; the only way to survive this caste-specific experience of abjection was to hope that children would migrate out of poverty. But despair too emerged, in brief flashes, when mothers were forced to face the inadequacy of Malayalam-medium schooling for the pursuit of desirable higher education, secure employment, land ownership and a respectable house.

Meanwhile, faced with the phenomenal increase of uneconomic schools, the Kerala state reworked its relationship with marginalized groups through a curious mix of managerial enterprise and pedagogic compliance. The state hailed families remnant at uneconomic schools as managers. But in the absence of any resources to manage, this extracted unpaid domestic labor from marginalized mothers. At the same time, pedagogically, the state mandated an oracy-focused English pedagogy (next chapter).

From Colony to Colony

Like the colony houses described earlier, St. Thomas School was also a dilapidated building with a handful of ancient blackboards, benches and desks separated out by screens to form classrooms. Overrun by pigeons and deprivation, the once-bustling school had become a symbol of social and material abjection as the village had migrated *en masse* into new worlds of ease. For instance, the school had no running water. Teachers, the cook, and I drew water from the church well located across the road for all the needs of the 12 students. Conversely, English-medium schools had indoor plumbing. Likewise, children at English-medium schools rode to school on buses and autos or on their parents' motorbikes while students enrolled in uneconomic schools walked to and from school with their mothers. Moving from a colony house to St. Thomas was but a meandering back into the familiarity of deprivation.

Mothers at St. Thomas were acutely aware of their exclusive presence in a normative past. Jessy described her walking to school routine as exclusive [*njan mathram*] and fatiguing [*maduthu*]. Others articulated their unease with walking to school in terms of safety. Walking children through the torrential downpour of the monsoons was neither easy nor safe. Younger children often had to be carried. Lightning strikes had become harsher with changing monsoon patterns. Further, when mothers fell sick and could not walk their children to school, students missed school, sometimes for weeks. Beyond the actual safety of the walking, the practice was marked temporally (of the past) and demographically (by Dalits). It was common earlier, but (almost) nobody did it anymore. Thus, walking to a Malayalam-medium school with children in tow as well as spaces such as uneconomic schools, colonies and roadside water taps produced a stasis in everyday life that was easily but painfully recognized.

Fatigued by the material and affective labors uneconomic schooling demanded, tired of living beyond the margins, Jessy wanted to end her life. Others were already in the future Jessy yet hoped intently for. And what had once been a 'difficult' and 'impoverished' past for most other Edanadu residents was Jessy's continuing present. Jessy often voiced the punishing nature of her everyday life saying, 'I don't even get to sit down for a minute [*oru minite kuththi irrikkan neramilla*]'. *Kuththi irrikan neramilla* [no time to sit down] is the same phrase non-elite mothers at low-fee English schools in Edanadu used to describe life a decade earlier, a time when they also toiled the whole day just to get routine chores done. In Dalit colonies and uneconomic schools, this feeling of being stuck in the normative past of the village heightened stasis – changelessness suggestive of inaction despite fervent and arduous action – collapsing the past, present and future into one long saga of labor and precarity. But Jessy felt that her bodily death, the only legitimate form of protest in certain contexts (Girija, 2011; Morrison, 1987), would betray her children to a loveless world. She asks, 'Who will they have if I'm not there? Will anybody else take care of them?' Love and nurture prevailed as a form of defiant resistance to corporeal death, and the social death of life beyond the margins.

At the other end of the spectrum was Sindhu. Dressed impeccably in cotton-silk *salwar kameez* from the upscale Roseons store, Sindhu stood out as someone who did not 'belong' at an uneconomic school. She had a bachelor's degree and often took up part-time consulting projects with the panchayat office. Her husband worked as a chef in the Gulf. Most fathers attached to St. Thomas were daily-wage laborers. Sindhu's family's migration experience was immediately visible since theirs was the only family at St. Thomas with a brand new house, built on a recently purchased plot of land. In Sindhu's case, economic upliftment reached its limits at caste borders and her movement out of a Dalit colony and uneconomic schooling was thwarted.

Sindhu had sent her oldest son Abhinesh to a low-fee private English-medium school, but teachers complained that he wasn't a 'teachable student'. On their advice, the boy stayed in Upper Kindergarten (UKG) for two years, but teachers were still dissatisfied with his progress. A certified teacher herself, Sindhu began to wonder if 'something was wrong' with her son; or maybe it was because she 'hadn't paid enough attention at home [*njan shradikkathathano*]'. Sindhu transferred Abhinesh to the uneconomic school St. Thomas in Class 1. At St. Thomas, Abhinesh blossomed. He was in Class 3 when I started my fieldwork, and he was the undisputed star of St. Thomas, winning district-level prizes for elocution, classical singing and light music. He made his debut on the stage [*arangettam*] as a classical singer in 2013.

Like Abhinesh's transfer from the non-colony space of the English-medium school to the colony-like material space of St. Thomas, Sindhu's transition out of a Dalit colony followed a similar meandering back into caste-segregated spaces. Sindhu's family had till recently lived in the same Dalit colony as Raghu's (Chapter 3). Her husband's 15 years of emigrant work had eventually amassed enough economic resources for them to buy land outside the colony. The plot they bought belonged to a respected high school teacher; it bordered a Dalit colony but was itself not in a colony. Work commenced on a new house, and by mid-2013, Sindhu's new house was ready, gleaming white, with traditional wood gables, and all modern conveniences. But by this time, the non-Dalits who lived in the vicinity had sold out their properties to Dalits like Sindhu and moved elsewhere. The border neighborhood had become a segregated Dalit middle-class neighborhood.

Obsessive Hope, Punishing Love

Though mothers articulated a terrible discontent and fatigue with living in the normative past of the village, they rarely spoke about desires for good futures, whether it be commodities, new residential spaces or English-medium schooling. But they obsessed over academic performance – a socially sanctioned and 'appropriate' orientation to good futures. One morning when I reached St. Thomas, I saw Jaisy at the door, hugging her mother, weeping. First graders and preschoolers routinely sobbed and wailed as mothers left, but Jaisy was in third grade then and I had never seen her cry to see her mother leave. I tried to comfort her, but she refused my offers and clung on to Jessy. I had witnessed enough bickering to know kids can be exceedingly mean to each other and I went in to find out what had happened. The other mothers were sitting in their usual spot chatting. They told me that Jessy's daughter had come to school without doing her homework, and Jessy had slapped her full across the face. When her daughter burst out crying, Jessy immediately hugged her, consoled her, and dried her tears and blew her nose. But when a teacher went to Jessy soon after, Jessy burst out crying. She was broken hearted to have hit her child, but the only way any desirable future could even be imagined as possible was if Jaisy did well in school, which she usually did.[1] When social norms purport schooling and academic success as the only way out of material destitution, hoping became obsessive, punishing and heartbreaking.

Annu was the soft-spoken mother of three, of whom the oldest Aneesha was in my 2nd grade cohort in 2014–2015. Annu's husband was a daily-wage laborer who also took up plumbing and other jobs, and they lived in a rented shack about a kilometer from school. Annu walked Aneesha to and from school every day, carrying her youngest and walking the others. The one time Annu fell sick during my fieldwork period, there was nobody to walk Aneesha to school and she missed a week of classes. But unlike Jessy, Annu rarely complained about her hardships. During one of the parent–teacher meetings when I commented on how diligent and hard working her daughter was, Annu responded, 'She is good at studies, but these days she isn't paying attention (to her studies). You should hit her, teacher, if she doesn't pay attention'. Orienting to good futures in a temporality of stasis was characterized by labor and pain for the children. If little Aneesha had to have a good future, she had to work harder and harder. Like Jessy, Annu too pushed her child hard. Both mothers solicited the help of more literate cousins or neighbors to monitor their children's reading of the picture books I sent home for reading practice. Any slip up was met with harsh and definitive punishment, the students confided. Mothers were fiercely optimistic about the academic success and possible futures of their children. They had to become hopeful to survive.

Stepping Into the Future

If considering the possibility of endless abjection, even momentarily, was agonizing for Jessy, stepping into yearned for futures – feeling, smelling and touching the future – made Jessy confront the inadequacy of hope in producing radical material and social change. In August 2014, Jessy's cousin moved into a new house near St. Thomas, and in the week that followed, Jessy's two children had a sleepover at their aunt's new house.

Though Jessy did not accompany them, she gushed about the new house after the sleepover. 'It's a wonderful house. You should see the tiles, they sparkle [*entho thelakkama*]'. Entering her cousin's new house seemed to be a momentarily stepping into the future, not just in the imagination but also in the corporeal body with all its sensorial consumptions.

When I was invited to see the new house, the smooth sparkling tiles, the fresh gleaming white paint and the fan whirling silently overhead seemed vastly different from Jessy's rough patchy cement floor, unpainted walls and the whirring table fan that sat clumsily on a roughly hewn wooden table. If the past was rough edged, cement colored and mud smelling, the future was smooth, white and without slush. As she took her children back home after the sleepover, Jessy said, 'I wish we had a house like that. But she has brothers in the Gulf (Middle East) who help her out. I don't have any brothers, let alone brothers in the Gulf'. When she saw others leave, like her cousin who had earlier lived next door, her resilient optimism revealed itself as insufficient. Hope was not enough. Emergent literacies in primary school were hardly adequate to climb out of abjection, buy land and build a new house. But Jessy persisted.

One morning, when we were among the earliest to arrive at school, Jessy came to me and said softly, glancing around to make sure nobody heard us, 'Didn't you ask me once what I hoped for Jaisy? I want her to become a doctor'. Only elite upper castes in Edanadu have become doctors in the past or the present, and to become a doctor in Edanadu is to embody unquestionable social worth. While children of upper-caste elites in Edanadu are naturally accorded this respect and worth on the strength of their inherited material and social capital, Dalits at uneconomic schools find themselves segregated out to perform abjection. And yet, yearnings for a different world are whispered about and carried secretly in the depths of a mother's heart.

We Were Developed

On 14 March 2013, St. Thomas School celebrated its 118th anniversary. The distinguished guests in attendance included the parish priest who was also the school manager, the panchayat president who, as the elected representative, was the manager of all state-owned schools in Edanadu, and Dr Varghese George, the Chairman of the Plantation Corporation of Kerala. A motely crowd of Dalit mothers sat on the low wooden benches, listening to guests reminisce their school years and the glorious histories of Kerala's school education. Dr George talked about modernity [*adhunikatha*], societal progress and individual self-actualization, proposing education as the liberatory agent:

> Once upon a time, there was poverty, starvation, superstition and illiteracy. All that has changed with modernity. We used to be a caste-fettered

society [*jathi kettu undakiya samuham*]. We were liberated from this through education. ... Kerala society has no slavery, social hierarchy or caste discrimination. Everybody studies here like siblings. Education brings you into a fuller humanity [*purna manushatwam*].

Faced with a group of Dalit mothers at an uneconomic school, Dr George stayed firmly in the glorious past, without ever venturing out to the contemporary. Kerala was a casteist society. We were liberated. The past is cut off from the present so that development can remain glorious.

While the state's larger development narrative tries to extend the glorious past into the contemporary, the steady increase of uneconomic schools complicates this claim. On the one hand, Kerala's female literacy rates are 94.3%, sex ratio is 1084, school dropout rates are less than 0.2% and incidence of poverty is 11.3% (GoK, 2018). The Human Development Report elaborates:

Kerala's achievements in human development indicators are often considered unparalleled in the whole developing world and is often compared with the development indices of advanced countries. Kerala's particular development experience of high human development achievements against low per capita income level was mainly attributed to the State's public intervention in health and education sectors. Throughout the discussion on the State's achievements in human development, education has occupied a prime place. In fact, education has always had a central role in determining Kerala's performance in social development. (GoK, 2015: 161)

On the other hand, uneconomic state-funded schools have been steadily increasing. In 1987–1988, there were 650 uneconomic schools (GoK, 1988: 78). By 1999, the number had increased to 1950 (GoK, 1999: 160), and by 2012–2013, just before I started fieldwork, the number of uneconomic schools in the state stood at 5573.[2]

Interestingly, the state attributes the cause of uneconomic schools to another development index: demographic decline. The birth rate, that is the number of births per 1000 of population per year, declined from 32 in 1970–1971 to 16 in 2001 and has hovered around 15 since then (GoK, 2018: xii). The comparable figure for India for 2017 is 20.4. However, while demographic decline reduces total number of enrollments, Arokiasamy and Retnakumar (2006) point out that this decline cannot explain the low numbers in state-funded schools. The number of students enrolled in state-funded lower primary schools in Pathanamthitta decreased by 28,819 from 1996 to 2001. But it was accompanied by an increase of 14,563 students enrolling in private, non-state-subsidized schools (2006: 240). They conclude that fertility decline may have led to a marginal change in enrollment patterns, but 'increasing enrollment trends in private schools have been a major factor for the declining enrollment' in state-funded schools (2006: 241).[3]

More recently, the state has shifted its narrative, ever so slightly, retaining the glorious past while introducing aspiration as the potential problematic. The website of the General Education Department of Kerala (2020) states:

> Kerala's achievements in social development and quality of life are, no doubt, inspiring and encouraging. The state has achieved a human development index comparable to the developed countries of the world. The society attaches so much importance to education that the school in Kerala is really the nucleus of the social microcosm. Better education kindles the aspirations of the people and the main concern is on how to improve the quality of education.

As Chapter 3 explained, shaming the aspirations of those who have left the state-funded system is a widespread practice. This locates uneconomic schooling as a problem caused not by the discriminations of educational development but by the aspirations, or greed, of low-income, consumer-parents. But how does the state respond to families remnant at uneconomic schools? While the pedagogic response of the state (improving quality of education) is analyzed in the next chapter, the following section explores how the state transforms the abject parent into a manager parent, only to reinforce gender and class roles for manager mothers at St. Thomas.

Manager Parents: Gendered Labor and the Uses of 'Community'

The Kerala Right to Education Act 2010 (RtE) legislated into being a 'school management committee', constituted primarily of parents, to monitor and direct the functioning of the school. According to the Government of Kerala RtE (2010: 5–8), 75% of the school management committee (SMC) should comprise of parents or guardians and the SMC should monitor the working of the school, prepare and recommend the school development plan, oversee the utilization of grants and ensure that teachers conduct their duties regularly. The parent will oversee the commitments of the state: inform the local state of school requirements, plan and conduct maintenance work and monitor the work of the state's permanent employees (teachers).

In her insightful analysis about the assumptions of 'community' in current educational policy, AR Vasavi (2020: 97–100) notes that the term has become a 'referent to an idealized social world of small primary relationships which are characterized by a high degree of personal intimacy, emotional depth, moral commitment, social cohesion, and continuity in time'. This romanticized notion of a harmonious institution overlooks the real conditions of village communities, as sites of caste-based conflict, tensions and exclusion. Depending on the kinds of economic, cultural and symbolic capital they can mobilize, actually existing parent 'communities' associated to schools refract and subvert the social relationships they are embedded in. The deprived 'community' at St. Thomas did not have any resources to manage; instead, they were coopted to do unpaid domestic work.

First, as a privately managed state-funded school, St. Thomas was not eligible for the maintenance grant or capacity building the state offered its schools. This is not an anomaly. About 56% of elementary schools in Kerala are state-funded but privately managed (GoK, 2018: 173–174).[4] The panchayat president tried to accommodate St. Thomas through loopholes in the law and sanctioned a laptop and computer training for families. Whenever he was invited as chief guest for an event, the headteacher put forward a litany of old demands in his welcome address: drinking water facilities, running water, fans, benches for students and a kitchen to cook midday meals in. As for the mothers, the supposed new managers of schools, they cleaned and cooked and served.

During every important event at the school – Onam and Christmas celebrations and the anniversary of school establishment – mothers at St. Thomas came together to sweep the school and its surroundings, wash and scrub the floor, clean the cobwebs and wipe down the meagre furniture in the school. Then, they went back home to cook the feast that would be served during the function. Before Dr George arrived to grace the auspicious function, mothers had already performed their required roles. The school was clean though sparse. The food was ready to be served after the speeches and student recitals finished.

Ammini, Drishya's mother, was formally engaged by the school to cook the midday meals and to do the general cleaning of school premises. While the other mothers, especially Sindhu, cooperated [*sahakarikkum*] with the teachers to clean and cook for festive days, Ammini did this on a daily basis and had become resilient to expectations of unpaid labor. On a particularly trying day, a fuming Suja, the first grade teacher, launched into a tirade:

She has no respect for me as a teacher
When I asked her to draw water from the well, she told me to knock it off
[*po teachere*]
and went off
Ajin vomited today
There was no water
Ammini hadn't come back
Whenever there is any program here,
She does not cooperate
She won't come
She won't sweep
She won't draw water

You should not draw close (to people like them)
They'll use you [*mothaledukkum*]

Like at any lower primary school, regardless of its public or private status or fees charged, young children in attendance are still being trained in basic social life, including eating and using the toilet. Accidents are common, children throw up, they wet themselves in the classroom and so on. Private schools engage *ayahs* in early grades to attend to such eventualities. At St. Thomas, Ammini was expected to help out whenever required though her job was to clean the school before classes and to cook the midday meal. Refusing to perform unpaid labor, Ammini came across as an uncooperative mother.

The Right to Education garnered mothers' unpaid labor to sustain the daily workings of the school. In doing so, it reinforced gender roles and class positions as active, responsive parenting. If the New English School expected mothers to perform unpaid pedagogic labor for the school, the Kerala state obliged mothers to perform unpaid domestic labor at the school. Mothers took up these roles out of ethical commitments to their children. While laboring at the school was one avenue to display commitment to children, the other, more pleasurable avenue was through market participation.

Ethics of Consumer Parents

During October 2014, as I walked up to school in the morning, I noticed that Jessy was busy keying numbers into a brand new phone, encased in a blue phone cover. She had bought a cellphone, or rather, as she explained to everyone, her mother had got one for her for Rs. 1000, and she was keying in everybody's phone numbers. Jessy had been one of the few mothers who had never brought a cellphone to school. Except for Sindhu, none of the families of the children I taught had a land phone. They had cellphones, which were cheaper and easier to maintain. When I called students at home to remind them of any books they had to bring for the class I taught, I typically spoke to fathers who were out at work. Mothers only had the cellphone with them when husbands had not left for work. But, as far as possible, they tried to bring the family cellphone to school during special events such as school anniversaries, Christmas celebrations and so on, to take photographs and videos of their children's performances. Jessy had never been able to participate in this sociality of mothering. She had never shared a video of her children singing silly songs, or a picture of them doing their many antics. To be able to do so now, afforded her great pleasure and delight.

Meanwhile, purchasing for the self rather than the child or the family invited moral censure, except in the case of Sindhu who had the economic and cultural capital required to excuse herself from many local norms.

This became clear in the barbs directed at Radhika, the only mother other than Sindhu who came to school in *salwar kammez*, with *kajal* drawn eyes, cellphone in hand. Mothers who lived closer to school typically walked their children to and from school in their nighties, draping a *thorthu* towel or a *dupatta* for modesty. Jessy, coming from further off, wore *salwar kameez* since she had to walk the main roads, but Jessy's *salwar kameez* were worn and torn from her incessant labors. With the exception of Sindhu, who alternated between nighties and expensive *salwar kameez* depending on her daily schedule, others moved freely between their domestic spaces and the school without any attire changes. Jessy often speculated where Radhika got the money for her many *salwar kameez*. Articulations of disapproval, however, were directed at Radhika's mothering practices rather than her choice of attire, though on rare occasions, they were intertwined. For instance, on hearing that Radhika's son had done poorly in his lessons that day, Jessy remarked: 'dressing up is not enough, you also have to teach your children'. Mothers' consumer practices had to be directed toward children, and when it was not, their sincerity in mothering was called into question.

While mothers (and children) self-censored and policed each other, children were acutely aware of the limits of consumer parenting. One of the beginner readers I used at St. Thomas was the UNICEF published *Father, I want* authored by Aruna Thakkar and Rao Bel. The short seven-page picture book illustrates a middle-class orientation to responsible consumption. In the narrative, a father and son duo visit a fair, where the father indulges the son's demands for ice candy and pinwheels only to find that indulgence made the child more demanding. The boy initially asks for 'only one' but later asks for 'one more, one more'. The father nips the demand in the bud the next time. When they chance upon a pair of goggles, he refuses to buy it in order to teach the son to become more moderate and responsible in his demands and desires. But readers at St. Thomas did not fit the normative expectations of the book. Jessy's daughter Jaisy read through the book and suggested that the father did not buy the goggle because he had run out of money. In her world, there was no expectation of responsible consumption since consumption itself was uncertain. Rather, the rare instances of consumer parenting were experiences of familial bonding.

To summarize, the state responded to the most deprived sections in its educational spaces through expectations of managerialism. But with no resources to manage, mothers turned into unpaid domestic workers. Mothers accommodated demands for unpaid labor even as they pursued the pleasures of consumerism in their struggles to become ethical in deprived spaces. But it was their preoccupation with education itself that afforded them pathways to become ethical in the midst of abjection. Meanwhile, the differential precarity experienced by mothers and teachers draw attention to the intersections of class and gender. All the teachers

attached to St. Thomas were female. With the school becoming uneconomic, they stood to lose their jobs and the economic security and spatial
mobility it afforded. The state expected them to be enterprising and
actively work toward attracting student enrollment in failing schools. But
when they had to 'sacrifice' their own children to shore up a failing
Malayalam-medium primary school system, the cost was unbearably
high. The same heartbreaking cost was considered negligible when it
came to Dalit mothers. As noted in Chapter 2, the 'exceptional' development of Kerala is built on this hierarchical ordering of citizen futures.

The Enterprising Teacher: Trading in Futures

For the parish priest and the headteacher of St. Thomas, the crisis of
uneconomic schooling was urgent and catastrophic. Reverend Kuriakose
began the 118th anniversary program saying:

> Your headmaster often speaks from despair [*nirasha*]. It is not difficult to
> understand, one look is enough to know [*otta nottathil nokkiya ariyam*].
> I try to tell him it's okay, that things will be different next year.

One look is enough to know that the existence of the school has become
uncertain. If the enrollment numbers cannot be brought around, the
118-year-old school will have to close. For the time being, the teacher who
concluded the events expressed her 'heartfelt gratitude [*hrdayam niranja
nandi*]' to the families in attendance for selflessly offering their children
to a Malayalam-medium school, a sacrifice nobody else in the vicinity was
willing to make:

> At *Plavelikadu* School, there are no new enrollments, no children coming
> into first grade. *Chettimukku*, it's the same. It's not that there are no
> children. But parents will only send their children to English-medium. We
> expect support from the parent teachers association (in ensuring enroll-
> ment at our school). Thank you for your big heartedness [*maha manas-
> kataykku nandi*], we express our thanks and gratefulness [*nandi,
> kadappadu parayunnu*].

Behind this heartfelt gratitude for the big heartedness of deprived groups
lies an open secret. Most teachers attached to privately managed, state-
funded schools had bought their jobs. To lose it due to school closure[5]
would also mean the loss of that capital investment.

Though enormously skilled at her job and thoroughly dedicated to the
children whom she taught, the teacher who thanked the parents had to
pay one month's salary in 1995 to procure her job, which amounted to Rs.
6000. A few years later, at the neighboring single management school, the
newly recruited teacher paid Rs. 700,000. Since St. Thomas was under a
corporate management, the auction rates for a teacher's job were lower

than at single management schools such as St. Johns. Teachers' salaries in 2014 at the lower primary level were in the range of Rs. 13,210 to 20,240 per month, to which a dearness allowance of 73% as well as a house rent allowance would be added. A crude calculation, say 35,000 per month over 30 years of service, put the job value at Rs. 12,600,000. In addition, there is retirement pension. Meanwhile, the 'volunteer' who filled in for the transferred teacher, who had managed a transfer to a more secure workplace, was paid Rs. 2000 per month in cash.

Sheena, one of the volunteer teachers who passed through St. Thomas, had attended a job interview for an upper primary schoolteacher's post the previous month. All the applicants waiting with her had Master's degrees and an additional Bachelor's degree in Education (B.Ed.). Sheena had completed a certificate program in teacher training in addition to her Bachelor's in Commerce. Regardless of the qualifications, the job would go to the candidate who could pay the most. According to Sheena, the going rate was around Rs. 1,000,000. If the core utility of education as exemplified in the development story had to do with self-actualization and social reformation, in practice, it was accompanied by a crude commodification of teaching jobs.

The conditions for this trade were put together by the education reforms of the Kerala government, which culminated in the Kerala Education Rules 1959 (KER). The KER is hailed as a corner stone of Kerala's development story. Through this legislation, the Kerala government assumed financial responsibility for teacher salaries in schools in order to make education accessible to all. If the state paid for education, it could demand that schools serve all citizens. As per the KER, school managements could not charge tuition or admission fee (GoK, 1959: chap. 12). While teacher salaries and terms of employment were thus made secure, in order to serve non-elite students, recruitment was left to the discretion of the school management, albeit according to specifications laid down by the government. Vacancies were defined according to the number of students and 'fixed' by the Educational Officer 'based on the effective strength of the class as on the sixth working day from the reopening date in June' (1959: 159). Teacher recruitment became a monetary bargain between the school manager and teacher candidates, calculated on the basis of the number of student bodies. This relationship has defined public education in Kerala since the KER came into force.

Jwalin shifted to St. Thomas in the second year of my fieldwork. As the sixth working day loomed closer, the headteacher and teachers worried that his earlier school would refuse to process his transfer certificate. 'What if they give him more things and make him stay there?' St. Thomas had given all incoming students new school bags and a set of notebooks. Along with the first graders, Jwalin too had received a bag and a full set of notebooks. Lower primary schools in the region followed a similar trading logic, exchanging student bodies for free schoolbags, books and school bus rides. Jwalin's transfer certificate was processed by the sixth working day and a precious body was added to the list of enrolled students at St. Thomas.

Toward the end of my fieldwork, a high school teacher from a state-funded high school in Thiruvalla visited St. Thomas to recruit students for her fifth grade class. Unlike primary schools, high schools were scarce and did not typically face enrollment issues. But even a small drop in numbers could lead to a 'division fall', that is, reduction of the number of sections/divisions in the grade. A division fall would result in the recalibration of number of sanctioned teacher posts and teacher(s) stood to lose jobs they had paid so much to procure. This particular school was over 10 kilometers away, and mothers were reluctant to send young children so far away. The teacher had come after a long day's work at her own school. She looked exhausted, and her face was as strict as her starched brown cotton saree. She promised the mothers that she would arrange for free rides on the school bus. The girls in fourth grade were promised to the girls' school in Edanadu, without whom that school would shut down. That exchange had been promised earlier. Women's bodies are more easily amenable to such exchanges. The only student left in fourth grade was Appu. He was ready for adventure, and the promises of an English-medium high school education in Thiruvalla. His mother agreed anxiously but hopefully. The teacher's mission was a success.

Meanwhile, Asha was the only teacher in the neighborhood whose child studied at the same uneconomic school that the mother taught at. Teachers' children had attended St. Thomas in the recent past but had graduated and moved on to English-medium state-funded schools where they were doing well. The day I visited her school, Asha told me her son was free: Of the two students enrolled in his class, one was unwell. As the only student in his class, he didn't have much to do. She explained that there had been a lot of opposition from her family against enrolling her son at the uneconomic school. But with the numbers so drastic, she felt morally compelled. Her son had attended lower kindergarten in a private school, where he had learned in the conventional way (Chapter 5). Therefore, he came to the uneconomic school familiar with English letters and ready to read beginner-level picture books. Asha made sure that he received additional training at home. There were plenty of picture books [*othiri word picture books*] and computer games at home, which mitigated the isolation of the uneconomic school. But the seclusion troubled Asha:

> When there was competition, he was coming along well. Now again, it's down to one person. So it's gone a bit down [*pinnem down ayi*].

As a teacher-mother, Asha embodies the contradictions of social reproduction: should the family focus on Asha's job to accumulate economic capital that could be put in the service of the child's future? But then, would four years of Malayalam-medium primary schooling at an uneconomic school ruin the future of their only child? Should they sacrifice the pensionable, secure job? It was a hard decision that was lived out in the everyday.

To summarize, the teacher who emerged out of the Kerala development story was one who procured an auctioned job, regardless of sincerity or competence. Due to the specifications in the KER, this trade is defined around student bodies, whose numbers are formalized on the sixth working day of every academic year. The differential valuing of citizen futures within the development story became visible only when non-abject bodies were subject to the same trade.

Conclusion

This chapter described the social and affective worlds of mothers attached to St. Thomas and the state's responses to uneconomic schooling. Mothers attached to St. Thomas hoped obsessively to survive abjection. But despair emerged intermittently when mothers were forced to face the inadequacy of Malayalam-medium schooling for the pursuit of desirable higher education, secure employment, land ownership and a respectable house. Meanwhile, the state hailed families remnant at uneconomic schools as managers. But in the absence of any resources to manage, this extracted unpaid domestic labor from marginalized mothers. The next chapter describes the pedagogic mandates of the state, which promoted an oracy-focused English pedagogy. Forced to reconcile the contradictions of deeply deprived contexts, teachers and students responded with embodiments of shame and desire.

Notes

(1) The best academic performances at St. Thomas were still significantly below expected grade level competencies, and I describe curricular violence in detail in the next chapter.

(2) Biju Prabhakar (2013: 4) clarifies that the definition of uneconomic schools was fixed in 2011 as schools with less than 25 students per class and which were therefore financially unviable for the state in terms of payment of teacher salaries. When the number of uneconomic schools under this definition was found to be 4614, the state revised its definition. Now uneconomic schools are schools with less than 15 students per class.

(3) There was an increase of 32,575 students from 2017–2018 to 2018–2019 in lower primary grades even though birth rate had declined to 14 (GoK, 2018: 174). The state attributed the shift to an ambitious '*Pothu Vidyabhyasa Samrakhshana Yajyam*' [Public Education Rejuvenation Campaign] (2018: 175). However, TA Ameerudheen (2018) points out that the Kerala state had served closure notices to 1585 private unaided unrecognized schools and the Director of Public Instruction is quoted as saying that these students might have joined state-funded schools. Arokiasamy and Retnakumar (2006: 240) note a similar pattern for 1999 where students enrolled in

private unaided schools dropped sharply due to the government's decision to close down all unaided schools having limited infrastructure.

(4) Only 36% are state-owned and state-funded, and 8% are fee-charging private schools.

(5) During my fieldwork period, schools were closed only on zero student enrollment. Teachers from such schools would get their basic pay but not other allowances. This almost halved the total salary they received in-hand. Additionally, they were deputed to challenging and demanding positions to support pedagogic innovations. The increased workload at half the salary led some teachers to take leave without pay.

7 Mandated Resistance

Every morning at St. Thomas School began with a morning assembly, one of the key features of which was 'news reading' by students. With only 12 enrolled students, each student from second to fourth grade was expected to do this activity. Students had to write down three or four news items from any daily Malayalam newspaper in a specially designated notebook and read these out during the assembly. This performance of reading, writing and re-reading was one of the key mechanisms through which students were taught to read and write in Malayalam. The school subscribed to one newspaper, and those who did not have newspapers at home came to school early to do this work. Teachers too came in early or took time out during the day to read the newspaper with struggling readers, identifying letters that students did not yet recognize. During the morning news reading too, students, especially younger students, fumbled with recently learned consonants and required help, day after day. Only by the fourth month or later did second graders typically read with some level of fluency. While reforms advocated a 'non-conscious' language-learning strategy (SCERT, 2009: 7, 15), reading was learned intentionally and laboriously.

Jwalin transferred to St. Thomas in 3rd grade, from another state-funded school. When he came to school in brand new jeans and brightly colored trendy T-shirts, his classmates put him in place by ridiculing his inability to read Malayalam. For the third grade teacher, the requirement to begin from the Malayalam alphabet for one of her four students was an unexpected setback. Jwalin knew most of the consonants. However, he had trouble recognizing consonant vowel combinations, since the vowel-shape transforms when it combines with a consonant. After a few weeks, his teacher noted that that he could identify the transformed vowels but couldn't read the consonant-vowel combinations together [*kutti cherthu vayikkathilla*]. That is, he could read 'k' and the transformed 'i' separately but hesitated to read it together as 'ki'. The teachers agreed that 'somebody had to do the grunt work [*arengilum menakkedanam*]' and expected his mother to be that person [*avande amma menakkedanam*]. On the one hand, Jwalin's unexpected and interruptive entry into a localized literacy economy illuminated the crucial work performed by first and second grade teachers and the extent of work entailed in literacy teaching and learning. On the other hand, it also reanimated the easy slippage of pedagogic responsibility from teachers to mothers.

While St. Thomas was successful in teaching students Malayalam literacy, which other state-funded uneconomic schools nearby seemed to have given up on, it struggled with the teaching of English. Though most of my teaching work at St. Thomas was with second graders, others too dropped by during recess, to look through the reading materials I was slowly accumulating. I describe fourth-grader Appu's encounter with *The Greedy Mouse* in some detail below. Appu picked out *The Greedy Mouse* from among a bunch of new books that had just come in from the Delhi publisher *Pratham*. *The Greedy Mouse* is the story of a mouse that finds a bun and wants to take it home to eat it all by himself. He pushes the bun from the back, he pulls it from the front, he tries pulling it with a string, but when the bun remains unmovable, he finally eats it where he found it. His stomach gets too big from eating the entire bun, and he finds himself unable to get into his house.

Appu looked at the front cover and tried out the words he knew – 'rat' and 'biscuit' (the illustration of the bun did look like a *Good Day* biscuit). But 'rat' and 'biscuit' did not map on to the letters he saw – m-o-u-s-e and g-r-e-e-d-y. Annoyed, he flipped through the pages, but there were too many words he did not know – 'front', 'back', 'push', 'take'. The story didn't make much sense to him without the words. He decided to try another book. But every book he flipped through did not meet his criteria for comprehension, and soon enough, Appu left the glossy shiny books to go play outside. It is important to note that Appu later passed the competitive Kerala state Lower Primary School Scholarship Exams and was a 'bright' student. But he had been betrayed of the proficiencies his counterparts at the New English School acquired, albeit with much work.

The previous chapter described the hopes and aspirations of mothers and explained how the state managed uneconomic schooling through the labor of mothers and the enterprise of teachers. This chapter focuses on the pedagogic management of uneconomic schooling. State produced textbooks, standardized exams and teacher training programs located pedagogic expertise in the enterprising labor of English-speakers, and in the process, downplayed the requirement for material resources and literacy learning. Theoretical linguistic justifications were put forward to bolster demands for expressive, speaking selves who would build a socialist democratic society. Like with the NCERT and the CBSE, the Kerala state also defined ethical English teaching and learning around the negation of rote and its alleged alienating labors. Meanwhile, in the sparse classrooms of the uneconomic school, teachers struggled with textbooks that required them to be English-speakers rather than English-users. Governed by the activist agendas of the academic Left in Kerala (Chapter 8), unmitigated by the ambivalences of the market (Chapter 4), the uneconomic state-funded school taught pedagogies of shame and desire.

Protection Against Rote: Fragmenting the Textbook

The mandated teaching learning materials in Grades 1–4, from 2008 to 2014, consisted of a student textbook and a teacher's sourcebook for each grade (Table 7.1). The teacher's sourcebook had two parts; a first part detailed conceptual underpinnings, and the second section compiled the texts to be taught in the classroom. The reforms sought to protect the English classroom from rote pedagogies and, therefore, fragmented the textbook such that it would not, or could not, be taught at home. The textbook for primary school grades was a compilation of fragments from the sourcebook.

Table 7.1 Reformed pedagogic materials

Teacher's sourcebook	<u>Part 1</u>: Theoretical assumptions and conceptual frameworks
	<u>Part 2</u>: Pedagogic materials: Five units, each comprising • Interaction (scripted questions) • Narrative (story proper, about 50 to 300 words each) • Process (activities, exercises)
Student's textbook	Narrative fragments, activities, exercises

To give an example from second grade materials, Unit 3 in the sourcebook consisted of one story titled *In the Lap of Nature* that ran from page 85 to 111, with sections titled Interaction, Narrative and Process. Unit 3 has 15 narratives interspersed with 25 interaction sections and 12 process sections (Table 7.2).

In the teacher's sourcebook, *In the Lap of Nature* begins with an interaction. Interaction typically lists scripted interactions to introduce the story, provide space for predictions and so on. Textbook writers explained that scripted interactions were provided so that teachers did not interact in 'wrong' English. The introductory *Interaction* in Unit 3 is as follows:

How many members are there in your home?
Who are they?
Elicit responses.
Let the pupils say in mother tongue (Amma, Achan, Aniyan...)
Teacher may megaphone them in English.
Don't you have grandparents at home?
Whom do you love the most? Why?

Table 7.2 Grade 2, Unit 3, *In the Lap of Nature* (a single story)

Teacher's sourcebook (pages 85–111)	• 25 interactions (scripted questions) • 15 narratives (about 50 to 300 words each) • 12 process sections (activities, exercises)
Student's textbook (pages 30–42)	5 narrative fragments (illustrated text, about 11 to 28 words) 1 song 2 activities and 4 exercises

Give them enough time for free interaction.
Today, let's listen to the story of a boy who loved his grandma very much.
His name starts with the letter M. Can you guess the boy's name?
Let the pupils guess and say the name.
Then introduce Manu.

While the questions (in English) listed in the *Interaction* focused on vocabulary related to families, the student textbook began with an illustration of
Manu in a pond, playing with fish, along with the lines: 'Manu is a smart
boy. He loves flowers, butterflies, and birds'. The interaction was misaligned
with the illustrations and descriptions in the student textbook.

Back to the sourcebook. The interaction is followed by a narrative.
The 'narrative' is the story proper, in monolingual English. The first
Narrative about Manu read as follows:

One morning, Manu was sitting on the veranda of his house.
Red, blue, yellow, black. He saw many butterflies flitting in the garden.
Woh! How colorful they are!
"Today, I'll catch one" he thought.
Manu walked into the courtyard.
The dew drops tickled his feet.
He slowly walked towards the garden.
The butterflies were on the shoe-flower plant!
They come to the flower to collect honey.
'Today I must catch one.'
He went near the butterflies.
They were busy enjoying honey.
'How can I catch one? Which one will I catch?
Yes, that big one, that big yellow one.'
His fingers almost touched the wings of it.
'Hi, here I got it.'
'Manu, what are you doing?'
Grandma called out from veranda.
Manu turned and looked at grandma.
'Ho, my grandma! I was about to catch one. But it flew away.'
'Manu, we can catch it in the evening.
Don't you have school today?
Now, come and take bath.'
Grandma went near Manu with a towel.
'Grandma, let me bathe in the pond.'
'No, not today Manu, you can take bath here itself,' his mother came out
from the kitchen and warned him.
'No, no, I want to go, please grandma, take me to the pond.' Manu began
to cry aloud.

Unlike the picture books we saw in Chapters 3 and 4, which were comprised of limited and comprehensively illustrated text, for instance, one
sentence per illustration, this narrative is a long text with no illustration.

No part of this interaction is available in the student textbook. Additionally, the state pedagogy expressly disallowed translations. How then were students like Appu, who had minimal exposure to English words, expected to understand and stay engaged?

Each of the 15 narratives in the sourcebook ranged from 67 to 277 words, most averaging around 150 words. These are largely descriptive in nature, meant to be read aloud by the teacher so as to evoke 'mental images' in children. To clarify, Grade 1 textbooks used bilingual narratives, and key plot elements were narrated in Malayalam. In Grade 2, the first two units attempt the same technique, but peripheral details rather than key plot details were narrated in Malayalam. From Unit 3, materials were monolingual, in English. Of the 15 narratives in Unit 3, small excerpts from five narratives were compiled in the textbook and illustrated. The remaining are to be delivered aurally by the teacher with appropriate gestures and emotions but without translation. Textbook writers clarified that the majority of the narratives were *excluded* from the textbook to thwart 'traditional' teaching at school, home or in the community: choral reading and the repeated writing of dictation words, word meanings or the like as described in Chapter 4. Instead, narrative fragmenting sought to mandate listening. However, without illustrations, simplification or translation, the sentence-level interaction of the learner and the textbook degenerated into meaning-less noise.

After another *Interaction,* the unit moved into a *Process* section. The 'process' sections in the sourcebook contained activities, exercises and picture reading guidelines for the illustrated narrative fragments. Activities varied from concept mapping to making paper fish, with a constant flow of scripted teacher talk in English. Exercises however were standardized and expected literary proficiencies. Four exercise items (1) writing a conversation, (2) writing thoughts of a protagonist, (3) writing a picture description, and (4) writing a rhyming poem, accompanied every unit. For instance, after a word web and fish-making activity, students are expected to write a conversation between Manu, and a neighbor Januchechi (SCERT, 2008: 29). In the sourcebook, the expected (written) conversation is provided as follows:

Januchechi: Manu, why are you so early today?
Manu: There is a programme in my school.
Januchechi: What is that?
Manu: Storytelling.
Januchechi: Are you participating?
Manu. Yes.
Januchechi: Then, all the best.

Student proficiencies were tested by centralized, standardized examinations conducted thrice a year. The second grade curriculum consisted of five units, and the District Education Office periodically communicated a 'scheme of work' to all teachers, indicating which units had to be taught for each of the three exams.

Through scripted interactions and narrative fragmenting, pedagogic materials not only reified oracy as the appropriate way to *know* English but also recognized teachers as English users with limited speaking abilities. Over 70% of the material was intended solely for listening. As for reading, opportunities for practice were severely limited. In Unit 3, only 5 of the 15 narratives that too small excerpts were included in the student textbook for reading. However, exams were written tests even though pedagogical emphasis on writing is minimal.

To summarize, unlike the literacy pedagogy of private schools where the textbook lesson was transformed piecemeal into the notebook and reassembled meaningfully at home by mothers and afterschool tuition teachers, aural lessons dissipated in the deprivations of the uneconomic school and the Dalit colony. The following section examines the theoretical arguments deployed to oppose reading writing practice, glossed as rote, and the next chapter describes the sociopolitical mores within which linguistic theories were interpreted and refashioned.

Mandating Resistance

The first section of the sourcebook, which details the conceptual logic of the reforms, articulates an emphatic resistance to the structural method of language teaching and behaviorist pedagogy (SCERT, 2009: 7–12, 15–18). The sourcebook explicitly places earlier pedagogic materials within the paradigm of Behavioral Psychology and Structural Linguistics (2009: 7). These supposedly present language at the 'sentence level or word level' rather than at the meaning level (2009: 19), for instance, practices such as 'beginning with ABC' (2009: 8), 'beginning with words or sentences' such as 'This is a pen' (2009: 9–10), 'teaching rhymes' (2009: 11) and 'teaching formulaic expressions' such as 'May I come in' (2009: 12) fragment language and erode meaning (2009: 18).

What is unstated but implicit throughout is concern for the literacy-literary divide, for all the literacy activities picked out for comment and prohibition are of the survival English variety. These are not the literary textbooks Tickoo (1986: 47) describes which too professed to teach pre-selected grammatical structures but 'hid and clothed' structures in narratives and 'exciting story lines'. The most popular of these was the *Gulmohur* series edited by Tickoo himself from 1974. The *Gulmohur* textbook had grammar exercises, but these were not the main lesson, they were the exercises that came after. Meanwhile, for less privileged counterparts studying in state-funded schools, the exercises had stood in for the lesson itself. This was true for the coordinator of the textbook writing committee, and he described a lesson on 'prepositional phrases' from the first English textbook he had encountered as a student, the 1997 Kerala English Reader for fifth grade. English was introduced in fifth grade during the 1990s. Unit 5 titled 'A Rat in a Hat' required students to 'look at the pictures' and 'read the phrases': 'a dog on a log', 'a cat on a mat', 'a cup on a saucer', 'a mug on a table' and so on (SCERT, 1997: 9–10). While this lesson is explicitly labeled 'prepositional phrases', it is also a classic example of the 'literacy in English' textbook described by Ramanathan (2005: 49–50).

The reforms thus translated sociolinguistic pedagogic hierarchies into a theoretical distinction between form and meaning. Though textbooks with 'meaningful' texts rather than form-based fragments prevailed in privileged private schools, these were elided to crystalize distinctions between form and meaning, and mechanical practice and spontaneous interaction. The coordinator of the textbook writing committee explained:

> Textbooks approached language as a bricklaying process. They didn't put forward language pedagogy. Letters are taught through mechanical drill. It was animal training. A for Apple. Can A be only for 'apple'? We are still in colonial times? What is 'hot cross buns'? Does anybody know? There was no meaningful transaction in language classrooms. Wren and Martin will have 101 sentences to demonstrate different conjugations for the word 'love': 'I am loving a girl', 'I am being loved by a girl', this is to teach form. Wren and Martin were grain merchants! Language is not about form, it is about ideas and meaning. Meaning is paramount. So we wanted to shake everything up, bring about a paradigm change. Importance is given to linguistic discourse. Both input and output have to be in discourse form.

That textbooks for privileged students were assembled to be more eclectic (and meaningful) than what was prescribed by theory is conveniently forgotten.

This brings me to the last point. The reforms index the 'traditional' through both theory and practice registers, assuming coherence between linguistic theory and textbook writer/teacher practice. As we have seen, textbook writers and editors happily deviated from theory. But they are absent in reform tirades; laments about theory are reserved instead for teachers. The sourcebook, for instance, writes that 'most teachers still take recourse to mother tongue translation' and on asking comprehension questions that elicit 'fixed answers', which result in 'teacher-dominated' (SCERT, 2009: 19), 'undemocratic' classrooms that force children to be 'passive' (SCERT, 2007: 15). Thus, structuralism and behaviorism allegedly produced fragmented, non-meaning-full pedagogic materials, which teachers and students embraced in practice (Table 7.3). On the contrary, Tickoo (1990: 413) explains that the official method, which supposedly focused on the teaching of form through mechanical drills, had never found favor with classroom teachers in India and that there was a 'total mismatch between curricular expectations and classroom practice'. In fact, while reforms assume that the structural method disallowed

Table 7.3 Kerala SCERT on rote and interaction

	Rote	Interaction
Theoretical frameworks	Structural linguistics, behavioral psychology	Natural language acquisition
Pedagogic practices	Mechanical repetition, memorization	Spontaneous/scripted interactions and narratives, activities
Student orientation	Intentional but passive	Unintended but active
Teacher	Authoritative	Democratic

meaning, teachers may have translated 'each lesson and every sentence in it into the regional language' (GoI, 1967: 46 as cited in Tickoo, 1990: 413) due to their preoccupation with meaning.

In effect, reforms prohibited all 'traditional' practices such as the teaching of the alphabet, words and rhymes, choral reading and writing drills (Chapter 4) in the name of resisting structuralism and behaviorism. Unlike the NCERT materials which assumed a voluntary abstinence from rote, Kerala SCERT pedagogies actively prohibited rote pedagogy and its accompanying literacy instruction. As we saw in the SCERT lesson, *In the Lap of Nature*, the textbook was designed to thwart literacy-based practice. Though reforms attempted to correct the literacy-literary divide, the elision of a sociolinguistic issue into a theoretical-linguistic problem superimposed a literacy-oracy divide onto the literacy-literary divide.

Biologizing the Social

While the social (literacy-literary divide) was implicitly evoked but erased, the theoretical underpinnings looked to nature and biology to justify the paradigm shifts in English pedagogy. With specific reference to English learning, the human was qualified as a 'natural' and biological human. The teachers' sourcebook (SCERT, 2008: 17) states the 'basic principles of learning a language' as:

(1) The child has an innate language system. Language learning is a natural growth of this innate language system.
(2) Language learning is a non-conscious process. This is radically different from the conscious learning of linguistic facts.

SCERT (2009: 7) further clarifies:

All that we mean by "innateness" is simply this: The human child is biologically equipped with language system. This gets unfolded as the language system of the speech community in which she lives. This is a natural process, a process that takes place without any conscious attempt from the part of the learner. Nor is there any special effort made by the mother or others to teach her the mother tongue.

Explaining his theoretical positions, the chief consultant of the Kerala English reforms, Dr K.N. Anandan (2014) explains:

> I am a Chomsky linguist. And Chomsky linguists are a very rare species. ... Chomsky has a claim regarding language. He says that every human being is genetically endowed with language. In those days it was called Language Recognition Device. Now it is called the Universal Grammar. ... After it was known for a few months, some ELT experts said that Chomsky's theory is regarding L1 – mother-tongue learning. And it doesn't apply to L2 [second language]. So for L2, students need this rigorous practicing and drilling. L1 will naturally develop, they said, because there is a linguistic ambience for that. In L2 however, you don't have a speech amenity, so it doesn't work. ... Chomsky has said that though I claim that humans have an inbuilt capacity to learn language, I am not claiming that language pedagogy can be worked out on this. ...
> I started producing a number of materials for lower primary, primary, middle school, high school and colleges. ... And everything followed a new paradigm where [traditional] teaching was stopped. ... Basically, it was based heavily on interactions – just interactions. Dialoguing, making students think – thinking is the only tonic for language. Make them think. And dialogue. Somebody expresses an idea. [So, you ask the students] Do you agree with that? Do you have any other opinion? It's a dialogue; nothing else.

While Chomskyan linguistics has been critiqued by sociolinguists, who place the ahistoric, universal, Chomskyan mind in bodies, and further, in social relationships and power hierarchies, as explained in Chapter 4 theoretical linguistics elides the distinctions between second language acquisition and second language learning. What the sourcebook and K.N. Anandan articulate are assumptions about second language acquisition, which fall apart if second language learning is considered.

What the sourcebook and K.N. Anandan forget to mention are that human beings are not 'biologically equipped' or 'genetically endowed' for literacy. Literacy does not unfold naturally or take place without 'any conscious attempt from the part of the learner' and 'efforts made by the mother or others to teach her'. As Romeo (2000) points out, proponents of natural acquisition convert processes that second language acquisition theory attempts to explain – how a child achieves spontaneous and appropriate use of language for everyday purposes – into 'uncontroversial observations' that then become a framework for (oracy-centered) classroom instruction. The evocation of nature and biology equate English learning with aurality and oracy. As K.N. Anandan notes, the pedagogy is 'based heavily on interactions – just interactions. [d]ialoguing'. Once spoken interaction is equated with 'thinking', literacy practice, that too repetitive drills, become 'unnatural'. Teachers who are non-speakers but users of English become 'authoritative' and 'undemocratic' by default.

It is from this biologized position of authority that the reforms mandated resistance to traditional literacy practices. SCERT (2009) forbids the teaching of the alphabet (A–Z), words (pen, table), spelling drills or dictation, and phrase-/sentence-level practice (grammar exercises) as mechanically repetitive 'pseudo-literacy' practices that have no place in the revised curriculum (2009: 9–11, 25–26). In addition, all question answers were also eliminated from state textbooks to prohibit mechanical repetition and memorization.

Emotional and Expressive

To ensure aurality/oracy-centered language learning and to foreclose any attempts at conventional (literacy-oriented) teaching learning practices, student textbooks were produced as compilations of 'narrative fragments'. For Dr K.N. Anandan, a narrative has both positive and negative functions. As we have seen, the narrative – by virtue of its fragmented form – resists rote. The positive function, according to Dr K.N. Anandan, is that it evokes an emotional excess which can be channeled into and results in language learning. Anandan (2014) writes:

> Oral narratives are extremely useful tools for acquiring language. Just present a narrative with emotive aspect. My hypothesis is that language experiences sustain in the human mind as emotional gestalts. Other things just fade out. You must have talked to many people round-the-clock but you can't recall. But there are certain things that you carry till death – those things that touched you – which emotionally touched you. … So any learning experience is like that. You have to link emotions. And neurobiologists also say the empathetic nerves have to be fired. …
> So here the story is given in very small text. It is a narrative.
> *It's getting dark.*
> *Jillu must be hungry.*
> *He is alone in the nest.*
> *Will he be afraid?*
> *I should get home soon* the mother squirrel thought.
> And then, what will Jillu's mother do now?
> Listen to your teacher.
> A curiosity and expectancy is created – a communicational expectancy – and you are filling it. That's all. At that point, you can predict, elicit their response. They can make predictions on what will happen. And that prediction – you can tap on that, where the reading text will appear again. After this, Now what will Jillu ask his mother?
> What may be her reply?
> And here the child has to build a conversation.

While the NCERT and private publishers designed pedagogic material around opportunities for repeated revisiting of the same linguistic item, K.N. Anandan replaces meaningful repetition with a generalized theory of affect. For him, language experiences that sustain as 'emotional gestalts' will be retained and those that do not will 'just fade out'. A long-time member of his team recalled that the initial narratives scripted by the team were 'terribly emotional [*bhayankara emotions aa*]' and the scripting team favored pathos to evoke emotional excess. In the narrative cited by K.N. Anandan, Jillu's mother has to encounter pathos to elicit the required linguistic-affective response from second graders. The handbook (SCERT, 2008: 6) instructs: 'Narratives are not meant to be explained or translated. Present them as such with proper feel and voice modulation'. The specificities of this directive (feel, voice modulation) are reminiscent of *katha prasangam* traditions, in which solo artists performed highly theatrical monologue-stories to musical accompaniment. Trivedi's (2015: 2) description of the performative style of V Sambasivan, an accomplished *katha prasanagam* artist, reveals the performative depth integral to *katha prasangam*:

> To make the narrative come alive, he also enacted all the roles of the characters, putting on and modulating different voices, tones, pitches and gestures suitable for various roles. Hence, his act was not just solo stand-up singing or narration but a fuller, more dramatic experience of the whole, where one singer-actor performed the roles of all the characters, harnessing into his show the energy and viscerality of the 'liveness' of theater.

A similar 'extravagantly emotional' performance (Trivedi, 2015: 5) is required of teachers, since the Kerala SCERT (2008: 8) asks them to assemble 'learning experiences which influence (children's) emotional orbit'. The 'dramatic emotionalism' that lies at the heart of *katha prasangam* (Trivedi, 2015: 5) had to become everyday English language pedagogy. All the information and affective landscape crucial to story comprehension had to be extra-linguistically coded in the performances of the *katha prasangak* teacher.

Meanwhile, this emotional excess is understood to generate linguistic production in English. Anandan (2014) states:

> So the output can be in the form of any number of one of the discourses – either conversation, or the narrative is continued, or a description or a letter – depending on the academic standard. No vocabulary exercise, no comprehension question, no grammar exercise – nothing is needed. When our society will understand that I don't know; it may take years. … I revised the curricular objectives in terms of discourses. A class one child has to construct and produce – both orally and also later in written form – description/conversation. …The output is defined in terms of discourses – not in terms of some structures or some vocabulary items. This is a basic thing that happened.

This obligatory 'discourse', for the practical purposes of teaching and testing, was defined at the 'upper limit of structural organization' – like a coherent stand-alone conversation (Stubbs, 1983: 7). Primary school English learning, and most importantly standardized testing, was structured around student production of four specific 'genre' discourses (Polanyi, 1988: 604): conversations, descriptions, rhymes and thoughts (SSA evaluation criteria, 2011, 2012, 2013, 2014). NCERT (2006: 16) points out that emergent learners' spontaneous production of language progresses from 'a one-word, mostly nouns, stage to the production of multi word sentences with verbs, auxiliaries, determiners, adjectives, prepositions, perhaps through a two-word stage'. For the Kerala SCERT primary textbooks, however, there are no stages of learning. Students progress from hearing rhapsodic narratives to discourse production in the written form, regardless of comprehension.

Prabhu (1987) describes the allures of learner discourse construction for 'meaning focused' pedagogies but cautions that insistence on production can be counterproductive. Though he had begun his Bangalore Communicational Project (1979–1984) with what he calls 'opinion gap tasks' – which involved 'identifying and articulating a personal response, feeling or attitude in response to a given situation', e.g. story completion (1987: 47) – he had eventually abandoned them. He writes:

> The value of open-ended activity for linguistic development can perhaps be realized better with advanced learners in a second language but in early stages of second language learning, open-ended activity too often leads only to learners' verbal imitation of one another, or of the teacher, and thus ceases to be genuinely open ended. (Prabhu, 1987: 48)

He goes on to explain what opinion gap activity involves:

> ... stating meaning which is very much one's own – and of a kind (for example feeling or attitude) which is neither well defined nor easy to articulate [...] leads to a high level of uncertainty, diffidence, or anxiety, though it offers a correspondingly high level of pleasure from success. ... [It] calls for both meaning and language which is one's own, and for that reason can seem daunting. (Prabhu, 1987: 49)

Interestingly, Prabhu used 'reasoning gap' activities that allowed his learners to progress from 'a one-word, mostly nouns, stage to the production of multi word sentences through a two-word stage'. For Prabhu, learners' 'sense of security' and perception of potential success was crucial for language learning. Necessarily beyond the linguistic repertoires of students, opinion gap activities caused 'uncertainty, diffidence, anxiety' and even frustration to the point of learners' disinclination to make the effort (1987: 47, 50, 56).

For Kerala state pedagogy however, opinion gap tasks and learner construction of genre discourses are mandatory evidence for language learning. Kerala pedagogy is built on principles of constructivism and critical pedagogy; for both, learners' active 'construction' of their own knowledge is crucial to learning. As Anandan (2014) explains:

> Elevate the learner from the level of a recipient to the level of a creator. He is a co-author of the textbook. Every learner is a co-author of the textbook. Understand this. And respect that child.

Thus, instructional design claims to respect and affirm learners and seeks to create opportunities for learners to 'co-construct' the story and thus 'construct' their own knowledge and language proficiencies. But to do so, teachers had to demand the impossible from learners, or manufacture expected results. It is important to reiterate that reading instruction is distressingly low in the pedagogic designs discussed above, be it rhapsodical narratives or discourse construction. Opportunity for fluency in word recognition (extracting sound and meaning from graphic symbols) is scarce. This configuration of an oracy-centered pedagogy that nevertheless demanded literacy proficiencies made teaching English an impossible activity.

Instead, what it generated was pedagogies of shame. The next section presents the twin components of pedagogies of shame. I describe a mandatory standardized test I administered to students in second grade and a compulsory teacher training session I attended as a teacher. For students, the test measured literacy proficiency though it was not taught. For teachers, the training modelled techniques for English speakers, not users. These did not teach English; they taught us to be ashamed of what we 'lacked'.

Pedagogies of Shame

It was December 2014. Before St. Thomas celebrated Christmas with carols, steamers and children dressed in white, students and teachers had to wrap up the term exams. Thrice in an academic year, centralized exams were held to check student progress. After the usual morning assembly, the headteacher handed me the question papers in a sealed brown envelope, ceremoniously, wrong side up, to display that the envelope was indeed un-tampered. Indexing the larger-scale institutions and practices associated with centralized exams, the envelope was marked with several bureaucratic notations: the district and the sub-district that located the school, the grade and subject of the examination, the name of the school, the number of answer scripts (5) and question papers (2) contained inside, a serial number, and another set number.

Ironically, inside the elaborately annotated envelope was a pale-green *Instructions to Teachers* sheet that began: 'The teacher should create a child friendly environment before starting the evaluation process', contradicting the numerical and administrative specificities of the envelope.

While the sealed envelope evoked discourses of fair and impartial evaluation of individual student ability, the instructions acknowledged the enterprise of evaluation as always potentially unfair and partial. Meanwhile, the five-page answer sheet began with the typical demand for student and school name. The four students, all girls, spread themselves out on the single low wooden bench, and began writing their names. They knew the performances expected of fair evaluations.

In keeping with the textbook format, the test was organized in the form of a singular narrative, which had four 'narrative gaps' or 'slots'. Building on the characters in Unit 3, this newly scripted narrative had slots for a conversation, thoughts, poem and a description. The pale-green question sheet, available only to the instructor, began in the following manner:

Interaction

- Do you like picnic?
- Which place do you like to visit?
- With whom do you like to go?
  (Elicit free responses)

Narrative
Gopi nerathe ezhunettu. Avan nalla santhoshathillanu. He is going to visit zoo today. *Avan yathrakulla orukkangal thudangi. Appozhanavanorthathu* "Oh! I didn't say Manu about this". He ran to the telephone and called his friend Manu.
[My translation: Gopi woke up early. He was very happy. He is going to visit zoo today. He began preparing for the journey. Then he remembered "Oh! I didn't say Manu about this". He ran to the telephone and called his friend Manu.]

The answer sheet continued the question with a picture of two boys talking on the telephone followed by the conversation exercise in a fill in the blanks format:

Activity I – Conversation
Write the conversation between Gopi and Manu
Gopi: Hallo, Manu Good morning.
Manu: ....
Gopi: How are you?
Manu: ....
Gopi: I am going to visit a zoo.
Manu: ....
Gopi: ....
Manu: ....

I had accompanied the students on a zoo visit the previous year and knew they would engage the interaction questions enthusiastically. Unlike the survival English exercises described by Ramanathan (2005: 54–56), the test sought to provide students with opportunities to develop their own 'writing voice'. I quickly scanned the rest of the narrative.

The second exercise however had nothing to do with the zoo trip; it introduced a puppy that Gopi was pining for, in order to situate the mandatory 'thoughts' exercise. The third narrative came back to the zoo trip, but in the form of the compulsory 'writing a poem/song' exercise. It would require much affective management to turn off students' interaction and steer them to the next exercise. Even more would be required to transform students' oral interactions in Malayalam and English into written products in monolingual English. The task was daunting. I read out the narrative without using the 'interaction questions' and moved into the conversation-bit students had in front of them.

Me (reading aloud): Hello Manu, Good morning
Aneesha (responds): Good morning
Me: How are you?
Aneesha: *evideyanennano?* [Does this mean, where are you?]
Me: No, (trying again, pretending to initiate a genuine conversation) How are you?
Aneesha: I am *nallathanennu enganna?* [How do you say 'fine'?]
Emilia: Beautiful
Jis: Happy?
Me: Okay, 'I am happy.'
I select "happy" from the two English responses because 'beautiful' would pose them greater difficulties in writing. I wait for them to write. Students copy 'Good morning' from the conversation-bit given in the answer sheet but get stuck with the next line, unsure of how to write 'happy.' Frustrated, Aneesha writes 'Hallo' instead of 'I am happy,' again copying the spelling from the question paper. Ajin attempts 'happy' and writes it as 'I am nppy.' Emilia hesitates till Jis, on a sudden epiphany, writes 'I am happy.' Emilia copies the spelling from Jis.
I read the next line from the answer sheet.
Me: I am going to visit a zoo.
Aneesha (to Emilia): *njan tourinu pova, ni varunno?*
[I am going on a tour; you want to come?]
Emilia: *nga* [yes]
Ajin (recalling a phrase from a picture book we had read together): I am playing.
Emilia: *Varunno ennu chodikku* [Ask if she wants to come].
Aneesha: Yes, *njanum veram* [I will also come].
There is no provision in the narrative to accommodate Manu joining Gopi on the trip. The 'thoughts' question that follows is scripted around Gopi and a puppy who is introduced after the conversation.
Ajin starts doodling.
Aneesha: *nivaa, engane parayum?* [How do you say 'come'?]
Ajin writes 'ox' in the slot after 'I am going to visit a zoo.' I think she means 'ok.' She continues writing. She carefully and painstakingly writes

'Larng is' on the next line, and finally *'This is Mlpr'* on the final blank line.
The others' answers are as follows:
Jis: ork
Aneesha: I am going to visit a zoo (copied from the conversation bit)
Emilia: I am halying (I think she means 'playing')
Manu is come (I think this was meant to be 'Manu, come')

The exam went downhill as we proceeded, each new section burdened by frustrations from previous sections. The girls became fatigued, trying to produce words, sentences and spellings they had not previously encountered (see also Prabhu, 1987: 49). In the previous cohort, one of the students typically responded to these demands with rage, and then tears. This cohort doodled, giggled and meandered into play. But while the others talked and laughed, Ajin maintained an almost stoic silence that I found deeply metaphoric. Ajin's performance of writing is careful and painstaking even when the letters themselves do not come together into a legible form for others. Though reader uptake may be negligible, the act is undertaken with utmost sacrality. As her activity indicates, (solitary) writing became legitimate language use, for the answer sheet erased everything else. The answer scripts were to be marked by an 'impartial' outsider, and there was nothing but non-sense awaiting her. Shame and anger flooded through me. I knew what students *could* do. I knew the books they read, and their engagements with and critiques of these texts. Further, I knew the obsessive hope mothers invested in their children's education and how much they looked to tests to validate their dreams. How could I face mothers with an answer sheet that recorded only absences?

The dire need for more appropriate materials led me to survey the children's books market in India and I began sourcing beginner-level reading materials. In what follows, I describe the responses of the four students to one such book, titled *Come*, published by Tulika. I choose this book for two reasons: First, it was one of students' favorite books; they repeatedly asked for it. Second, in the test described earlier, one of the words produced in both its spoken and written forms is 'come'.

Every time I handed out a picture book to the class, students read it with their hands, tracing the lines of the pictures and the words. Emilia had also taken to hugging and smelling the books. State textbooks are printed in cheap color, and the luxuriousness of picture books heightened the dullness of our books and the cheapness of our wall materials. I typically asked students to look through the pictures and write down words they thought they knew. They wrote down 'the' and 'to' as they leafed through the book, spending time on each page to soak in the colors and the pictures. Picture after picture reinforced the singular theme of the book, indicated by the simple word, 'come'. Night turned to day, flower became fruit, clouds brought rain. 'Come, said the big yellow leaf to the tiny green leaf'. The students, all girls, paused on the 'yellow' leaf but decided that they did not know the word.

Emilia: *Ithariyamallo?* Yellow?	***Emilia***: Don't we know this? Yellow?
Jis: *Ithu* yellow *ano?*	***Jis***: Is this yellow?
Parichayamunde	It (the word) looks familiar
Aneesha-*nu ariyamo?*	Aneesha, do you know it?
Aneesha: *Illa*	***Aneesha***: No

'Egg', on the other hand, did not pose any trouble. Aneesha wrote it down as soon as she saw it. Emilia said: 'Egg *muttaya* [Egg is egg]', and Jis promptly responded, '*njanum ezhuthatte* [let me also write it down]'.

These word recognition instances were punctuated by an intermittent commentary about the pictures. The long strange beard streaked with white, in particular, drew some laughter and ridicule. Black hair grayed and became white, but nobody had that long a beard! By the time they finished, their combined list had eight words. After the picture walk, I read the book, slowly, finger on each word. 'Come, said the stars to the sun'. Aneesha's puzzled face prompted some explanation and I said: 'Stars *ba paranju,* sun *vannu* [stars said come, the sun came]'. Aneesha turned to Jis and said, 'come'. Jis nodded. We continued reading. Much to my embarrassment, they liked to repeat after, at the top of their voice. I had learned that my middle-class sensibilities of 'proper' reading did not match their desired performances. By the second reading, they could recognize the patterns and Emilia told me '*teachere vayikkale* [teacher, don't read it yet, let me try]'. We ended the session with a drawing activity. They drew four of their favorite illustrations from the book and captioned each picture, 'come'. Desperate for more writing and re-reading practice, I insisted that they also label the pictures: 'bird', 'egg', 'star', 'sun' and so on. I filled in the pattern words in case they wanted to read at home. That evening, as we got ready to leave, Aneesha called out to Ajin, who was idling behind, 'come, come'. Ajin broke out into a hop and they began their walk back home.

Even though I found our routine reading of picture books productive and affirming, the limits of teacher work that is not aligned with state-sanctioned methods were painfully evident. Our interactions and students' emergent reading skills could not be converted into the reified written responses required by state-mandated tests and students were forthright in requesting 'traditional' drill exercises like dictation [*kettezhuthu*]. The more interesting a picture book, the more eager students were to have dictation words. The activity involved identifying key words, which would then be written out five or six times, vertically, in a notebook. The writing had to be accompanied by the saying of the word, letter by letter. The process was incomplete without a written test. Writing out the words from hearing, rather than by copying, afforded them access, albeit partial, to legitimate performances in satisfying ways. While the state-mandated test produced them as ignorant and my reading sessions generated a community of learners, it was solitary, accurate writing that permitted them to produce themselves as legitimate learners.

Students further re-figured the 'lacks' characterizing their classroom instruction by foregrounding a crucial discarded object, the blackboard. Every Friday evening, the four girls enrolled in second grade crowded around the prolific hibiscus plant adjacent to the school verandah to pick wilting flowers. They took these flowers to the old, decrepit blackboard that stood in one corner of the classroom and wiped it down, crushing the flower to release its sap. The tallest of the four, Emilia, stood on tiptoe to wipe down the top borders. I rarely used the blackboard. For one, it was so old that any writing was barely legible, even for a four-student class. Second, neither the state method nor my informal picture book methodology had much role for blackboard work. The state method was oracy centered, and the picture book work was focused on a different material object, the picture book. In contrast, at the New English School, literacy practices were regimented to produce functional language ability and students' primary classroom obligation was copying off the blackboard. While this task was undertaken with absolute sacrality, it was also marked by a banal disregard for the blackboard as well as ardent loathing for practice drills and testing (Chapter 4). This dialectic – disregard for a much-used object (blackboard) and practice (copy writing) at the non-elite English-medium school and longing for the same at the uneconomic Malayalam-medium school – reveal the relational nature of desire. As Motha and Lin (2013: 344) point out, desire cannot exist in isolation or out of a social context.

I move on to the second pedagogy of shame, this one of teachers. A one-day mandatory teacher-training program had been held a few months prior to the exam at the District Institute for Educational Training. According to the program plan, teachers had to conduct a pre-test with their students, which would inform the day's work. The pre-test consisted of a picture of a temple festival along with a prompt to write a description of the festival. When teachers came in for the program, the day's plan was explained to us. The morning session would identify 'errors' within students' written responses, and the afternoon session would focus on teaching methods that would rectify these errors. Fourteen teachers from the sub-district attended the program that day. We formed groups with about four teachers and were given student responses from another group. As we pondered over the responses handed to us, a demure teacher dressed in a starched yellow cotton sari stated matter-of-factly, in a voice that carried:

All four are the same. *Ithezhuthipichatha. Kuttiyude* level spelling mistakes-*il ninnu manasilakkanam.*

[These are not "authentic" student responses. You can make out differences in student learning levels only from the spelling mistakes students made while copying down the teacher-made answer.]

She stated what was obvious but never spoken out loud in 'official' spaces; teachers administering the test had manufactured student answers to satisfy state demands for students' linguistic production. As teachers nodded in agreement, I sensed an opportunity to formally discuss some of the central issues teachers faced in their everyday teaching practice. As a resource person, I was familiar with the lead facilitator, Rani, and during tea break, I shared the observation with Rani. However, I returned uneasy, remembering an earlier program where my efforts to bring in data from my classroom had come to a humiliating end. All the 'mistakes' in students' written responses had been attributed to my 'lack' of English usage in the classroom. As the day progressed, this deficit model resurfaced in individualized and collective forms.

After tea break, the groups were invited to present their error analysis. When it came to our group, Rani called on the teacher in the yellow sari. The teacher was asked to read out student responses. As noted earlier, the responses did not have many errors, except for spelling mistakes. So instead of an error analysis, Rani picked the sentence 'We are going to a temple festival' and began asking why it was meaningful.

Rani: Why is the sentence meaningful?
Teacher: Structure
Rani (interrupting): Structure *mathrameollo?*

"We are going to a temple festival" meaningful *anu*
Enthu kondanathine meaningful *ennu parayunnathu?*
"Are-going"; plural-"we"; "to"-a preposition; "a" village festival-article, indefinite article; *enthu konde* the *paranjilla?*

Specific *ayittum* teacher *ariyanam.*
Teacher: Preposition
Rani (Correcting pronunciation): Pri-position *alla,* pre-position

Rani: Why is the sentence meaningful?
Teacher: Structure
Rani (interrupting): Is there only structure?
"We are going to a temple festival" is meaningful.
Why is it meaningful?

"Are-going"; plural-"we"; "to"-a preposition; "a" village festival-article, indefinite article; why didn't the child use "the" (instead of "a")?
You have to be specific in your answer.
Teacher: Preposition
Rani (Correcting pronunciation): Not pri-position, it's pre-position

Questioning the pronunciation and grammatical competence of the teacher, Rani effectively silenced her. Throughout the rest of the day, the teacher in the yellow sari stayed quiet, invisible and yet hyper-visible.

While one teacher's critical response was thus transformed into an individual lack, a more banal collective lack was articulated in the afternoon session, when facilitators moved from the error analysis to the 'solution' through a demonstration lesson. Gita, the lead facilitator for the afternoon, explained to the assembled teachers:

> When we discuss the problems in the morning, we are convinced that lack of interaction in the classroom. That is why they (students) fail to use expressions, prepositions, ask questions. They fail to use these because we fail to use these in the classroom.

Students' 'errors' were thus transformed into teachers' pedagogic and linguistic 'lacks'. Students did not produce (written) responses because teachers did not use (spoken) language in the classroom.

During his 2014 talk, Dr Anandan was asked a question about the implications of his curriculum for teachers in state-funded schools.

> *Question*: In the Kerala textbook, the teacher's manual or the teacher's guideline, from how you explained it, seemed a very scripted kind of a manual where the exact dialogue is scripted for the teacher – this much in Malayalam, this much in English. Is it then a very scripted curriculum? And how much teacher autonomy is there to do something different? If it is not a scripted curriculum, and if there is teacher autonomy, then what is the status of the teacher's knowledge of the English language and their comfort in transacting an open-ended curriculum?
>
> *Answer*: There was an anxiety that when the teacher has to present a narrative, she cannot develop a narrative herself. She doesn't have that much linguistic competence. So we gave this as an oral narrative to be presented. … teachers were not able to frame a question. They would say "Where you going?" rather than 'Where are you going?' "This your book? Or this is your book?" rather than 'Is this your book?' There was no auxiliary inversion. So there were a lot of problems of such nature. Unless you frame the questions in the right way, the children will miss correct input.
>
> Teacher autonomy is of course a very valid question. But that autonomy has to happen when the teacher can manage a language class herself. Before that, there is a kind of gestation period which takes three to four months. After that, they will gain confidence.

According to Anandan, only those who can speak fluently and accurately in English can be enlisted as autonomous and responsible English teachers. His curriculum foregrounds this definition of knowing English and invisibilizes other ways of knowing English.

All 14 teachers who attended the training program were English users. Most teachers had Bachelor's degrees, and a few also had Master's degrees, and all their post-10th grade education was in English. Meanwhile, only about 4 of the over 160 teachers practicing in the district were fluent

English speakers; they had been inducted as resource persons by the District Institute. I was one of them. Like me, the other three selected teachers also had migration experiences; two had spent considerable time in other Indian states, and one frequently traveled to the Middle East where her husband worked. Unlike the more typical non-elite migration to labor colonies in the Middle East, where Malayalam rather than English tended to be the inter-ethnic language of contact (Gardner, 2010), we were embedded in privileged emigrational linguistic geographies. The normalization of English proficiency as the ability to speak English made the other more readily available resources invisible.

Rani ended the day's program with a demonstration lesson, where interestingly, she did not use the state-mandated textbook. Preferring a more spontaneous interactional classroom to the scripted textbook, she chose a boat-making activity where she could deliver a continuous flow of teacher-talk. Thus, though teacher educators did not affirm state materials, they did foreground oracy. The demonstration lesson did not have any reading or writing tasks. The teacher development program was thus conceptualized with the twin assumption that (1) oral interaction in the classroom is the primary teaching method and (2) student proficiencies in English can only be evaluated if they are written.

While both teachers and school families embedded in this pedagogy had ample reasons to exit a school system that marginalized and humiliated them, their differential social locations is perhaps most poignantly illustrated by their varying costs of exit. To leave a system that shamed them, teachers in state-funded schools, most of whom were women, would have to court economic dependence and spatial immobility in a deeply patriarchal system. For students remnant at state-funded schools, the only exit option was dropping out of the school system, which was too high a price for Dalit mothers whose hopes of climbing out of poverty were singularly located in the education system (Chapter 6). For Dalit mothers whose lives were already marked by spatial segregation, economic deprivation and sociocultural marginality, exit foreclosed the possibility of hope itself.

The next section illustrates the most common method of exiting the resistance pedagogy of the Kerala state. Learners and parents thwarted state pedagogies, but after graduating primary school. Within uneconomic primary schools, disciplined as they were by frequent exams, inspections, teacher 'training' and a generalized lack of economic, social and cultural capital, such deviations were harder.

Moving Across Borders

When Appu graduated lower primary school, unmindful of systemic failures, he enrolled at a state-funded English-medium school in Thiruvalla. The state insisted on mother tongue education only in primary grades and all state-funded high schools in and around Edanadu had English-medium sections, and one token Malayalam-medium section. Appu came to me for homework help on Saturdays during his transition phase, and I was amazed at how rapidly his vocabulary had enlarged. He read the story *The Mirror* in his English textbook as well as the section on photosynthesis in his *Basic Science* textbook with very little assistance. What he had earlier known as '*prakasha samsleshanam*' had now become photosynthesis, and he read how plants absorbed water and minerals to produce food. He had trouble with 'storage' but otherwise read the text unassisted. He told me that his regular tuition teacher made him write everything five times. Appu had written out the entire text of photosynthesis five times, like students at New English School had done for all their subjects from their earliest years of schooling. Appu had transferred to similar 'labor-full' pedagogies, but as his mother pointed out, it was still early to know how much difficulty [*budhimuttu*] was involved in the transition, and if he would have to eventually transfer to the Malayalam-medium section at the high school.

Exiting the state's pedagogy of resistance was mediated by two extraneous challenges. First, students like Appu would be found 'lacking' in comparison to classmates who had trained in rote pedagogies from earlier grades. This was compounded by a second challenge. Malayalam-medium schooling in earlier decades had taught technical words in English, for instance, the mathematical technique of 'addition' or the commercial instrument called 'cheque', and these had produced a subterraneous vocabulary in learners. Current schooling practices replaced these with 'proper' Malayalam words. Moving from *prakasha samsleshanam* to photosynthesis, as we saw, was a laborious and disproportionately consequential process for Appu. To do this for all school subjects, with others in the same class excused from this work, was not an easy undertaking.

'It was very difficult [*budhimuttu*] for me, I had come from Malayalam-medium; it was very difficult for me to follow what was being said'. Ponamma teacher reminisced of her own linguistic transitions from Malayalam-medium to English-medium instruction several decades ago, at the college level. 'English-medium students will "grasp" everything quickly', she explained. Similar to how first grade students at the New English School could 'grasp' the lexicon of *Big People*, and perform accurate phonological and semantic extractions, English-medium students were equipped with the lexical foundations [*adisthanam*] necessary to grasp classroom knowledge. Mothers at the New English School had similar memories of their pre-degree/plus-two education, which was the site of linguistic transition for the vast majority of them. Talking about her transition from Malayalam-medium schooling to English-medium, Anuja said:

> Only five or six of us were from Malayalam-medium. The first week, we didn't understand anything. Everything is in English. And those who have come from English-medium, they were so proud [*jada*]. But our

instructor was kind. He encouraged us, told us it will be difficult initially, but then you will pick up. I had calculated [*kanakku kuttal*] to choose to write all my examinations in Malayalam[1] but when I saw how evaluation worked, that option also petered out. Skills became *naipunyam*. All the bank terms (she was enrolled in a Commerce course) that you are familiar with in English – cheque, account opening – all of them had such strange Malayalam terms.

The artificiality and unfamiliarity of domain-specific terms in Malayalam compounded the difficulties of transitioning from Malayalam-medium to English-medium education. Talking about her teaching certification, B.Ed, Sheena said: 'If you look at the terms in Malayalam, you won't understand anything. But if you look at the terms in English, all the terms are familiar'.

The production of domain vocabulary in Malayalam was undertaken after the formation of the United Kerala [*aikya keralam*] state in 1956. Ponamma teacher called this corpus building *Malayalikaranam* or making something Malayali. Her own schooling had been prior to this corpus building, which had provided her with the crucial affordances of a lexical foundation in English even though she attended a Malayalam-medium school. She said:

The words were not in Malayalam, do you understand? All subjects. So I did not have lexical poverty [*wordsinu daridryam*]. That is how I can teach everything in English. I do not have a paucity of words. Even if I have to teach Math, I know how to say 'multiplication' and 'division'. All the four operations (addition, subtraction, multiplication, division[2]), I know them in English. So I don't find it difficult [*budhimuttu illa*]. Even today, I don't know the Malayalam term for multiplication; it is true [laughs]. That was one 'benefit' I had.

Children who inherit these lexical foundations from their families, and those who acquire it laboriously in schools, turn into teachable students even as the others fall away as *arkum vendathavar* [unteachable, those whom teachers don't want].

Conclusion

This chapter described the pedagogic worlds of uneconomic schooling. Legitimizing resistance through theory and biology, the state strangled the learning opportunities of the most marginalized learners by fragmenting the primary resource available in the classroom – the English textbook. The convoluted design foregrounded emotional excess but with little opportunity for meaning-making. Literacy practice was prohibited altogether, but it was tested, that too through very formalized testing practices. The oracy bias of linguists found an exceptionally sharp manifestation and engendered widespread pedagogies of shame. Exiting this formation was possible, for Dalit families, only on exiting the physical space of the primary school. And then, new challenges awaited.

This chapter is a cautionary tale about zealous expertise. In the case of Kerala state pedagogy, the arguments I made in this chapter are not new. Chomskyan linguistics has long been critiqued as inadequate for language pedagogy. As I argue in the next chapter, what allowed this dated language theory to persist was the sociopolitical context in which it was deployed. The Kerala state's resistance pedagogy of English Language Teaching was an extension of its generalized resistance pedagogy to marketization and neoliberalism. It is in this context and from this moral ground that rote was defined as detrimental to democracy and marked for annihilation. Further, though NCERT's cognitive linguistic theories and CBSE's communicative language orientation diverged substantively from the Kerala state's biological claims and emotional mandates, they too elided language as oral expression. The convergence of diverse language pedagogies around oracy assembled a formidable moral geography around rote and interaction.

Notes

(1) The provision exists to learn in English but be evaluated in the regional language. This was more popularly taken advantage of in non-Science subjects.
(2) The Malayalam equivalents are *kuttuka, kurakkuka, gunikkuka, harikkuka*.

8 Rote to Interaction

The previous chapters described how non-elite students, teachers and their families encountered English in classrooms, and by extension, at homes. Given the nature of classroom pedagogy in India, the discussion focused on textbooks-in-use, the theoretical assumptions of textbooks and the implications of these for non-elite classrooms. But if all three pedagogic engagements analyzed earlier insisted on oracy-based pedagogies, why were they so different? This chapter suggests that differences in (1) political contexts and (2) policy processes help us understand the variations between the oracy-focused pedagogies of the National Council of Educational Research and Training (NCERT), the Central Board of Secondary Education (CBSE) and the Kerala state.

The key government agencies involved in school-level English language pedagogy are the NCERT, the CBSE and State Councils of Educational Research and Training (SCERT). I begin with a brief overview of the three agencies to set up the analysis that follows. Following, I describe and analyze the contexts and processes that constituted the three reforms, which produced the textbooks analyzed earlier: the 1988–1997 CBSE reforms (*Interact in English Main Course Book*), the 1993–2014 Kerala English reforms (*Kerala state textbooks*) and the 2005 NCERT reforms (*Marigold*).

NCERT, CBSE and States in the Indian Union

Education is primarily the responsibility of states in the Indian union. The state of Kerala was formed in 1956, merging the erstwhile princely states of Travancore and Cochin with the Malabar region, which had earlier been part of the Madras Presidency. The Republic of India came into being in 1950, but the states in the union were reorganized later along linguistic lines. The first elected Government of Kerala instituted education reforms, legislating into being the Kerala Education Rules 1959 described in the previous chapters. There are considerable inter-state variations in educational provision and policy. The histories of development described in Chapter 2 have already introduced the colonial, post-independence and post-2000 educational development landscapes of Kerala.

To set up an academic infrastructure for school education at the national level, the National Council of Educational Research and Training was set up in 1961 as the apex academic body in all matters related to school education. Seven institutions established in the initial decades after independence, including the Central Institute of Education (1947), the Central Bureau of Textbook Research (1954), the Central Bureau of Educational and Vocational Guidance (1954) and the All India Council for Secondary Education (1955), were merged to form the NCERT (NCERT, 2011b). Since education is the responsibility of states in the union, national-level agencies primarily advised and supported the states in the union. One notable exception was the CBSE.

In 1962, the CBSE was re-constituted[1] to especially serve the children of transferable central government employees. However, since the CBSE was an affiliating and examining board with little or no pedagogic responsibility, in the same year, the Second Pay Commission of India recommended the establishment of a federal-state funded schooling system called Central Schools Organization for the same student population, which would be affiliated to and examined by the CBSE. The CBSE was distinct from local-state school boards such as the Kerala Education Board, especially when it came to language of instruction. To manage the linguistic transitions that would otherwise have impeded the schooling of children of transferable central government employees, the CBSE offered English-medium schooling. The states were expected to provide regional-medium schooling. Therefore, the English-vernacular schooling divide, at least in the initial decades of independence, fell along CBSE (including central state-funded schools) and regional state-funded schools. As explained in Chapter 2, local elites managed this educational deprivation by pressurizing Kerala state-funded high schools to open English-medium sections.

Table 8.1 provides a partial timeline of the political events that situated the formation of the NCERT, CBSE and the Kerala SCERT. The initial decades after independence, the 1960s, 1970s and 1980s, were decades of 'planned neglect' for school education as state resources were earmarked for higher education in technology and science (Sherman, 2018). It is with the District Primary Education Program (DPEP) that a national program for universalizing primary education was set up in India.

Though the DPEP and the CBSE English reforms were undertaken around the same time, their target population, objectives and outcomes could not have been more different. This is because the CBSE and the states have very different educational mandates, roles and responsibilities. As noted in Table 8.2, the CBSE catered to the elite, and its English reforms tried to shift rote to interaction in secondary grades for already proficient students. The Kerala DPEP English reforms, on the other hand, introduced English in primary grades in the most 'backward'

Table 8.1 Timeline of political events, formation of the three agencies and key reforms

Independence and partition of British India	1947
Constitution comes into effect, formation of the *Republic of India*	1950
Formation of *Kerala state*, following the States Reorganization Act 1956	1956
Kerala Education Rules, drafted and legislated into being by the Communist Party led Govt. of Kerala, elected to power in the first general elections in 1957	1959
Merger of 7 institutions to form the NCERT	1961
Reorganization of CBSE in its post-independence form	1962
First *National Policy of Education*, based on the recommendations of the National Education Commission (1964–1966)	1968
District Primary Education Program, first concerted national program on school education	1993
Reformulation of the State Institute of Education into the *Kerala SCERT*	1994
National Curricular Framework in effect during fieldwork period, drafted by the NCERT, under the directorship of Krishna Kumar	2005
Kerala Curricular Framework initiated by the Communist Party led Govt. of Kerala elected to power in 2006, under the leadership of education minister MA Baby, by the Kerala SCERT under the directorship of MA Khader	2007

Table 8.2 Reform agencies, roles and implications for English pedagogy

	Roles and responsibilities	Implications for English pedagogy
CBSE reforms	Be responsive to the educational needs of students whose parents were employed in the Central Government and have frequently transferable jobs	Align English-medium instruction of privileged students in secondary grades with international standards
Kerala DPEP	Improve quality of primary school education, especially for marginalized	Initiate English teaching in primary grades in backward districts
NCERT reforms	Create a common program of school education for the nation	Produce English textbooks for CBSE schools, which also function as model textbooks for states.

districts in the state to its most marginalized student groups. Meanwhile, its immediate role as academic advisor to the CBSE meant that the NCERT reforms produced new textbooks for central government-funded CBSE schools. At the same time, as the apex body for school education, these textbooks also became model textbooks for all states in the Indian union.

To summarize, the contradictory but overlapping roles of the NCERT (mandated to serve well-resourced central-government funded schools but also model pedagogy for the most marginalized groups), the CBSE and the state governments shaped the ways in which reform pedagogies took shape. The following sections analyze the political contexts and policy processes of each reform in greater detail.

Kerala English Reforms

Activist professionals

I met O.M. Sankaran, or O.M.S. as he is popularly called, at his home in Kannur, North Kerala. At his Laurie Baker-style house, a mixture of spirals and arches, beautiful yet spartan, O.M.S. patiently described the experiments in pedagogy and democracy that he had been a part of for several decades now. O.M. Sankaran had been the Kerala State Program Officer for the District Primary Education Program (DPEP), the World Bank funded program that set in motion a series of education reforms, spanning over two decades. Trained in education at the prestigious Regional Institute of Education (RIE), Mysuru and in democratic politics by the Kerala Shastra Sahitya Parishad (KSSP), O.M.S. embodies the tensions and contradictions of the activist professional.

The KSSP was founded as an organization of professionals interested in pedagogic activism. Known in English as the People's Science Movement, the Kerala Shastra Sahitya Parishad (Parishad hereafter) was founded in 1962 by a group of social activists, science writers and scientists to educate ordinary people in science. Kumar (1984: 1082) contends that 'people's science' is a misnomer because the Parishad was committed to taking 'the scientist's science to the people' rather than in codifying the science people practiced. The Parishad's rationale was not unique. Bhikhu Parekh (1991) reminds that the Nehruvian model of development for newly independent India was modernization centered on industrialization, socialism and scientific temper. But, offering a corrective to the Nehruvian development project, Parishad activists attempted to re-orient scientific research to benefit 'common people' (Kumar, 1984; Parameswaran, 1996). The Parishad's principal focus remains science education and development, but its expansion into state governance came out of Parishad members taking on leading roles in the Communist Party when socialism was waning globally.

The growing importance of the Parishad in the Communist Party of India Marxist (CPI-M or CPM) has its beginnings in the Emergency proclaimed by Indira Gandhi (1975–1977) but acquired significance later, with the decline of socialism. Though many early Parishad members were Communist Party members, it was during the Emergency[2] that the Parishad became radicalized. Williams (2008: 123) clarifies that since the Parishad was a cultural organization, it was not targeted during the Emergency; what had earlier been a community of progressive scientists and teachers became a 'safe haven' for Communist Party members in Kerala. Similarly, Zachariah (1989: 16) notes that during the Emergency, the Parishad achieved 'almost overnight', a 'mass membership'. Crucially, Zachariah (1989) also records that in 1987, approximately 60% of Parishad members were teachers in Kerala's schools and colleges. The Communist Party has a long history of teacher involvement, with prominent leaders like A.K. Gopalan, Joseph Mundasherry and P.K. Chathan Master having worked as educators. A.K. Gopalan is said to have remarked that in the Malabar region, teachers in most of the schools had been his students (Jeffrey, 1978).

Meanwhile, the mass influx of Communist Party members into the Parishad radicalized the organization on the one hand and altered the dynamics of power within the Communist Party on the other hand. In particular, the transitions of the late 1980s – a collapsing economy at home and the decline of socialism worldwide – precipitated a process of 'ideological and practical re-orientation' (Williams, 2008: xvii). Recognizing that its traditional militant labor unionism was becoming inadequate, the Left was forced to look for alternatives. In this context, the phenomenal success of the 1988–1989 Ernakulum Total Literacy Project decisively shifted Left politics away from trade unionism in favor of reformist developmental projects that 'empowered' the 'masses' (Devika, 2007; Törnquist, 1995).

The District Collector of Ernakulum district, a former vice president of the Parishad, undertook a mass adult-literacy project in the district with close cooperation and logistical support from the Parishad (Joseph, 1996; Sivadas, 1991). The Parishad's experience with popularizing science education was harnessed to ensure both pedagogic and administrative support for the project, as well as to generate the volunteerism entailed in covering roughly 600,000 households across the district. The project was able to gather unprecedented support, and on 4 February 1990, in a meeting attended by the then Chief Minister of Kerala E.K. Nayanar, the Prime Minister of India V.P. Singh formally declared Ernakulam to be the first totally literate district in India. Enthused by the success of the Total Literacy Project, Parishad leaders pushed Communist Party leaders to adopt participatory democracy, or 'democratic socialism', as the Left's new development agenda. The success of the Total Literacy Project gave the Parishad an upper hand within the Left.

During this time, in 1993, the 73rd Constitution Amendment Act devolved power along a three-tiered Panchayati Raj system (district, taluk and village). CPM-Parishad leaders like Thomas Isaac spearheaded the People's Campaign for Decentralized Planning. The KSSP proposed participatory democratic socialism to rectify the hierarchies that had come to characterize the CPM. Democratic socialism was predicated on empowering local communities to become an oppositional civil society, which would govern both the state and the market. This entailed training in democratic leadership through the development of organizational and institutional resources. Williams (2008: 11) explains that the Left's Parishad-inflected pedagogy re-defined socialism as the 'dominance of civil society over state and economy' rather than as a negation of capitalism. The Left approached devolution as the mechanism through which an oppositional civil society could be crafted. Unlike decentralization, which entails the transfer of decision-making authority to regional offices or delegation, which involved the transfer of authority for particular tasks, devolution called for the institutional transfer of authority, resources and power to plan development projects (Williams, 2008: 49; see Tharakan, 2000). However, the power of the pedagogic state was devolved to a specific sub-community of activist professionals, not parents or teachers.

During the same period, in 1993, the national government launched the DPEP. The 1991 economic crisis in India provided leverage to the World Bank to insist that India adopt a debt-led strategy for educational development. Along with economic reforms and structural adjustment, the nation moved into an international-aid based educational development policy for primary education even as higher education began to be privatized. The year 1993 was also the year when the *Learning Without Burden* report was tabled under the chairship of noted scientist and educator Prof. Yashpal. O.M.S. recalls that educators working in Kerala in the early 1990s felt 'a tremendous sense of possibility [*bhayankaramaya romanticism*]'. They felt that the DPEP could be used to bring about the kinds of changes they envisioned in the formal school system.

From their work with the Ernakulam Total Literacy Project, O.M.S. recounted that the Parishad had come to believe that 'the formal state machinery will not be able to do the (DPEP) work [*sarkar samvidhan-athinu ithu chaiyyan pattukela*]'. The Parishad had followed up the adult literacy program with a study on school learning outcomes. Titled *Vidyalayathile Niraksharatha* [School Illiteracy], the report illuminated the alarmingly low learning levels in state-funded schools to the extent that graduating high school students did not know the Malayalam alphabet. Responding to this crisis in first language literacy, O.M.S. had initiated a literacy program for primary school children in Kasargode's Malayalam-medium schools. Realizing that '[he] was part of the system' and that the system was starting to do things, hostility to the World Bank was tempered with ambivalence. He recalls:

> We were protesting against World Bank funding at that time. It was a soft loan at 2.5% interest over 40 years, it could be wasted [*nashipichu kalayam*] but the people would still have to repay it [*janangal thirichadakkanam*].

The Left took up the DPEP in Kerala and approached O.M.S. to head the program. O.M.S. joined DPEP as the State Program Officer in 1996.

The DPEP's assumptions and objectives fit awkwardly with the educational landscape of Kerala. The DPEP was a targeted program. In 1994, DPEP covered 42 districts in 7 states. The selection criteria – districts with female literacy levels lower than the national average – meant that not a single district in Kerala would fit the criteria. Similarly, the DPEP sought to improve access to schooling and to universalize primary education.

Colonial and post-independence educational policy had already achieved this goal to a large extent in Kerala. Recontextualizing DPEP for its socio-historic context, the Kerala state focused on the DPEP's objective of 'enhancing professional and managerial capacities for the delivery of primary education' (Kumar *et al.*, 2001: 562). O.M.S. was in charge of materials development and teacher training. This entailed a shift from (re)distribution to capacity building.

O.M.S. had moved from the Kasargode District Institute of Education and Training (DIET) to Kannur DIET by then and had already begun experimenting with textbook production. Working with the existing Minimum Levels of Learning (MLL) textbooks, his team had produced a series of teachers' handbooks for primary grades. DPEP offered an opportunity to mobilize resources for textbook preparation and teacher training. O.M.S. began work on both. He instituted the first residential teacher training program in the state, a seven-day program for Master Trainers. Avoiding seniority as the primary criteria of selection, O.M.S. assembled a cadre of 'committed' educators at the state level. The training day began at 9 am and went on till 12 midnight. O.M.S. soon came to be called *orakkam mudakkunna sankaran* [the taskmaster who will not let you sleep]. The new Malayalam textbooks were irreverent, utilizing 'street Malayalams [*theruvu bhasha*]' instead of canon poetry.

English was not offered in primary grades during this time. Since the DPEP was a primary education program, English became the last subject to be considered for curricular revision. However, parental desires for English schooling were already evident, and Sankaran approached K.N. Anandan to develop English language pedagogic materials for the DPEP. Anandan, a Chomskyan linguist with a PhD from the prestigious Central Institute of English and Foreign Languages (CIEFL), was appointed the chief consultant. Subsequently, Anandan designed the Second Language Acquisition Program for DPEP schools, with Classes 4 and 5 constituting the beginning level (Nair, 2004). Following the rigorous teacher development model set in place by Sankaran, Anandan identified and nurtured a team of teachers to become 'resource persons' for the Second Language Acquisition Program.

Activism thus dovetailed with professionalization. Fournier (1999: 7) describes occupational professionalism as 'exclusive ownership of area of expertise and knowledge', the power to define the nature of problems and solutions and a pervasive image of 'collegial work relations of mutual assistance and support rather than hierarchical, competitive or managerialist control'. The induction of certified experts committed to democratic socialism and the production of a trained cadre of educators through intense, frequent, non-competitive interaction assembled an affective pedagogic institution comprised of activist professionals. Authority, resources and power to plan pedagogic projects were devolved, but in favor of privileged, English-educated, educated-English speaking, activist

professionals, who demanded allegiance to their vision for an oppositional civil society. This framework of participation eliminated the possibility of parent or non-English-speaking teacher participation. Thus, the
Left's agenda of devolving power to local communities was achieved by
defining 'community' in specific ways.

Affective institutions

The 2008–2009 textbooks were due for revision. The Joint Review
Mission had visited Kerala and recommended guidelines for revision. One
of the primary concerns had been the fragmented textbook. The new
textbooks therefore had to conform more closely to the NCERT's model
textbooks, the *Marigold* series. By 2014, the textbook writing team had
assembled. The residential textbook writing workshop was held at the
state capital Thiruvananthapuram. When I reached the venue, I thought
I had the wrong address. The venue was a large marriage hall cum auditorium complex. I inquired with the watchman. He nodded his head
vigorously and led me past the auditorium to a nondescript building.
Here, in small motel-style rooms that could barely hold a bed and a table,
activist pedagogues were writing new English textbooks.

Underwear hung out to dry on makeshift clotheslines inside the
rooms. Male colleagues walked in and out in *lungis* and *mundus,* sometimes congregating for impromptu discussions. Women teachers were
fewer. Dressed in *salwar kameez,* they were equally gregarious and
involved. Though I did not see any women's underclothes hanging out to
dry, women moved around the rooms late into the night, discussing, writing, debating or just chatting about shopping schedules. Intimately familiar with the deep patriarchies of Kerala, I was surprised and even envious
of the freedom women participants seemed to enjoy at the residential
workshop.

Unlike the NCERT *Marigold,* which was a one-time exercise in experimental pedagogy put together by a group that dispersed soon after, the
Kerala textbooks were the product of a sustained pedagogic engagement
undertaken by a long-standing, cohesive community. The 2007–2008
textbooks that were in use during my fieldwork period, as well as the
textbooks of 2013–2014, were written by a 'core group' who had worked
together for at least a decade. Though the Left lost power in 2001, pedagogic reforms progressed with external funding continuing in the form of
the *Sarva Shiksha Abhiyan* (Education for All) project. The continuity
offered by federally earmarked funding for individual state education
projects allowed the formation of a close-knit community of language
pedagogues who shared Anandan's pedagogic vision and commitment.

This core group was first assembled institutionally when the Left was
voted to power in 2006. The new government initiated work on the Kerala
Curricular Framework, in accordance with the recommendations of the

National Curricular Framework (2005) and invited Prof. M.A. Khader from the NCERT to head the Kerala SCERT. The pedagogic experiences of the DPEP were consolidated in consultation with the National Curricular Framework, and like at the national level, work commenced on textbooks that exemplified the new curricular framework. Subject English was extended to primary grades for the first time, and textbooks for Classes 1–4 were prepared with Dr K.N. Anandan as chief consultant. Anandan and his core group worked devotedly to infuse classroom practices with their oppositional pedagogy.

The production of this expert community afforded a few practicing teachers, including women, unparalleled opportunity for professional development and personal belonging. Though the team members readily acknowledged my critiques of the textbook, they diffused blame away from their theoretical assumptions. Leafing through the Swedish book series *Mamma Moo and Crow* that I had brought, a writer noted wryly that the curriculum committee would not appreciate the illustrations: 'all they'll have to say (about this wonderful book) is that the rat is not wearing underwear [*eli jatti ittitilla, ithanavaru parayuka*]'. All the six writers I met articulated loyalty to their community as well pride in the pedagogic work they undertook: 'this kind of special work happens only here (in Kerala) [*evide mathram kandu verunna prathyeka work*]' said a writer from a north Kerala district. But it was when one of the teacher-writers referred to Dr Anandan in familial terms (like a father, *achane pole*) that I realized the significance of this community for their personal lives and sense of self.

During my fieldwork period, the Left was not in power, and it was the Congress government that had undertaken textbook revision. Anandan had resigned from his consultancy position and moved to work with the neighboring Andhra Pradesh government. A few of his core team members had similarly dispersed from the SCERT to return to classroom teaching or more localized teacher training institutes. The core group did not exist institutionally. But they existed as an affective institution, bound together by the care work and the obligations that had developed out of their prolonged relationship.

Despite their formal dispersion, the core team assembled virtually for the English textbook revision. There was nobody else with the necessary expertise in language pedagogy. The official writing team produced the new materials in consultation with Anandan and the dispersed team. Core team members who were part of the official textbook writing workshop would do the actual writing. These materials would then be sent off to the virtual team for feedback. The comments affirmed the work or gave suggestions for improvement. Both affirmations and suggestions were important for the textbook writing team. For this empowered, resource-enriched, close-knit community of activist professionals, their moral intentions were enough to achieve an egalitarian society. But for those outside of this community, this pedagogy largely afforded experiences of humiliation and alienation.

Expressive citizens

So far, we have seen how the academic Left in Kerala spearheaded the World Bank-funded primary education reform program, assembling a core cadre of activist professionals who designed a pedagogy of resistance. I have shown how reforms proposed an indigenous version of second language acquisition, organized around resistance to the colonial/imperial. This section elaborates the textbook production process in terms of its content.

Shaped by this political and ideological backdrop, the Kerala Curricular Framework crafted an 'issue based' curriculum for all subjects including English, rather than a 'theme based' curriculum as recommended by national frameworks, in order to build an egalitarian, socialist, democratic society (SCERT, 2007: 16). The SCERT (2008: 30) writes:

> We should sensitize the learners about the numerous issues faced by our society as the learning material itself. Then the learners could intervene directly in social changes.

The English textbooks used in primary grades during my fieldwork period were thus composed around eight issues. The chief consultant Dr K.N. Anandan (2014) explained in a public talk:

> The Kerala curriculum is an issue-based curriculum – not theme-based. We have identified eight issue domains like marginalization, mismanagement of land and water and so on. And every subject is woven around these social issues. And every child has to take up a social issue. The lessons are designed in this manner. Before this, we had very clean textbooks. An unreal society – a sort of 'prettified' society. But it is an ugly society that we are bringing into textbooks.

Thus, though the Kerala state reform concurred with NCERT's theoretical orientations vis-à-vis second language acquisition, the textbooks produced in Kerala were remarkably different.

First, the decision to craft an issue-based curriculum meant that English textbooks for primary grades had to be written rather than compiled. Since children's books typically gloss over social inequality or present an unreal, prettified society, they were deemed inappropriate. This severely limited the quantity of pedagogic material to one state produced textbook per grade. Second, the criteria for textbook writing shifted from pedagogic design to issue coverage. As described in Chapter 7, the reformed textbooks had several quality issues: fragmentation, length and coherence of narrative, and lack of repeated encounters with linguistic items. But these were not taken up seriously. One of the core group members explained:

> Social issue is presented in a way that it evokes feeling in the student [*kuttikke* feel *chaiyunna avasaram*]. The learner should understand, should respond [*prathikarikkuka*]. Why should the child read? To understand the issue. When is language produced naturally? From a communicative yearning. The narrative is a tool for that.

Language learning was thus understood to naturally result from the emotional intensity attached to a real social issue. As explained in the previous chapter, the learner's obligation to 'intervene' in society became a mandate to 'respond' to the issue presented in the narrative, in monolingual English in the opinion gap format (conversation, thoughts, poems and picture description). To intervene in society, the learner had to become an *expressive* citizen.

One of the incidents narrated by O.M.S. was an evaluation visit conducted by the European Union, one of the funders of the reform program. The dignitary had expressed interest in visiting schools. From fieldwork, I knew that specific state-funded schools are primed as visit schools. Schools with adequate number of students, teachers who have been inducted as resource persons and are responsive to pedagogic reforms and expressive students typically make the cut. O.M.S. noted that the third standard students at the visit school interacted with the visitor, greeting her 'Good morning, Ma'am' and asking, 'What is your name?' O.M.S. remarked: 'They were communicating'. According to O.M.S., the EU dignitary wanted to compare this experience with a CBSE school. She was taken to a CBSE school run by the Nair Service Society. 'She met sixth standard students. There was no communication. After 15 minutes, "your name?"' Regardless of what actually transpired at the two sites, note what O.M.S. regards as successful English pedagogy: the production of a confident, expressive student. The antithesis is the shy, silent CBSE student. However, as described in Chapter 5, parallel hierarchies were being constructed around academically proficient, confident, polite speakers and (academically weak) expressive but rude speakers.

While learners were thus inducted into (hierarchical) expressive identities, the reforms relied heavily on expressive pedagogues. Like with the *kathaprasangam* training noted in the previous chapter, expressive excess became a practical criterion for teaching. The academic coordinator for the 2008–2009 textbook production insisted that the textbooks crafted by the team have 'magical power in the hands of a resourceful teacher'. For him, the expressive capacity of the teacher-presenter was as important as the material itself. Meanwhile, one key criterion for teachers to be inducted as resource persons was expressive ability. Resource persons remarked that they were selected because they verbalized their responses frequently [*prathikarikkunnavare pidichu idum*]. Thus, on the one hand, an expressive self became valorized as a pedagogic qualification and requirement. On the other hand, it was recognized as a citizenship duty expected of students in the classroom.

Tiered expert communities: Coherence across difference

The core team was one small, dispersed, but influential community within the sprawling educational bureaucracy of the pedagogic state. True, they had disproportionate power as designers and writers of the textbooks mandated for study in state-funded schools. Yet, the coherence of oracy as pedagogic common-sense was achieved in a more dispersed fashion. Table 8.3 details the multiple agencies and activities I encountered as a teacher associated with a state-funded primary school during 2013–2014.

Primary schoolteachers in state-funded schools in Edanadu encountered two agencies repeatedly and frequently, the Block Resource Center (BRC) and the DIET. The SCERT and the core team were distant entities who only materialized as authors of the prescribed textbooks. The bulk of the training was carried out by locally inducted teacher-trainers and by BRC and DIET faculty as explained in Chapter 7. Though the BRC and DIET frequently disagreed with the SCERT and the core team albeit from a distance and with no real effect, and though the BRC and DIET were often at odds with each other, resource persons earmarked for English pedagogy at all the agencies were English speakers with varying levels of exposure. The slippage around oracy as the self-evident indicator of expertise in English language proficiency and pedagogy cohered across different tiers of the administrative bureaucracy.

To summarize, the Kerala English reforms were shaped by electoral politics and the restructuring of the Left in Kerala, international aid, new

Table 8.3 Tiered expert communities

Activity	Conducted by	Conducted at	Organizational oversight
Textbook writing	Anandan's core team	Residential workshop, Thiruvananthapuram (State level)	SCERT, State Curriculum Committee
Teacher training for textbooks	District- and block-level resource persons with BRC and DIET faculty	Government schools, BRCs	BRC
Workbook preparation		DIET	DIET (Activity suggested by District Panchayat President)
Teacher training for workbook			
Preparation of question papers		Residential workshop, Kozhencherry (District level)	DIET, BRC

administrative infrastructures and re-conceptualizations of democratic citizenship. The convergence of activism and professionalization, the affective ties of the core group and the coherence of oracy as proficiency across tiered systems generated a specific pedagogic illiberalism, according to which resources typically available only to elites were central for building an egalitarian society.

CBSE Reforms

Unlike the Kerala state's pedagogic illiberalism, which ironically stemmed out of its zealous commitment to non-elite empowerment, the CBSE's English reforms completely ignored the prospect of non-elite participation in its pedagogic promises. To recap from Chapter 5, the CBSE reforms designed teaching along allegedly progressive, international standards (IELTS) but aligned testing with supposedly regressive but efficient rote. In practice, a foreign-led, professional team designed teaching materials but was overruled by the native executive team. This section describes the contexts and processes of transnational collaboration that resulted in the production, and failure, of the *Main Course Book*. It chiefly analyzes internal reports and documents associated with the CBSE English reforms discussed in Chapter 5. The most candid among these is the 1988 report authored by the British consultants of the English reforms, Ray Williams and Sarah North, during their initial, three-week, formulation-stage visit to India.

The reform timeline and agencies help situate the sections that follow. The CBSE undertook the English Language Teaching (ELT) reform project in 1988 to renew its secondary English curriculum for Course A. Financial support was available from the Overseas Development Agency (later Department for International Development, DfID) through the British Council, and academic support came from the College of St. Marks and St. Johns (Marjons), Plymouth, UK. Based on the recommendations of the Marjons specialists, a process of change was initiated, which involved the training of 57 CBSE teachers at Marjons (Mathur, 1995: 306). The teachers assisted Marjons experts in producing reformed teaching materials, a three-book Communicative package titled *Interact in English*. The reformed textbooks were introduced in the 1993–1994 academic year in Class 9 and board exams were conducted in March 1995 for Class 10. Meanwhile, a Curriculum Implementation Study was commissioned to the CIEFL.

CBSE reforms: Transnational commensurability for elites

Williams and North (1988: 2) state that the CBSE is the 'most influential Board of Secondary Education in India'. The CBSE is funded directly by the Ministry of Human Resources Development, it is autonomous, and it advises the Ministry on all matters related to secondary education in India. Further, the Chairman of the CBSE is the statutory Executive Chairman of the Council of Boards of Secondary Education, which is comprised of all 32 secondary school boards in the country. Williams and North (1988) note that during the time of their visit, there were 31 Boards of Secondary Education at the regional state levels and one at the national level: the CBSE.

Though CBSE schools were actually very diverse even in 1988, the British consultants were invited only to elite schools in their preparatory visit. The diverse CBSE schools were divided linguistically along an English-vernacular divide and Ray Williams and Sarah North visited only English-medium schools. During 1992, CBSE-affiliated schools consisted of government schools in union territories and states which do not have their own secondary school boards (1042); central schools for mobile civil servants (517); defense personnel (19); the rural elite (250) and 'independent' schools (1033). Fee-paying private schools are called 'independent' by virtue of their independence from the state, which organizes the other categories of CBSE schools. Within this diverse population, English Course A is offered in schools where the medium of instruction from Class 1 has been English. English Course B is offered in regional-medium schools where English has been taught from Class 6 (Williams & North, 1988: 4–5). The CBSE English reforms were limited to English Course A. The core clientele of the CBSE reforms was its English-medium schools, which catered to 'the children of the comparatively prosperous, upwardly mobile sector of Indian society'; these students are also recognized as 'potential academic 'high fliers' who [were] likely in their future careers to hold responsible posts in a variety of professions' (Williams & North, 1988: 5).

Since Communicative Language Teaching during this time was organized around 'needs analysis' (Williams & North, 1988: 32), the terms of reference of the project included 'a preliminary assessment of the English language study skills requirements of Class 10 leavers (TOR 3)' (p. 19). It is to articulate this need that the report explicitly established the CBSE's A track as comprised of children of professionals and oriented toward a professional education.

To define the terms of reference and objectives of the reforms, the British team articulated the CBSE's association with elites through English's relationship with the professions and professionals. The British Council report (1992) about the reforms states under Point 9:

English is the language of higher education, especially for scientific, technological, medical, legal, economic, and management studies. It is also the language of pan-Indian communication in Business, Administration and Research in Pure and Applied Sciences and Technology. Competence in English language therefore is a necessity for employment at middle and upper levels of management and administration in all private and public sectors.

The Marjons report echoes the British Council appraisal. The report goes on to make specific observations and comments about the professional middle class in India and English. What then were the 'needs' of this professional class? In terms of English proficiency, there did not seem to be any pedagogic need. Williams and North (1988: 11–12) were 'impressed by students' oral proficiency', and students seemed to 'enjoy English and doing things in English' like reading novels and writing stories. The 'problem' was the postcolonial, academic/scholastic nature of English in India, which had to be re-formed for transnational commensurability. The resolution of an 'Indian' problem by a foreign team did not pan out well, and as explained in Chapter 5, the reforms were thwarted by testing designs that were rote based. However, about a decade after the reforms, the professions were globalized in the context of liberalization, and the need for transnational commensurability became more urgent. To resolve the national-international tensions that plagued its earlier reform attempts, the CBSE – an affiliating and examining body for diverse students in secondary grades – had to establish a new school board that catered specifically to elites.

CBSE international

Though the CBSE ELT reforms 'failed' during the 1990s, reform objectives were picked up in the post-2000 years with greater depth and breadth. If the initiation of professional English in IELTS formats failed during the 1990s, a more substantive transformation became possible when elite Indians crossed transnational borders in greater numbers. From 1999 to 2011, the number of Indian students studying in foreign universities, predominantly in institutions in the English-speaking countries of US, UK and Australia, increased by over 200% (UNESCO Institute for Statistics, 2016). Additionally, the ascendance of the new professional – imagined as a high-net worth individual who is culturally at ease in both the West and the East (Searle, 2013) – drove aspiration and acceptance. The actual lives of transnational elites are more complicated (Amrute, 2016) and caught in translation (Punathambekar, 2005).

The CBSE established a new school board in 2010, unambiguously named *CBSE International* or CBSE*i*, specifically to meet the needs of an emerging class of 'global citizens'. In its *FAQs for Parents*, the CBSE*i* states that the new curriculum provides a 'globally sensitive curriculum that would help Indian learners either to pursue their higher studies in countries abroad or interact meaningfully with global markets for ensuring active participation in the development process' (CBSE, 2010: 1–2). The CBSE*i* claims that this internationalization will prepare India's 'future citizens to become global leaders in the emerging knowledge society' (CBSE*i*, Mission & Vision). To do so, the CBSE re-structured itself from a secondary school examining agency to a K-12 pedagogic body, but only for globally oriented, wealthy Indians. According to Resnik (2010), curricular internationalization entails the valorization of cognitive skills (problem-solving and innovation), emotional skills (adaptability and cultural empathy) and sociocultural skills (cooperation, collaboration and communication). As the CBSE internationalized, it too mandated the teaching and evaluation of problem-solving skills, values and conversational skills (ASL described in Chapter 5) in English in affiliated schools, whether they prescribed to the national or international version.

The crucial distinction between the international and the national version is rote. The CBSE*i* categorically states that it will not prescribe textbooks, in order to circumvent 'routine textual learning'. Instead, it will produce an assemblage of resources that teachers can adopt and adapt for their individual classrooms. The CBSE*i* *FAQs for Parents* describes that students will learn research orientations, critical humanities, community service, performing arts and cross-cultural and communicative skills through active, learner-centered curricular situations. Further, scoring was shifted from numerical/alphabetical indicators to 'descriptive profiles'. But even as the CBSE*i*'s international orientations shape the CBSE general curriculum, the CBSE's focus on science and math education, and now informational technology skills, shapes the CBSE*i* as a thoroughly Indian internationalism.

The CBSE*i*'s pedagogic services were, of course, not available to all. CBSE*i* affiliation fees were set at Rs. 250,000, over three times more than the Rs. 75,000 charged for a CBSE affiliation. CBSE*i* schools similarly had to guarantee a mandatory reserve fund that is five times more than what is required for CBSE schools (CBSE, n.d.). Reports suggest that the CBSE's newfangled commitment to internationalization, a decade after the initial steps were taken, was triggered by changing education markets. A materials producer for CBSE*i* described the CBSE*i* as 'India's answer to International Baccalaureate'. The Times of India reports the unprecedented growth of international programs such as the International Baccalaureate program, the Cambridge International Exam and Edexcel UK in metro cities in India (Mukul, 2015). Facing attrition from its core elite community, the CBSE had to do what it could not during the 1988–1997 reforms and *become* international.

With the CBSE explicitly locating a national constituency and another, separate, international constituency, even the notional idea of equity seemed insignificant. Perhaps this discomfort is part of the reason why all the pedagogic and administrative innovations of the CBSE during the 2010s were abruptly discontinued in 2017–2018. The CBSE*i* was dismantled. The Communicative English Course *Interact in English* was discontinued. In keeping with the CBSE's *modus operandi*, these decisions came to affiliated schools in the form of circular CBSE/ACAD/JS(ARTI)/2017 Notification number Acad-06/2017 dated 31.07.2017 and CBSE-Acad/DS-AHA/Cir/2018/ Circular number Acad-07/2018 dated 09.03.2018, respectively. The information is meant to be 'disseminated to all concerned teachers, students, and parents', and all concerned schools are asked to 'note accordingly for strict compliance'.

NCERT Reforms

In comparison to the well-intentioned illiberalism of the Kerala state and the classed reforms of CBSE, the NCERT reform processes were too fragmented to have a coherent ideology. Though the immediate context of the reforms was morally and affectively charged, the burden of national representation, the contradictory institutional location of the NCERT and the transitory nature of the design team coupled with an over-ambitious pedagogic agenda limited the scope of ideological commitments.

The NCERT reforms of 2004–2007 are by now viewed by progressive educators as an epochal shift in pedagogic paradigms. The National Curricular Framework and its associated position papers and textbooks embody the shift from behaviorism and top-down expertise to constructivism and participatory reform. However, rather than a planned paradigm shift, the reform emerged out of a political crisis at the national level. Second, unlike the Kerala reforms which were located in the deep affective bonds of the core team, the nature of collaboration within the NCERT was fleeting, fragmentary and procedural. This trivialized an ambitious pedagogic design (Chapter 4).

Similar to the economic reforms of 1991 which were at the time of the reforms a form of crisis management, the national education reforms of 2004–2007 were initiated in response to a topical crisis: the Hinduization of school curricula attempted by the National Curricular Framework for School Education 2000 (NCFSE). Drafted by the NCERT under the directorship of Prof. J.S. Rajput during the tenure of the BJP-led government, the NCFSE 2000 sought to Indianize, nationalize and spiritualize school curriculum, especially by re-writing Indian histories in ways that normalized India as a Hindu nation (Akhtar, 2005; CABE, 2005; Guichard, 2010; Kumar, 2000; Visweswaran et al., 2009). Outraged at this blatant 'saffronization' of education, or what Krishna Kumar (2000: 1057) called 'indigenous fascism', the Left, minorities and several state governments such as Delhi and Kerala opposed the NCFSE 2000 and a public interest litigation was filed in the Supreme Court of India to stall the implementation of NCFSE 2000.

When the BJP-led coalition lost to the Congress-led United Progressive Alliance (UPA) during the general elections of 2004, the UPA government promised to de-saffronize school curriculum and appointed Prof. Krishna Kumar, one of India's foremost critical educators, as the Director of the NCERT. Under Krishna Kumar's directorship, the NCERT reviewed the NCFSE 2000, its affiliated textbooks, and began consultations for a revised National Curricular Framework. Though Social Science especially

History textbooks were at the center of debate (Guichard, 2010), all subject pedagogies including language pedagogy were re-considered. For
English language pedagogy, the National Focus Group chaired by Prof. R.
Amritavalli, a noted linguist, drafted the National Position Paper, which
laid out pertinent pedagogic concepts and curricular expectations
(Chapter 4). Simultaneously, work commenced on textbooks that would
exemplify the recommendations of the Position Paper.

Between activism and professionalization

Dr Usha Dutta's involvement with the NCERT *Marigold* textbooks
and her later trajectory at the publishing giant Malhotra Book Depot
(MBD) is an interesting illustration of the tensions between NCERT's
participatory ideals and the professionalization it eventually advanced.
During the time of the reforms, Dr Dutta was the NCERT's member
coordinator for the *Marigold* series for primary grades. She coordinated
the textbook writing work of practitioners and experts and was ultimately responsible for pulling these different forms of participation into
a coherent textbook within the allotted time.

When I met her, Dr Dutta had retired from the NCERT and had
joined the textbook giant, the MBD, as consultant. The MBD corporate
office in New Delhi, where she had her office, reflects the aspirations of an
industry leader. Similar to transnational Information Technology companies that work in a 'knowledge economy', MBD does not allow visitors to
bring in cellphones or computers. It is careful with its proprietary rights
over intellectual property. MBD had recently gone transnational, producing textbooks for school students in South Africa. Dr Dutta sat in her air
conditioned office, in an imposing office chair, and moved back and forth
between her involvement with the South African textbooks and the 'donkey's work' she had to do as the NCERT's member coordinator. She
acknowledged that she 'became popular with the *Marigold*', and her transition to the private textbook publishing industry was mediated by the
recognition that the *Marigold* garnered.

Krishna Kumar's vision of practitioner-driven textbook design had
unintended consequences, such as the appreciation of Dr Dutta as an ELT
professional and her integration into the private textbook market. Usha
Dutta's secession from the public to the private is not unique. In fact, the
structural location of the NCERT amplifies this paradox. As an advising
agency, the NCERT's potential for action is largely symbolic. The only
substantive pedagogic mandate the NCERT has, in the form of textbook
production, is to cater to the needs of the federally funded, central school
system affiliated to the CBSE. For the NCERT, this paradox – its aspirations to serve under-resourced communities and its institutional mandate
to serve well-resourced groups – finds expression in myriad ways. Usha
Dutta's pathway to MBD is but one effect.

Complying with Krishna Kumar's vision of textbook production as a practitioner as much as an expert endeavor, the NCERT sent out invitations to practicing teachers to participate in the textbook production process. A current NCERT faculty put it this way: 'we write to many people and whoever has time responds'. The 13 practitioners who responded for the primary section (Classes 1–4) are listed on the *Marigold* acknowledgements page: 5 worked on Books 1 and 3 and all 13 worked on Books 2 and 4. Of the 13, all 9 practitioners who worked within formal school systems were affiliated with CBSE schools, particularly to federal-state funded schools such as Kendriya Vidyalayas, Army Public Schools and Demonstration Schools attached to Regional Institutes of Education. National reforms thus inadvertently became a CBSE affair.

The chief advisor of the *Marigold* textbook production committee for Classes 1–4,[3] Prof. Lalitha Eapen, described the textbook writing process as a two-year, episodic, teacher-training program rather than as a textbook writing workshop. She remembers that 'teachers who were writing this didn't know the a-b-c of ELT' and she had to 'train them'. She began sessions with lectures, but the intermittent meetings of the group were attended by different participants. Meanwhile, the deadline was 'severe', and the textbooks had to be ready in six months.

As the NCERT member on the team, Usha Dutta had to pick up the flak. She managed the chaotic nature of the project by imposing a structure on the textbook. Amrit had defined it loosely as the child encountering '10 good poems and 10 good stories'. Dutta elaborated this brief into a poem followed by a story, packed with exercises of various kinds and concluded with 'teacher's pages'. The teacher's pages would provide practical guidelines on how to approach the paradigm shift the *Marigold* aimed to bring about.

Cognizant of future timelines – books for Grades 2 and 4 had to be written in a second phase – and the potentially disruptive nature of any scandals, Dutta stayed away from contentious issues and stuck legalistically to the themes identified in the National Curricular Framework. She was adamant that the textbook would not feature any icons or topical issues: 'cats and dogs are better. What if Sachin (Tendulkar) gets into a scam?' As for themes such as gender parity and diversity, she accommodated them through artwork that specifically included the requisite number of women, minorities and 'others'. She remembered that the book had gone to publication when she realized that it did not address one of the themes (peace and harmony). 'There was no activity on peace. So I put a friendship band on the last page. Nobody can say we have missed out on peace'. The pedagogic ambitions and participatory aspirations of the NCERT were operationalized by a fleeting, fragmented community of practicing teachers and pulled into place by the practical ingenuity of Usha Dutta.

Textbook writing for the NCERT is always a fraught affair. First, it shoulders the burden of representing the whole country. Second, the NCERT's proximity and accountability to the ministry and the parliament makes it especially susceptible to 'questions in the parliament' which must be responded to, sometimes with revised versions of the textbook. While these hold true for all NCERT work, the 2005 reforms had an additional burden. The English textbooks were expected to bring in a paradigm change but also be written by practicing teachers who were embedded in 'traditional' pedagogic practices. The position paper had put forth a radically different approach to language pedagogy, one that opposed traditional teaching practices in many ways. A motely group comprising seven teachers, four school leaders and two children's book writers had assembled to craft the most ambitious English textbooks the NCERT had ever attempted. For the practitioner members, as well as for the NCERT member coordinator, Dr Usha Dutta, the learning entailed was significant.

During my interview with her, Dutta reminisced that the *Marigold* was an 'extreme deviation' from what was then prevalent, and she was uncertain if it had been too 'experimental'. This hesitation, as well as the chaotic organization, is evident in the textbook. Bhattacharya *et al.* (2012: 24–25) find the Class 3 *Marigold* textbook 'arbitrary and disconnected' and 'abrupt and isolated'. Further, the market mitigated the *Marigold*'s ambitions to a great extent. As explained earlier, the CBSE school system is closely integrated with the market (Chapter 4); most private schools prescribe privately published textbooks, which are not inspected or regulated by any state agency (CABE, 2005). It is only in Grades 9–12 that CBSE schools follow a uniform English pedagogy and that was prepared by the CBSE, not the NCERT. As I have detailed in Chapter 4, private textbooks did not make oracy central to the textbook but blended it into a literacy-centered curricula. Only non-elite private schools with the unusual configuration of low-income parents and conscientious school leaders who sought out 'quality textbooks' such as at the New English School prescribed the *Marigold*. However, even then, the *Marigold* did not foreclose traditional literacy practices completely; teachers and mothers were able to subvert and circumvent reform mandates.

To summarize, the three English reforms emerged in very different contexts and pursued very different agendas. Therefore, it is not surprising that the textbooks produced through the reforms are very different. What is surprising is that despite the differences, there is a remarkable consensus around oracy as the default marker of ethical and efficient pedagogy. Chapters 4, 5 and 7 have examined the self-articulations through which each of the reforms justified oracy. The NCERT assumed oracy to be natural and universal. The CBSE desired oracy to become international. And the Kerala state believed language learning to be biological and therefore oral. This chapter has inserted these assumptions and desires into sociopolitical contexts and organizational procedures to flesh out how abstract assumptions took concrete shape. In the final section, I consolidate the analysis presented in earlier chapters to highlight the implications of oracy pedagogies for the ELT profession.

Teaching Reformed Pedagogy: The Labor of Enterprise

The 2014 English Language Teacher Educator Conference held at Hyderabad was jointly hosted by the British Council and the English and Foreign Languages University (EFLU), the two institutions that have directed English language pedagogy in the region since independence. EFLU was set up in 1958 as the Central Institute of English with British Council's J.G. Burton serving as the Director of Studies (Tickoo, 2012). About 2500 English language teachers and teacher educators from across the country, affiliated to the EFLU, NCERT and regional state institutions congregated for the 2014 conference. Those of us staying at EFLU traveled together on a rickety old bus that took us on the 22-kilometer bus ride across the city to the conference venue, Novotel Hyderabad Convention Center in Hitech City. This five-star hotel cum convention center, flanked by a swimming pool, existed in a placeless oasis cut off from anything that reminded one of India. We could well have been abroad. Like the liminal spaces of the airports that mediate the journey between the nation and the foreign, Novotel did not allow auto rickshaws on its sprawling property. The long bus ride back and forth gave us ample time to comment on the many journeys we undertook to travel from the situated realities of ELT in actually existing classrooms to the place-less, world-class, universality of market-driven, 'international' ELT.

The big players were all in attendance – Oxford University Press, Cambridge University Press, Collins, Trinity and of course the British Council. A large promotional map of India in a British Council stall proudly proclaimed that *English Partnerships*, the British Council's state partnerships initiated from 2007 onward, covered Punjab, Delhi, Assam, West Bengal, Bihar, Tamil Nadu, Kerala, Karnataka and Maharashtra. On the bus ride, a colleague from Kerala wryly commented that the British Council had replaced colonization with councilization.

The enterprising efforts of the British Council, and other agencies, are paralleled by a redefinition of the ELT field around enterprise. The aspirations erupting on to the educational landscape are to be met by the enterprising teacher who will design personalized teaching materials and bring them to coherence through intensive oral interaction. At the NCERT, Keerti Kapur's impromptu demonstration lesson (Chapter 4) veered off in all directions and included worksheets and plans that were far from the textbook narrative. In the training workshop at Thiruvalla DIET (Chapter 7), Rani too had abandoned the textbook and done a paper-folding activity as a model lesson. ELT in India now accepts interactional pedagogy organized around oracy and enterprise as common sense. It is no longer justified. Instead, what is justified is the shift from teacher training to teacher development.

Two of the three sub-themes of the 2014 conference spoke specifically to 'continuing professional development' for English language teachers. In her plenary talk titled *Teacher Development as the Future of Teacher Education,* Prof. Rama Mathew, who had earlier headed the CBSE ELT Curriculum Implementation Study, distinguished between 'teacher training' and 'teacher development'. Teacher training assumes that there are pedagogic techniques and skills that work in classrooms and seeks to impart these to teachers. Teacher development 'is seen to be a voluntary process, on-going, bottom-up, since the starting point is the teacher's own experience, where new information is sought, shared, reflected on, tried out, processed in terms of personal experience and finally "owned" by the teachers' (Slide 4). Teacher development expects teachers to be researchers, resource persons, materials developers, assessors, monitors and mentors (Slide 37). Teacher training is passé. Teacher development is in. The work undertaken for the book is perhaps an excellent example of teacher development and the labor of enterprise. But resources – money and time – are disproportionately distributed.

Conclusion

The unlikely convergences of activism and transnationalization mediated the shift from rote to interaction in the context of liberalization in India. This convergence came about through specific political contexts and policy processes. The political context of the Kerala reforms was embodied by the activist orientations of the Kerala state, which required an expressive student, regardless of comprehension. The protracted process of the DPEP and the SSA assembled the cadre of activist professionals who would zealously safeguard oracy against rote. The state's moral zeal to regenerate an egalitarian society generated its resistance to a crucial social resource and practice, rote. Participatory citizenship and deliberative democracy became conduits for marginalization when new hierarchies were superimposed on existing ones.

Meanwhile, an experimental pedagogy in one state became national policy when similar assumptions were consolidated by national agencies. Again, the political context of right-wing saffronization provided the impetus to draft a national curricular framework. But the policy processes that emerged out of the framework, led by the NCERT, were fragmented, fleeting and ambitious. Alongside, the CBSE assumed transnational mobility as the marker of full citizenship in national development projects. Partnering with the British Council and other British agencies, the CBSE's international version defined cosmopolitan cultural capital negatively, as the opposite of rote. Nevertheless, both the CBSE and private publishing houses crafted pedagogic opportunities to pursue rote while disowning it. Thus, the non-necessary convergences of activism and transnationalization shifted the norms of English proficiency from academic literacy to oracy and enterprise pedagogies.

Notes

(1) The CBSE was set up in 1921 as a local-state board for regions now located in Rajasthan and Madhya Pradesh.

(2) The Prime Minister Indira Gandhi declared a state of emergency across the country in June 1975 during which time elections were suspended, the press censored, political rivals imprisoned and civil liberties curbed. The order was withdrawn after 21 months in March 1977.

(3) Lalitha Eapen was the chief consultant for *Marigold* Books for Classes 1–5, which were completed over a three-year period. However, since the Kerala-state categorized primary grades as Classes 1–4, I only consider the production of *Marigold* Books for Classes 1–4, produced over a two-year period.

9 Conclusion: Linguistic Imperialism from Below

Revisiting his 1992 book *Linguistic Imperialism*, Robert Phillipson (2013: 5) suggests that analysis of linguistic dominance should 'shift from a colonial and postcolonial perspective to contemporary patterns'. If the colonial was marked by the binary (colonizer-colonized; native speaker–non-native speaker) and the postcolonial by the refusal of the binary, the contemporary discards the binary altogether and celebrates difference (Hardt & Negri, 2000). How is inequality produced in a political economic context where markets include (almost) everyone and celebrate diversity?

This book described the complex web of relationships and desires through which contemporary dominations are generated and upheld. While familiar arguments related to linguistic imperialism reappeared in the book, including the British Council's role in promoting English and non-elites' reconstitution of English in ways that made it serve their purpose, the context of Kerala posed the moral as a central thematic. The book described how English was newly constituted as a dominant language through the fervent ethical work of non-elites and the moral reforms of well-intentioned English Language Teaching (ELT) experts. I showed how non-elite mothers migrating from a subsistence economy to a consumer society turned to English-medium schooling to substantiate the radical social mobilities they had already experienced. Their ethical obligation to produce a similar experience of social mobility for their children advanced the business of low-fee private English-medium schooling. Meanwhile, actually existing regional-medium schools such as St. Thomas showed us the punishing hope of mothers to pierce the romanticized veil of Malayalam-medium schooling. New forms of domination operate through aspirations, which are driven by ethical-moral impulses.

Linguistic imperialism from below drew attention to the ways in which non-elite aspiration and action produced the dominance of English as well as the cruel irony of charging them with the power to subjugate and exploit society. Critical educators hailed non-elites as responsible for the injustices of English-medium education. They were portrayed as bad consumers whose irrational aspirations jeopardized the democratic possibilities of education. Additionally, national policy and pedagogy abhorred rote pedagogy and attempted to rescue non-elite children from their own parents. Here too, morality advanced action, but linguists' and policymakers' disproportionate access to resources allowed them to assemble far-reaching reforms.

To return to Phillipson's (2013) invocation, the analysis in the book revealed what is similar and different about the dominations of English in the post/colonial context and the contemporary. The colonial and postcolonial excluded the 'others', but the contemporary excludes *through* inclusion. Desires for progress through English have always existed, but their fullest manifestation across difference was made possible through market liberalization. The 'postcolonial condition' (Gupta, 1998: 10) was such that ordinary Indians reacted to 'the endless disappointments' of development 'not by questioning the desirability of progress itself, but rather by holding more closely to this prospect' (Pandian, 2008: 173). This devotion to progress reached its fullest force with liberalization. The deepening of consumer practices and its accompanying affective labors made English education obligatory for good mothering, across class and caste borders. Rather than romanticizing mothers' ethical work, I have attempted to describe it as a contradictory space marked by regimentation, peer-policing, humiliation and domination.

Alongside, I described how the actions of diverse elites across local, regional and national levels converged curiously to bring about a paradigm shift in English language pedagogy. What held this strange, disaggregated empire together was elite anxiety over loss of distinction. Local educators, regional policymakers, theoretical linguists at the national level and private publishers did not sketch out a coherent program of action together. In fact, they disagreed over theoretical claims and materials production. Despite the scattered and contesting nature of reform work, these advanced a specific notion of change that reworked the notion of language in ways that consolidated existing inequalities.

While research tends to posit the state and the market as antagonistic, their complimentary roles in consolidating elite privilege are worth reiterating. The NCERT and the CBSE cautioned against rote but to a core clientele that had defined its relationship to the state through the market. NCERT textbooks were produced for use in CBSE schools, which are largely private schools. These subscribed professionally designed, privately published textbooks, which amplified rote and supplemented it with a whole array of picture books that encouraged pleasurable repetition. Ethical citizenship was assumed to be the prerogative of the wealthy, whose very wealth made the upper end of the marketplace exclusive and moral. At the same time, lack of access to markets exacerbated marginality. At the uneconomic school, the Kerala state strangled the learning opportunities of the most marginalized learners by fragmenting the primary resource available in the classroom – the English textbook. The convoluted design foregrounded emotional excess but with little opportunity for meaning-making. Without the mediations of the market, the oracy bias of linguists found an exceptionally sharp manifestation and engendered widespread pedagogies of shame.

Two aspects I have tried to thread throughout the book are the specificity and processual nature of moral aspiration. The diverse aspirational locations and aspirations traversed in previous chapters – those of Dalit mothers, non-elite families, Left educators and language pedagogues, and internationally mobile elite Indians – urge close attention to the specificity of aspiration and morality. The book also attempted to rescue aspiration from reductive economic, static, universalistic or ahistoric interpretations. While literature on low-fee private schooling imagines an already existing, rational consumer as the ideal citizen, the book posits that aspirational consumer-citizens are made, not born.

Additionally, I have emphasized how the re-production of privilege is fraught and contradictory. I showed how oracy-focused pedagogy was riddled with its own contradictions. Proficient English speakers subjected to new standards encountered hyper-scripted formats that atrophied communication. Non-elite students at the New English School attempted to learn the cosmopolitan cultures of English communication through bilingual books, but they were too deeply rooted in the regional. The ease and fluency of positive politeness eluded them. The ease and fluency of translating communicative language pedagogy eluded the CBSE also, which attempted elaborate reforms that failed.

Diverse moral aspirations thus transformed the status and function of English in India from a second (academic) language to a first (communicative) language. Rather than intentional, strategic workings by an invisible, coherent, neoliberal market, the converging assumptions of Leftist, critical pedagogues and privileged elites re-aligned English proficiency along elite resources. To emphasize the historically contingent nature of these convergences, I described the political contexts of the reforms. The Kerala English reforms were undertaken by a communist state struggling to re-articulate socialist democracy through schooling reforms. Sustained funding assembled a tight-knit cadre of English-speaking, activist professionals, who offered participative, expressive citizenship as the alternative to consumer citizenship and the privatization of primary education. Their pedagogic reforms mandated expressive oracy (in English) in primary classes as the pedagogic route to build a socialist democratic society. The NCERT reforms too had activist aspirations but were caught up in institutional structures that served middle-class interests. The contradictions fragmented and trivialized pedagogy, but reformers expected oral interaction to bring it into coherence. Diverging from its activist counterparts, the CBSE sought to make domestic social interaction amenable to transnational standards. The most obvious modality of commensurability was proficiency in English-speaking skills. The unlikely convergence of activism and transnationalism thus assembled the conditions under which interaction became pedagogic commonsense even though literacy rather than oracy is the most readily available local resource.

Applied linguistic scholarship in the recent past has been preoccupied with language practices that challenge the enduring hegemony of monolingualism in the Global North (Blommaert, 2014; Canagarajah, 2018; García & Wei, 2014; Pennycook & Otsuji, 2015; Rymes, 2014) even as it grapples with the possibility that this criticality is uncannily aligned with market logics of flexibility, enterprise and innovation (Canagarajah, 2017; Flores, 2013; Kubota, 2014). The book extends this scholarship by describing similar tensions in the Global South about criticality and market logic.

On the one hand, ideas that critiqued dominant discourses of native supremacy and monolingualism became new hegemonic moral norms. Though Pennycook cautions that criticality should not produce new orthodoxies (2001: 8), the book showed that applied linguistics' valorization of the critical slips too easily into orthodoxy. Pennycook (2001: 8) writes that critical scholars should:

> maintain a greater sense of humility and difference and [to] raise questions about the limits of [our] own knowing. This self-reflexive position also suggests that critical applied linguistics is not concerned with producing itself as a new orthodoxy, with prescribing new models and procedures for doing applied linguistics. Rather, it is concerned with raising a host of new and difficult questions about knowledge, politics, and ethics.

I have presented one deeply troubling account of how intentions to question dominant (Western) knowledge, politics and ethics produced orthodoxy and violence. Furthermore, though discussions about criticality in language studies (Kubota & Miller, 2017) urge self-reflexivity to be accompanied with result-oriented action, in the reform contexts I have described in the book, praxis took on bizarrely perverse directions. I agree that research geared toward publication needs to be countered with the call to action. Further, I am deeply aware that the teaching work I did, if it can be called reflective action or praxis, is what allowed me to raise specific questions about knowledge, politics and ethics in this book. But the violence of reform praxis is a haunting reminder of the troubling consequences of well-intentioned action.

On the other hand, radical shifts in political economy have made the critical endeavor generally fraught. Recent scholarship has drawn attention to how neoliberal market logic evacuates the critical edge of radical theories (Flores, 2013; Inoue, 2007; Kubota, 2014; Mohanty, 2013). Ironically, the book described how non-elite mothers' ethical-political work emerged *through* marketization to simultaneously advance and undermine social justice. To imagine that 'the world could be otherwise' was the 'ethical analytical labor' critical scholars performed to denaturalize formations of power (Gershon, 2011: 537). But markets too teach those embedded in unequal systems that the world can be otherwise.

How then do we imagine social justice work? Critical applied linguists and feminists have long argued that politics emerges through the agency produced by domination. In her seminal work on the feminist politics of Islamic piety, Saba Mahmood (2005: 17) writes that 'the very processes and conditions that secure a subject's subordination are also the means by which she becomes a self-conscious identity and agent'. Meanwhile, feminists like Kathi Weeks (2007: 234) point out that in the neoliberal context, any 'notion of political resistance grounded in an outside' is untenable. Affect, morality/ethics, politics, all of these can no longer be separated out into a sphere that is outside capitalist production. What the book has attempted is a detailed account of the affective and moral politics of English aspiration and pedagogy that is fully integrated with the market but in unexpected and contradictory ways. Rather than an end to politics, it is the beginning of a new kind of politics.

References

Adam, B. (2008) Future matters: Futures known, created and minded. *Twenty-First Century Society* 3 (2), 111–116.

Ahmed, S. (2004) Affective economies. *Social Text* 22 (2), 117–139.

Akhtar, S. (2005) A critical note: Debating education. *Social Scientist* 33 (9/10), 37–40.

Ameerudheen, T.A. (2018) Why Kerala's public schools have seen a rise in student strength for the first time in 25 years. *Scroll*. See https://scroll.in/article/884082/why-keralas-public-schools-have-seen-a-rise-in-student-strength-for-the-first-time-in-25-years (accessed 20 September 2021).

Amritavalli, R. (2007) *English in Deprived Circumstances: Maximising Learner Autonomy*. New Delhi: Cambridge University Press India.

Amrute, S. (2016) *Encoding Race, Encoding Class: Indian IT Workers in Berlin*. Durham, NC: Duke University Press.

Anagnost, A. (2008) Imagining global futures in China: The child as a sign of value. In J. Cole and D. Durham (eds) *Figuring the Future: Globalization and the Temporalities of Children and Youth* (pp. 49–72). Santa Fe, NM: SAR Press.

Anandan, K.N. (2014) English language textbooks for primary classes: Some experiences of working in Kerala and Andhra Pradesh. Talk delivered at the 14th WATIS forum.

Aneesh, A. (2015) *Neutral Accent: How Language, Labor, and Life Become Global*. Durham, NC: Duke University Press.

Appadurai, A. (1986) *The Social Life of Things*. Cambridge: Cambridge University Press.

Appadurai, A. (2013) *The Future as Cultural Fact*. London: Verso.

Arnold, T.C. (2001) Rethinking moral economy. *American Political Science Review* 95 (1), 85–95.

Arokiasamy, P. and Retnakumar, J.N. (2006) Explaining school enrollment trends in Kerala, India. *Journal of South Asian Development* 1 (2), 231–248.

Asianet News (2014) Newshour: UKG student shut in kennel for talking in class. See https://www.youtube.com/watch?v=nV5OgEnuImM&list=PLZ47UtqJR_EG2R_LcM3yNdNi-e3pzAzUd&index=57 (accessed 20 September 2021).

Azim Premji Foundation (2013) Private schools are no panacea: Result of providing a choice of schools to parents of children in rural Andhra Pradesh. A preliminary report. APF.

Bartlett, L. (2010) *The Word and the World: The Cultural Politics of Literacy in Brazil*. New York: Hampton Press.

Bartlett, L. and Holland, D. (2002) Theorizing the space of literacy practices. *Ways of Knowing Journal* 2 (1), 10–22.

Baviskar, A. and Ray, R. (eds) (2011) *Elite and Everyman: The Cultural Politics of the Indian Middle-Classes*. New Delhi: Routledge.

Berdahl, D. (1999) '(N)ostalgie' for the present: Memory, longing, and East German things. *Ethnos* 64 (2), 192–211.

Bhattacharya, R., Madan, A., Basu, N. and Sarkar, S. (2012) *Notes of Running Feet: English in Primary Textbooks*. Bhopal: Ekalavya.

Bhatty, K., De, A. and Roy, R. (2015) The public education system and what the costs imply. *Economic and Political Weekly* 1 (31), 10–13.

Black, S.P. (2018) The ethics and aesthetics of care. *Annual Review of Anthropology* 47, 79–95.

Blommaert, J. (2014) Infrastructures of superdiversity: Conviviality and language in an Antwerp neighborhood. *European Journal of Cultural Studies* 17 (4), 431–451.

Bourdieu, P. (1977) The economics of linguistic exchanges. *Information (International Social Science Council)* 16 (6), 645–668.

Bourdieu, P. (1986) The forms of capital. In J. Richardson (ed.) *Handbook of Theory and Research for the Sociology of Education* (pp. 241–258). Westport, CT: Greenwood.

British Council (1992) *Central Board of Secondary Education: ELT Project Phase 2 Project Memorandum.* New Delhi: British High Commission.

CABE (2005) *Regulatory Mechanisms for Textbooks and Parallel Textbooks Taught in Schools Outside the Government System.* New Delhi: Committee of the Central Advisory Board of Education, MHRD.

Cameron, D. (2000) *Good to Talk? Living and Working in a Communication Culture.* London: Sage.

Canagarajah, S. (1999) *Resisting Linguistic Imperialism in English Teaching.* New Delhi: Oxford University Press.

Canagarajah, S. (2017) *Translingual Practices and Neoliberal Policies: Attitudes and Strategies of African Skilled Migrants in Anglophone Workplaces.* Cham: Springer. DOI: 10.1007/978-3-319-41243-6_1

Canagarajah, S. (2018) Translingual practice as spatial repertoires: Expanding the paradigm beyond structuralist orientations. *Applied Linguistics* 39 (1), 31–54.

CBSE (n.d.) *Self-Assess Package for 'Interact in English'.* Delhi: CBSE.

CBSE (n.d.) *Assessment of Speaking and Listening, Descriptors for Assessment of Speaking.* Delhi: CBSE.

CBSE (n.d.) *Assessment of Speaking and Listening, Specifications for Speaking, Class 9.* Delhi: CBSE.

CBSE (n.d.) *Handbook for Teachers: Interact in English.* Delhi: CBSE.

CBSE (1962) *Manual of Rules and Regulations.* See https://www.cbse.gov.in/cbsenew/rti_rules.html (accessed 20 September 2021).

CBSE (1994) *Interact in English Main Course Book* (1st edn). Delhi: CBSE.

CBSE (2009) *Interact in English Main Course Book* (5th edn revised reprint). Delhi: CBSE.

CBSE (2010) *CBSE International, FAQ for Parents.* Delhi: CBSE.

Chacko, M.A. (2020) English educated as 'ready-made' leaders: Re-inscribing distinction through the Student Police Cadet project in Kerala, India. *South Asia: Journal of South Asian Studies* 43 (4), 775–792.

Chalhoub-Deville, M. and Turner, C.E. (2000) What to look for in ESL admission tests: Cambridge certificate exams, IELTS, and TOEFL. *System* 28 (4), 523–539.

Chandra, S. (2012) *The Sexual Life of English: Languages of Caste and Desire in Colonial India.* Durham, NC: Duke University Press.

Chidsey, M.M. (2017) Mediated empowerments: An ethnography of four, all-girls' "public schools" in North India. PhD thesis, Columbia University.

Chidsey, M.M. (2020) Theatres of empowerment: Elite all-girls' Indian "public schools" and the production of performative altruism. *South Asia: Journal of South Asia Studies* 43 (4), 723–740.

CIEFL (1997) *CBSE ELT Curriculum Implementation Study Final Report.* Hyderabad: Department of Evaluation, CIEFL.

Cummins, J. (1979) Cognitive/academic language proficiency, linguistic interdependence, the optimum age question and some other matters. *Working Papers on Bilingualism Toronto* (19), 197–202.

Davies, A. (1981) Book review of "Communicative Syllabus Design" by John Munby. *TESOL Quarterly* 15 (3), 332–336.

Davies, A. (2013) *Native Speakers and Native Users: Loss and Gain.* Cambridge: Cambridge University Press.

De, A., Noronha, C. and Samson, M. (2003) Private schools for less privileged: Some insights from a case study. *Economic and Political Weekly* 37 (52), 5230–5236.

Desai, S., Dubey, A., Vanneman, R. and Banerji, R. (2008) Private schooling in India: A new educational landscape. In S. Bery, B. Bosworth and A. Panagariya (eds) *India Policy Forum* (pp. 1–58). New Delhi: Sage for National Council of Applied Economic Research. https://www.ncaer.org/publication_details.php?pID=159

Devika, J. (2006) *Engendering Individuals: The Language of Re-forming in Early Twentieth Century Keralam*. Hyderabad: Orient Longman.

Devika, J. (2007) Fears of contagion? Depoliticisation and recent conflicts over politics in Kerala. *Economic and Political Weekly* 42 (25), 2464–2470.

Devika, J. (2008) Post-demographic transition research on childcare in Kerala. *Economic and Political Weekly* 43 (5), 15–18.

Devika, J. (2010) Egalitarian developmentalism, communist mobilization, and the question of caste in Kerala State, India. *The Journal of Asian Studies* 69 (03), 799–820.

Dey, S. (2019) What are the implications of the English-language education policy of the Andhra Pradesh government? *Economic and Political Weekly* 54 (49). See https://www.epw.in/engage/article/what-are-implications-of-english-language-education-policy-of-andhra-pradesh-government (accessed 20 September 2021).

Donner, H. (2006) Committed mothers and well-adjusted children: Privatisation, early-years education and motherhood in Calcutta. *Modern Asian Studies* 40 (2), 371–395.

Donner, H. (2008) *Domestic Goddesses: Maternity, Globalization and Middle-class Identity in Contemporary India*. Delhi: Routledge.

Dreze, J. and Sen, A. (2002) *India: Development and Participation*. New Delhi: Oxford University Press.

Ellis, R. (1994) *The Study of Second Language Acquisition*. Oxford: Oxford University Press.

Faust, D. and Nagar, R. (2001) Politics of development in postcolonial India: English-medium education and social fracturing. *Economic and Political Weekly* 36 (30), 2878–2883.

Fernandes, L. and Heller, P. (2006) Hegemonic aspirations: New middle-class politics and India's democracy in comparative perspective. *Critical Asian Studies* 38 (4), 495–522.

Flores, N. (2013) The unexamined relationship between neoliberalism and plurilingualism: A cautionary tale. *TESOL Quarterly* 47 (3), 500–520.

Fournier, V. (1999) The appeal to 'professionalism' as a disciplinary mechanism. *The Sociological Review* 47 (2), 280–307.

Fraser-Gupta, A. (1997) Colonisation, migration, and functions of English. In E.W. Schneider (ed.) *Englishes Around the World, Volume 1* (pp. 47–58). Amsterdam: John Benjamins.

Freire, P. (1998) *Pedagogy of Freedom: Ethics, Democracy, and Civic Courage*. Lanham, MD: Rowman & Littlefield Publishers.

Fuller, C.J. and Narasimhan, H. (2006) Engineering colleges, 'exposure' and Information Technology: Professionals in Tamil Nadu. *Economic and Political Weekly* 41 (3), 258–288.

Gago, V. (2017) *Neoliberalism from Below: Popular Pragmatics and Baroque Economies*. Durham, NC: Duke University Press.

García, O. and Wei, L. (2014) *Translanguaging: Language, Bilingualism and Education*. London: Palgrave Macmillan.

Gardner, A. (2010) *City of Strangers: Gulf Migration and the Indian Community in Bahrain*. Ithaca, NY: Cornell University Press.

General Education Department of Kerala (2020) Website home page https://education.kerala.gov.in/

Gershon, I. (2011) Neoliberal agency. *Current Anthropology* 52 (4), 537–555.

Gilbertson, A. (2016) Cosmopolitan learning, making merit, and reproducing privilege in Indian schools. *Anthropology & Education Quarterly* 47 (3), 297–313.

Girija, K.P. (2011) On suicide, caste, and higher education. *Insight Young Voices*. See https://thedeathofmeritinindia.wordpress.com/2011/04/26/84/ (accessed 20 September 2021).

Government of India (1967) *The Study of English in India: Report of the Study Group Appointed by the Ministry of Education*. Delhi: Ministry of Education.

Government of Kerala (1959) *Kerala Education Rules*. Trivandrum: Government of Kerala.

Government of Kerala (1988) *Economic Review*. Trivandrum: Kerala State Planning Commission.

Government of Kerala (1999) *Economic Review*. Trivandrum: Kerala State Planning Commission.

Government of Kerala (2010) *Kerala Right to Education Rules*. Trivandrum: Government of Kerala.

Government of Kerala (2014) *Economic Review*. Trivandrum: Kerala State Planning Commission.

Government of Kerala (2015) *Economic Review*. Trivandrum: Kerala State Planning Commission.

Government of Kerala (2018) *Economic Review*. Trivandrum: Kerala State Planning Commission.

Grabe, W. (2004) Research on teaching reading. *Annual Review of Applied Linguistics* 24, 44–69.

Graeber, D. (2001) *Toward an Anthropological Theory of Value: The False Coin of Our Own Dreams*. New York: Palgrave Macmillan.

Guichard, S. (2010) *The Construction of History and Nationalism in India: Textbooks, Controversies and Politics*. London: Routledge.

Gupta, A. (1998) *Postcolonial Developments: Agriculture in the Making of Modern India*. Durham, NC: Duke University Press.

Halliday, M.A.K. (1973) *Explorations in the Functions of Language*. London: Edward Arnold.

Hardt, M. and Negri, A. (2000) *Empire*. Cambridge, MA: Harvard University Press.

Harklau, L. (2002) The role of writing in classroom second language acquisition. *Journal of Second Language Writing* 11 (4), 329–350.

Henry, O. and Ferry, M. (2017) When cracking the JEE is not enough. Processes of elimination and differentiation, from entry to placement, in the Indian Institutes of Technology. *Samaj* 15, 1–28.

Heyer, J. (2015) Dalit women becoming 'housewives': Lessons from the Tiruppur region, 1981-82 to 2008-09. In C. Still (ed.) *Dalits in Neoliberal India: Mobility or Marginalization?* (pp. 208–235). New Delhi: Routledge.

Holmes, J. (2012) Politeness in intercultural discourse and communication. In C. Bratt Paulston, S.F. Kiesling and E.S. Rangel (eds) *The Handbook of Intercultural Discourse and Communication* (pp. 205–228). Oxford: Blackwell.

Inoue, M. (2007) Language and gender in an age of neoliberalism. *Gender & Language* 1 (1), 79–91.

Irani, L. (2019) *Chasing Innovation: Making Entrepreneurial Citizens in Modern India*. Princeton, NJ: Princeton University Press.

Jain, M. (2018) Schools, market and citizenship in Delhi. In M. Jain, A. Mehendale, R. Mukhopadhyay, P. Sarangapani and C. Winch (eds) *School Education in India: Market, State and Quality* (pp. 191–226). Abingdon: Routledge.

Jakimow, T. (2016) Clinging to hope through education: The consequences of hope for rural laborers in Telangana, India. *Ethos* 44 (1), 11–31.

Jang, I.C. (2017) Consuming global language and culture: South Korean youth in English study abroad. PhD thesis, University of Toronto.

Jangid, G. (2004) A whole language approach to second language instruction: Literacy and language acquisition. PhD thesis, Central Institute of English and Foreign Languages.

Jayadeva, S. (2018) 'Below English line': An ethnographic exploration of class and the English language in post-liberalization India. *Modern Asian Studies* 52 (2), 576–608.

Jeffrey, R. (1978) Matriliny, marxism, and the birth of the Communist Party in Kerala, 1930-1940. *The Journal of Asian Studies* 38 (1), 77–98.

Jeffrey, R. (1994) *The Decline of Nair Dominance*. Delhi: Manohar.

Joseph, P.J. (1996) The total literacy project of Ernakulam: An epoch-making experiment in India. *Convergence* 29 (1), 10–19.

Kapur, D., Prasad, C.B., Pritchett, L. and Babu, D.S. (2010) Rethinking inequality: Dalits in Uttar Pradesh in the market reform era. *Economic and Political Weekly* 45 (35), 39–49.

Kapur, D. and Vaishnav, M. (2014) Being middle-class in India. *The Hindu*, 9 December. See https://www.thehindu.com/opinion/op-ed/being-middle-class-in-india/article6673580.ece (accessed 20 September 2021).

Karopady, D.D. (2014) Does school choice help rural children from disadvantaged sections? *Economic & Political Weekly* 49 (51), 46–53.

Kaur, R. (2016) The innovative Indian: Common man and the politics of jugaad culture. *Contemporary South Asia* 24 (3), 313–327.

Kaur, R. and Sundar, N. (2016) Snakes and ladders: Rethinking social mobility in post-reform India. *Contemporary South Asia* 24 (3), 229–241.

Kern, R. and Schultz, J.M. (2005) Beyond orality: Investigating literacy and the literary in second and foreign language instruction. *Modern Language Journal* 89 (3), 381–392.

Kingdon, G. (1996a) Private schooling in India: Size, nature, and equity-effects. *Economic and Political Weekly* 31 (51), 3306–3314.

Kingdon, G. (1996b) The quality and efficiency of private and public education: A case study of urban India. *Oxford Bulletin of Economics and Statistics* 58 (1), 57–82.

Kingdon, G. (2017) *The Emptying of Public Schools and Growth of Private Schools in India. Report on Budget Private Schools*. New Delhi: Centre for Civil Society.

Kipnis, A. (2001) Articulating school countercultures. *Anthropology & Education Quarterly* 32 (4), 472–492.

Koda, K. (2005) *Insights into Second Language Reading: A Cross-Linguistic Approach*. New York: Cambridge University Press.

Krashen, S.D. and Terrell, T.D. (1983) *The Natural Approach: Language Acquisition in the Classroom*. San Francisco: Alemany Press.

Krishnan, S. (2014) Making ladies of girls: Middle-class women and pleasure in urban India. DPhil thesis, University of Oxford.

Krishnaswamy, N. and Burde, A.S. (1998) *The Politics of Indians' English: Linguistic Colonialism and the Expanding English Empire*. Delhi: Oxford University Press.

Kuan, T. (2015) *Love's Uncertainty: The Politics and Ethics of Child Rearing in Contemporary China*. Berkeley, CA: University of California Press.

Kubota, R. (2014) The multi/plural turn, postcolonial theory, and neoliberal multiculturalism: Complicities and implications for applied linguistics. *Applied Linguistics* 37 (4), 474–494.

Kubota, R. and Miller, E.R. (2017) Re-examining and re-envisioning criticality in language studies: Theories and praxis. *Critical Inquiry in Language Studies* 14 (2–3), 129–157.

Kumar, K. (1984) 'People's science' and development theory. *Economic and Political Weekly* 19 (28), 1082–1084.

Kumar, K. (1985) Reproduction or change? Education and elites in India. *Economic and Political Weekly* 20 (30), 1280–1284.

Kumar, K. (1996) *Learning from Conflict*. New Delhi: Longman.

Kumar, K. (2000) Noise and design. *Economic and Political Weekly* 35 (13), 1057.

Kumar, K. (2010) Quality in education: Competing concepts. *Contemporary Education Dialogue* 7 (1), 7–18.

Kumar, K., Priyam, M. and Saxena, S. (2001) Looking beyond the smokescreen: DPEP and primary education in India. *Economic and Political Weekly* 36 (7), 560–568.

Kumaravadivelu, B. (2006) *Understanding Language Teaching: From Method to Postmethod*. New York: Routledge.

Kurien, P.A. (2002) *Kaleidoscopic Ethnicity: International Migration and the Reconstruction of Community Identities in India*. New Brunswick, NJ: Rutgers University Press.

Larsen-Freeman, D. and Long, M.H. (1991) *An Introduction to Second Language Acquisition Research*. New York: Routledge.

Liechty, M. (2003) *Suitably Modern: Making Middle-class Culture in a New Consumer Society*. Princeton, NJ: Princeton University Press.

Lieten, G.K. (1977) Education, ideology and politics in Kerala 1957-59. *Social Scientist* 6 (2), 3–21.

Lindberg, A. (2001) *Experience and Identity: A Historical Account of Class, Caste, and Gender among the Cashew Workers of Kerala, 1930–2000*. Lund: Lund University.

Liyanage, I. and Canagarajah, S. (2019) Shame in English language teaching: Desirable pedagogical possibilities for Kiribati in neoliberal times. *TESOL Quarterly* 53 (2), 430–455.

Lukose, R.A. (2009) *Liberalization's Children: Gender, Youth, and Consumer Citizenship in Globalizing India*. Durham, NC: Duke University Press.

Mahmood, S. (2005) *Politics of Piety: The Islamic Revival and the Feminist Subject*. Princeton, NJ: Princeton University Press.

Mathew, R. (2012) Understanding washback: A case study of a new exam in India. In C. Tribble (ed.) *Managing Change in English Language Teaching: Lessons from Experience* (pp. 195–202). London: British Council.

Mathew, L. (2022) The merit of medicine: Science aspirations in India. *Cultural Studies of Science Education*. See https://doi.org/10.1007/s11422-021-10088-y

Mathur, P. (1995) Curriculum change in process: The case of an ELT project. In R.K. Agnihotri and A.L. Khanna (eds) *English Language Teaching in India: Issues and Innovations* (pp. 301–315). New Delhi: Sage.

Mazzarella, W. (2003) *Shoveling Smoke: Advertising and Globalization in Contemporary India*. Durham, NC: Duke University Press.

McGuire, M.L. (2011) 'How to sit, how to stand': Bodily practice and the new urban middle-class. In I. Clark-Deces (ed.) *A Companion to the Anthropology of India* (pp. 115–136). Malden: Wiley-Blackwell.

MHRD (2016) *Educational Statistics at a Glance*. New Delhi: Ministry of Human Resources Development.

Mohan, P.S. (2005) Religion, social space and identity: The prathyaksha raksha daiva sabha and the making of cultural boundaries in twentieth century Kerala. *South Asia: Journal of South Asian Studies* 28 (1), 35–63.

Mohanty, C.T. (2013) Transnational feminist crossings: On neoliberalism and radical critique. *Signs: Journal of Women in Culture and Society* 38 (4), 967–991.

Moore, T. and Morton, J. (2005) Dimensions of difference: A comparison of university writing and IELTS writing. *Journal of English for Academic Purposes* 4 (1), 43–66.

Morrison, T. (1987) *Beloved*. New York: Alfred Knopf.

Motha, S. and Lin, A. (2013) "Non-coercive rearrangements": Theorizing desire in TESOL. *TESOL Quarterly* 48 (2), 331–359.

Muehlebach, A. (2012) *The Moral Neoliberal: Welfare and Citizenship in Italy*. Chicago: University of Chicago Press.

Mukul, A. (2015) International Baccalaureate schools in India post 10-fold growth in 10 years. *The Times of India*. See https://timesofindia.indiatimes.com/home/education/

news/International-Baccalaureate-schools-in-India-post-10-fold-growth-in-10-years/ articleshow/47349322.cms (accessed 20 September 2021).

Munby, J. (1978) *Communicative Syllabus Design: A Sociolinguistic Model for Designing the Content of Purpose-Specific Language Programmes.* Cambridge: Cambridge University Press.

Muralidharan, K. (2013) Priorities for primary education policy in India's 12th five-year plan. In *India Policy Forum* (pp. 1–61). Delhi: NCAER. https://ideas.repec.org/a/nca/ncaerj/v9y2013i2013-1p1-61.html

Muralidharan, K. and Kremer, M. (2006) *Public and Private Schools in Rural India.* Cambridge, MA: Department of Economics, Harvard University.

Naik, J.P. (1997) *The Education Commission and After.* Delhi: APH Publishing.

Nair, J. (2015) Dirty minds. *Economic and Political Weekly. Post Script* 50 (35), 1–2.

Nair, S.K. (2004) The teaching of English in government/aided primary schools in Kerala under DPEP. *Kerala Research Programme on Local Level Development Discussion Paper 58.* Thiruvananthapuram: Center for Development Studies.

Nakane, I. (2007) *Silence in Intercultural Communication: Perceptions and Performance* (Vol. 166). Amsterdam: John Benjamins Publishing.

Nakassis, C.V. and Searle, L. (2013) Introduction: Social value projects in post-liberalisation India. *Contributions to Indian Sociology* 47 (2), 169–183.

Nambissan, G. (2011) Low cost private schools for the poor in India: Some reflections. In *India Infrastructure Report* (pp. 84–93). New Delhi: Routledge. DOI: 10.4324/9781315538914

Nambissan, G. and Ball, S. (2010) Advocacy networks, choice and private schooling of the poor in India. *Global Networks* 10 (3), 324–343.

Nambissan, G. and Batra, P. (1989) Equity and excellence: Issues in Indian education. *Social Scientist* 17 (9/10), 56–73.

Naumescu, V. (2019) Pedagogies of prayer: Teaching orthodoxy in South India. *Comparative Studies in Society and History* 61 (2), 389–418.

NCERT (2000) *National Curricular Framework for School Education.* New Delhi: NCERT.

NCERT (2005) *National Curricular Framework.* New Delhi: NCERT.

NCERT (2006) *Position Paper: National Focus Group on Teaching of English.* New Delhi: NCERT.

NCERT (2011a) *Raindrops, English Textbook.* New Delhi: NCERT.

NCERT (2011b) *50 Years of NCERT.* New Delhi: NCERT. See https://ncert.nic.in/pdf/leading_the_change.pdf (accessed 20 September 2021).

Nossiter, T.J. (1982) *Communism in Kerala: A Study in Political Adaptation.* Berkeley, CA: University of California Press.

Osella, F. and Osella, C. (2002) *Social Mobility in Kerala: Modernity and Identity in Conflict.* London: Pluto Press.

Pandey, G. (2009) Can there be a subaltern middle-class? Notes on African American and Dalit history. *Public Culture* 21 (2), 321–342.

Pandian, A. (2008) Devoted to development: Moral progress, ethical work, and divine favor in south India. *Anthropological Theory* 8 (2), 159–179.

Panikkassery, V. (1970) *Dr. Palpu.* Thrissur: Current Books.

Parameswaran, M.P. (1996) Kerala shastra sahitya parishad: Yesterday, today, tomorrow. *Les Sciences Hors D'Occident Au XX Siecle, Sciences et Development 5,* 281–298.

Parayil, G. and Sreekumar, T.T. (2003) Kerala's experience of development and change. *Journal of Contemporary Asia* 33 (4), 465–492.

Parekh, B. (1991) Nehru and the national philosophy of India. *Economic and Political Weekly* 26 (1), 35–48.

Pennycook, A. (1994) *The Cultural Politics of English as an International Language.* New York: Routledge.

Pennycook, A. (2001) *Critical Applied Linguistics: A Critical Introduction.* Mahwah, NJ: Lawrence Erlbaum.

Pennycook, A. (2002) Mother tongues, governmentality, and protectionism. *International Journal of the Sociology of Language* 154, 11–28.

Pennycook, A. and Otsuji, E. (2015) *Metrolingualism: Language in the City.* New York: Routledge.

Phillipson, R. (1992) *Linguistic Imperialism.* London: Oxford University Press.

Phillipson, R. (2013) *Linguistic Imperialism Continued.* Hyderabad: Orient Blackswan.

Pine, F. (2014) Migration as hope. *Current Anthropology* 55(S9), S95–S104.

Polanyi, L. (1988) A formal model of the structure of discourse. *Journal of Pragmatics* 12 (5), 601–638.

Prabhakar, B. (2013) *Nammude school vidyabhyasam engotte? [Where is our school education headed?]* http://bijuprabhakar.com/wp-content/uploads/2013/09/DPI-article. pdf

Prabhu, N.S. (1987) *Second Language Pedagogy.* Oxford: Oxford University Press.

PROBE (1999) *Public Report on Basic Education in India.* New Delhi: Oxford University Press.

Punathambekar, A. (2005) Bollywood in the Indian-American diaspora: Mediating a transitive logic of cultural citizenship. *International Journal of Cultural Studies* 8 (2), 151–173.

Radhakrishnan, P. (1981) Land reforms in theory and practice: The Kerala experience. *Economic and Political Weekly* 16 (52), 129–137.

Radhakrishnan, S. (2011) *Appropriately Indian: Gender and Culture in a New Transnational Class.* Durham, NC: Duke University Press.

Rajan, R.S. (1992) Fixing English: Nation, language, subject. In R.S. Rajan (ed.) *The Lie of the Land: English Literary Studies in India* (pp. 7–28). Delhi: Oxford University Press.

Ramanathan, V. (2005) *The English-Vernacular Divide: Postcolonial Language Politics and Practice.* Clevedon: Multilingual Matters.

Resnik, J. (2010) Multicultural education–good for business but not for the state? The IB curriculum and global capitalism. *British Journal of Educational Studies* 57 (3), 217–244.

Rizvi, F. (2014) Old elite schools, history and the construction of a new imaginary. *Globalisation, Societies and Education* 12 (2), 290–308.

Rofel, L. (2007) *Desiring China: Experiments in Neoliberalism, Sexuality, and Public Culture.* Durham, NC: Duke University Press.

Romeo, K. (2000) Krashen and Terrell's "natural approach." Blog. See https://web.stanford.edu/~hakuta/www/LAU/ICLangLit/NaturalApproach.htm (accessed 20 September 2021).

Rudnyckyj, D. (2010) *Spiritual Economies: Islam, Globalization, and the Afterlife of Development.* Ithaca, NY: Cornell University Press.

Rymes, B. (2014) Communicative repertoire. In C. Leung and B. Street (eds) *The Routledge Companion to English Studies* (pp. 287–301). London: Routledge.

Sancho, D. (2015) *Youth, Class and Education in Urban India: The Year that can Break or Make You.* London: Routledge.

Sancho, D. (2017) Escaping India's culture of education: Migration desires among aspiring middle-class young men. *Ethnography* 18 (4), 515–534.

Sarangapani, P. (2018) Hyderabad's education market. In M. Jain, A. Mehendale, R. Mukhopadhyay, P. Sarangapani and C. Winch (eds) *School Education in India: Market, State and Quality* (pp. 161–190). Abingdon: Routledge.

Sarangapani, P. and Jain, M. (2018) Appendix, formation of pedagogy. In M. Jain, A. Mehendale, R. Mukhopadhyay, P. Sarangapani and C. Winch (eds) *School Education in India: Market, State and Quality* (pp. 218–226). Abingdon: Routledge.

Sarangapani, P. and Winch, C. (2010) Tooley, Dixon and Gomathi on private education in Hyderabad: A reply. *Oxford Review of Education* 36 (4), 499–515.

Sarukkai, S. (2014) Indian experiences with science: Considerations for history, philosophy, and science education. In M. Matthews (ed.) *International Handbook of Research in History, Philosophy and Science Teaching* (pp. 1691–1719). Dordrecht: Springer.

Satyanarayana, K. and Tharu, S. (2011) *No Alphabet in Sight: New Dalit Writing from South India–Dossier 1, Tamil and Malayalam*. New Delhi: Penguin.

Savignon, S.J. (1991) Communicative language teaching: State of the art. *TESOL Quarterly* 25 (2), 261–278.

SCERT (1997) *Kerala English Reader, Class 5*. Thiruvananthapuram: SCERT.

SCERT (2007) *Kerala Curriculum Framework*. Thiruvananthapuram: SCERT.

SCERT (2008) *English Sourcebook Standard 1*. Thiruvananthapuram: SCERT.

SCERT (2009) *English Sourcebook Standard 2*. Thiruvananthapuram: SCERT.

Searle, L. (2013) Constructing prestige and elaborating the 'professional': Elite residential complexes in the National Capital Region, India. *Contributions to Indian Sociology* 47 (2), 271–302.

Searle, L. (2016) *Landscapes of Accumulation: Real Estate and the Neoliberal Imagination in Contemporary India*. Chicago: University of Chicago Press.

Sherman, T.C. (2018) Education in early postcolonial India: Expansion, experimentation and planned self-help. *History of Education* 47 (4), 504–520.

Sivadas, S. (1991) *How Ernakulam Became the First Fully Literate District in India*. Paris: UNICEF.

Skeggs, B. (1997) *Formations of Class and Gender: Becoming Respectable*. London: Sage.

Sriprakash, A., Qi, J. and Singh, M. (2017) The uses of equality in an elite school in India: Enterprise and merit. *British Journal of Sociology of Education* 38 (7), 1022–1036.

Srivastava, P. (2007) Neither voice nor loyalty: School choice and the low-fee private sector in India. *Occasional Paper, 134*. https://ir.lib.uwo.ca/edupub/114/

Srivastava, S. (1998) *Constructing Post-colonial India: National Character and the Doon School*. Delhi: Routledge.

SSA (2011) *English, Annual Evaluation, Standard Two*. Thiruvananthapuram: Sarva Shikhsha Abhiyan.

SSA (2012) *English, Annual Evaluation, Standard Two*. Thiruvananthapuram: Sarva Shikhsha Abhiyan.

SSA (2013) *English, Annual Evaluation, Standard Two*. Thiruvananthapuram: Sarva Shikhsha Abhiyan.

SSA (2014) *English, Annual Evaluation, Standard Two*. Thiruvananthapuram: Sarva Shikhsha Abhiyan.

Stubbs, M. (1983) *Discourse Analysis: The Sociolinguistic Analysis of Natural Language*. Chicago: University of Chicago Press.

Subramanian, A. (2019) *The Caste of Merit: Engineering Education in India*. Boston: Harvard University Press.

Tanu, D. (2017) *Growing Up in Transit: The Politics of Belonging at an International School*. New York: Berghahn Books.

Tate, W. (2020) Anthropology of policy: Tensions, temporalities, possibilities. *Annual Review of Anthropology* 49, 83–99.

Taylor, L. and Weir, C.J. (eds) (2012) *IELTS Collected Papers 2: Research in Reading and Listening Assessment* (Vol. 2). Cambridge: Cambridge University Press.

Tharakan, M. (1984) Socio-economic factors in educational development: Case of nineteenth century Travancore. *Economic and Political Weekly* 14 (46–47), 1913–1928, 1955–1967.

Tharakan, M. (1998) Socio-religious reform movements, the process of democratization and human development: The case of Kerala, South-West India. In L. Rudebeck, O. Törnquist and V. Rojas (eds) *Democratization in the Third World* (pp. 144–172). London: Palgrave Macmillan.

Tharakan, M. (2000) Community participation in school education: Experiments and experiences under people's planning campaign in Kerala. *International Conference on Democratic Decentralization.* Thiruvananthapuram: State Planning Board.

Tharamangalam, J. (ed.) (2006) *Kerala: The Paradoxes of Public Action and Development.* New Delhi: Orient Longman.

Thiranagama, S. (2019) Rural civilities: Caste, gender and public life in Kerala. *South Asia: Journal of South Asian Studies* 42 (2), 310–327.

Thompson, E.P. (1971) The moral economy of the English crowd in the eighteenth century. *Past & Present 50* (1), 76–136.

Thorkelson, E. (2008) The silent social order of the theory classroom. *Social Epistemology* 22 (2), 165–196.

Tickoo, M.L. (1986) Syllabuses, scholars and schooling systems. *Sociolinguistic Aspects of Language Learning and Teaching, Occasional Papers, SEAMEO* 41, 9–23.

Tickoo, M.L. (1990) Towards an alternative curriculum for acquisition poor environments. In M.A.K. Halliday, J. Gibbons and H. Nicholas (eds) *Learning, Keeping and Using Language: Selected Papers from the 8th World Congress of Applied Linguists, Sydney, Volume 1* (pp. 403–418). Amsterdam: John Benjamins.

Tickoo, M.L. (1995) Reading-writing research and Asian TEFL classrooms: Providing for differentness. In M.L. Tickoo (ed.) *Reading and Writing: Theory into Practice* (pp. 259–279). Singapore: SEAMEO Regional Language Center.

Tickoo, M.L. (2012) Indian ELT at sixty plus: An essay in understanding. See http://www.teacherplus.org/indian-elt-at-sixty-plus-an-essay-in-understanding/ (accessed 20 September 2021).

Tobin, J., Hsueh, Y. and Karasawa, M. (2009) *Preschool in Three Cultures Revisited: China, Japan, and the United States.* Chicago: University of Chicago Press.

Tooley, J. and Dixon, P. (2003) *Private Schools for the Poor: A Case Study from India.* Reading: Centre for British Teachers.

Tooley, J., Dixon, P. and Gomathi, S.V. (2007) Private schools and the millennium development goal of universal primary education: A census and comparative survey in Hyderabad, India. *Oxford Review of Education* 33 (5), 539–560.

Törnquist, O. (1995) *The Next Left? Democratisation and Attempts to Renew the Radical Political Development Project: The Case of Kerala.* Copenhagen: NIAS Press.

Tripathy, R. (2015) Strategic lives: When the Indian knowledge migrant returns. *Economic & Political Weekly* 50 (24), 81–89.

Trivedi, P. (2015) Rhapsodic Shakespeare: V Sambasivan's kathaprasangam/story-singing. *Actes des Congrès de la Société Française Shakespeare* (33). DOI: doi.org/10.4000/shakespeare.3590

Tuxen, N. (2017) "It's about exposure": Elite Indian international students and the desire to accumulate cosmopolitan cultural capital. *Conference Proceedings TASA 2017 Conference.*

United Nations (1975) *Poverty, Unemployment, and Development Policy: A Case Study of Selected Issues with Reference to Kerala.* New York: United Nations.

UNESCO (2017) School enrollment, primary, % net – India. UNESCO. See https://data.worldbank.org/indicator/SE.PRM.NENR?locations=IN (accessed 20 September 2021).

UNESCO Institute for Statistics (2016) Education: Outbound, internationally mobile students by host region. USES.OF.56.40510. UNESCO.

Vaish, V. (2005) A peripherist view of English as a language of decolonization in postcolonial India. *Language Policy* 4 (2), 187–206.

van Ek, J.A. (1975) The threshold level. *Education and Culture* 28, 21–26.

van Ek, J.A. and Trim, J.L.M. (1991) *Threshold Level 1990.* Strasbourg: Council of Europe.

Vasavi, A.R. (2020) *Educational Differentiation and Disjunction*. Delhi: Orient Blackswan.

Vidakovic, I., Elliott, M. and Sladden, J. (2015) Revising FCE and CAE reading tests. *Researchers Note* 62, 8–14.

Viswanathan, G. (1992) English in a literate society. In R.S. Rajan (ed.) *The Lie of the Land: English Literary Studies in India* (pp. 29–41). Delhi: Oxford University Press.

Visweswaran, K., Witzel, M., Manjrenkar, N., Bhog, D. and Chakravarti, U. (2009) The Hindutva view of history: Rewriting textbooks in India and the United States. *Georgetown Journal of International Affairs* 10 (1), 101–112.

Vries, J.D. (2008) *The Industrious Revolution: Consumer Behavior and the Household Economy, 1650 to the Present*. New York: Cambridge University Press.

Weeks, K. (2007) Life within and against work: Affective labor, feminist critique, and post-Fordist politics. *Ephemera: Theory and Politics in Organization* 7 (1), 233–249.

Wilkins, D.A. (1976) *Notional Syllabuses: A Taxonomy and its Relevance to Foreign Language Curriculum Development*. London: Oxford University Press.

Williams, M. (2008) *The Roots of Participatory Democracy: Democratic Communists in South Africa and Kerala, India*. New York: Palgrave Macmillan.

Williams, R. and North, S. (1988) *Report on a Three Week Formulation Stage Visit to India, 16 October to 5 November 1988, in Connection with the CBSE ELT Project*. Plymouth: College of St Mark and St John.

Woods, P. (2009) British Council support for English in Africa: Past, present, and future. Talk given at British Council, Khartoum.

Zabiliute, E. (2016) Wandering in a mall: Aspirations and family among young urban poor men in Delhi. *Contemporary South Asia* 24 (3), 271–284.

Zachariah, M. (1989) Dilemmas of a successful people's education movement in India. *Paper Presented at the Annual Meeting of the Comparative and International Education Society*. See http://files.eric.ed.gov/fulltext/ED319095.pdf (accessed 20 September 2021).

Zyskowski, K. (2020) Aspiration as labour: Muslim women at basic computer training centers in Hyderabad. *South Asia: Journal of South Asian Studies* 43 (4), 758–774.

Index